The Color Bind

The Color Bind

Talking (and not Talking)
About Race at Work

Erica Gabrielle Foldy and Tamara R. Buckley

Russell Sage Foundation

The Russell Sage Foundation

Library of Congress Cataloging-in-Publication Data

Foldy, E. (Erica)
  The color bind : talking (and not talking) about race at work / Erica Gabrielle Foldy and Tamara R. Buckley.
    pages cm
  Includes bibliographical references and index.
  ISBN 978-0-87154-472-8 (pbk. : alk. paper) 1. Racism in social services—United States. 2. Social service—Practice—United States. 3. Social workers—United States. 4. Racism—United States. 5. Diversity in the workplace—United States. 6. Teams in the workplace—United States. I. Buckley, Tamara R. II. Title.
  HV40.8.U6F65 2014
  361.0089'00973—dc23

2013039634

Book design by Suzanne Nichols

RUSSELL SAGE FOUNDATION
112 East 64th Street, New York, New York 10065
10 9 8 7 6 5 4 3 2 1

EGF: To Roma, my mother, a civil rights activist
and the first person who talked to me about race.

TRB: To my parents, Ray and Cathy, for being
my first teachers about race.

~ Contents ~

~ List of Figures ~

~ About the Authors ~

ERICA GABRIELLE FOLDY is associate professor of public and nonprofit management at the Wagner School of Public Service at New York University.

TAMARA R. BUCKLEY is associate professor of counselor education, Department of Educational Foundations and Counseling, School of Education, Hunter College, the City University of New York (CUNY), and associate professor of critical social/personality psychology at The Graduate Center, CUNY.

~ Acknowledgments ~

A book about talking about race can't happen without a lot of talking—about race and many other things besides. Many, many colleagues, friends, and family members engaged with us in some way in this work, which sustained us, challenged us, and ultimately made this book possible.

We met as post-doctoral fellows working with Robin Ely and David Thomas at Harvard Business School on one of their research projects. We are eternally grateful to them, not only for introducing us to each other but also for providing some of the key intellectual scaffolding for the book with their work on diversity perspectives, as well as for their mentoring and encouragement along the way.

The Russell Sage Foundation has been a critical source of support, in many ways. We were Visiting Scholars at the Foundation in 2007–2008, which enabled us to spend a year analyzing our data, writing it up, and forming a true intellectual partnership. We thank in particular Eric Wanner, then president, for that opportunity. Suzanne Nichols, director of publications, through her continuing belief in the project as well as her steady, no-nonsense, spot-on advice, has been crucial to this book coming to fruition. The anonymous scholars who reviewed the manuscript made multiple unerring points that strengthened the final product.

Of course, this book could not have happened without the participation of the child welfare agency depicted here. We particularly thank the agency's commissioner, who generously opened the doors, as well as several key senior staff who handled all the details. We cannot name names for confidentiality reasons but we trust you know who you are. We are also grateful to the dozens of employees who made us welcome at their meetings and patiently engaged in multiple interviews.

Finally we thank Ji Chang and Tien Ung, who provided skillful research assistance with unfailing good cheer and a can-do attitude. They were both a delight to work with.

Erica's Acknowledgments

My father, Leslie, was an academic; my mother, Roma, spent most of her life as a social justice activist. Clearly, my work has been indelibly inscribed by both, as well as by my brother, Seth, steadfast in his pursuit of social change as a doctor and public health advocate.

A number of colleagues read chapter drafts and always had choice insights to offer. My writing group, Fulton 214, includes Rich de Jordy, Pacey Foster, Danna Greenberg, Tammy MacLean, Peter Rivard, Jenny Rudolph, and Steve Taylor. Not only are they a smart and perceptive crew, they are just really fun, and our usually boisterous meetings were a welcome break from long hours at the computer. Kate Kellogg read most of the manuscript and wrote astonishingly detailed and discerning notes. Vicky Parker and Jody Hoffer Gittell provided ongoing moral support and encouragement.

My long-time friend, Rachel Martin, not only read every chapter closely, but has been my ongoing and remarkably wise partner in exploring what it means to be a white person thinking, writing, and teaching about race and ethnicity. Up for everything from urgent consultations to hours-long conversations, Rachel has walked this road with me. I am blessed to have her as a friend.

I am fortunate to be part of several intellectual communities whose work has informed my broader thinking about identity and learning. The Wagner School of Public Service at New York University strives to be a place where race is discussable, and my colleagues have always been supportive of my research. The Research Center for Leadership in Action at Wagner explores the role of identity, including racial identity, in leadership as well as how to deepen and diversify the pool of people taking up leadership. The Center for Gender in Organizations at the Simmons School of Management is committed to understanding gender in the context of race, class, and other dimensions of difference. The Institute for Governmental Studies at the University of California, Berkeley, and Mills College both hosted me during my sabbatical in 2012.

Early in my academic life, I encountered the work of action science and action inquiry, which helped me see that curiosity and receptivity can be basic life orientations. This work has informed everything I have done since, including my thinking about broaching race. I am indebted to Bill Torbert and Diana McLain Smith for their guidance, and to Jenny Rudolph and Steve Taylor, my closest peers in this work, for our years of collective learning.

I regularly thank the fates for bringing me Tamara as a colleague and friend. I began this project largely on my own, but came to realize I could not complete it solo. Tamara generously accepted my invitation and ultimately became a full partner in the work. Not only does she have a profound understanding of people of all backgrounds, and a deep empathy for them, she is a model of self-awareness and self-reflection. I look forward to sustaining and enriching the professional and personal connections that lie before us.

Finally, my husband Roger is a thoughtful skeptic and researcher whose adherence to rigorous empiricism required identifying every possible alternative to the argument Tamara and I were developing. While making for some extremely animated discussions, it ultimately was provocative in the best sense of the word: it provoked me to question my assumptions, return to the data, and ensure our case was air-tight. For this and many other reasons, I could not have found a better life partner.

Tamara's Acknowledgments

My parents were my first teachers about race. My father, like many black men, often views the world through a racial lens; much of my early thinking about race was influenced by him. My mother, who is white, taught me another set of lessons about race. By insisting that my sister and I know and feel proud about being black, she demonstrated a comfort and security with her own race and deep sense of racial equality. Together they created a home where race talk was a common part of daily life. It is from this place that I have a deep belief that race is discussable—even across race.

My early teachings blossomed at Teachers College, Columbia University, where I found my second family. Robert T. Carter, a race and racial identity scholar, introduced me to theories and research to make sense of my personal experiences and concerns related to race. His steadfast commitment to understanding race, racism, and racial identity taught me that my own intellectual leanings were important and worthy of further pursuit. Being part of Robert's research team also connected me with a group of like-minded people who continue to support me personally and professionally.

The City University of New York has been my intellectual home for over a decade. Hunter College, known for its commitment to diversity in its broadest sense, across race, socioeconomic status, and citizenship, and my colleagues have always been supportive of my research. At The Graduate Center in critical/social personality psychology I am surrounded by a community of scholars and students committed to social justice.

It is not every day that two people from different racial backgrounds and academic disciplines come together to write a book about race. I am immensely thankful to have traveled this road with my coauthor, Erica. Our friendship and collaborative partnership has opened me to new ways of thinking and has been an example of the importance of learning and safety.

Finally, my family is an important source of love, support, and grounding. In my life partner, Merle, I have an ally with whom to talk about race. Her deep knowledge and candor about race as well as her insistence that I challenge myself to go further than I believe I can always inspires me. My daughter,

Cameron, who is vibrant and curious, began to see the world and all its colors at the early age of two. Recently we were on a New York City bus when she made reference to the driver as, "the white bus driver." After noticing the glares from others, then quieting her and suggesting she not include his race, Merle and I looked at each other and realized that she had just had her first lesson about racial norms—we do not talk about race in public. Not fully comfortable with that compromise, I imagine that as a family we will continue searching for ways to challenge those norms.

~ Chapter 1 ~

The Color Bind

The local office of the state's child welfare agency was difficult to find. Although it was located on a busy road, no signs indicated that the office was inside. In fact, the door from the street looked almost like a back entrance, without identification of any kind. Once inside, instead of a lobby, there were just a dark and somewhat dingy set of stairs leading up and a hallway leading to an elevator. The office of the agency was on the third floor.

In one of its conference rooms, a team of eight social workers sat in folding chairs around a long dun-colored folding table. The room was large and light, but spare, with faded gray and tan colors and little decoration save for several posters tacked on the wall. Like those advertised in airline magazines, one proclaimed Teamwork, accompanied by a photo of the Great Wall of China. Another announced Vision and included a picture of a lighthouse by a rocky coastline.

The workers were immersed in a conversation about a particularly challenging case. The members of this family were recent immigrants from West Africa who had witnessed terrible violence because of their country's civil war.[1] The agency was involved in the case because the fourteen-year-old son, living with his grandparents, had become too difficult for them to handle. He was currently at a group facility receiving treatment for posttraumatic stress disorder (PTSD).

One particularly troubling behavior was his tendency to move in very close to others, but the source of the behavior was unclear. Was it culturally informed or a sign of aggression? The lead caseworker, Dave, described what the boy would do. "He'll corner her [the staff person at the group facility]. Get right up into her face. He does that with other people. Did that with me, [with] every one of us in that meeting." His coworker, Chris, wondered about the boy's diagnosis: "Sounds to me like we don't have a lot of information on the kid. What's his evaluation say? To me PTSD is a throw away diagnosis. More going on." Arlo, another team member, agreed, raising the possibility of cultural misunderstanding or stereotyping: "[PTSD is] attached to every kid [that] comes from Africa." Chris built on this: "Culturally, from [West African country], talking close to someone might not be a boundary issue."

Katie, their team leader, picked up this theme, noting that their consulting psychologist had puzzled over the role of culture when doing a psychiatric evaluation: "He was debating [whether to give] him psychosis as part of his diagnosis, because we don't have a full understanding of his culture." "Or what he lived through," noted Katie's supervisor, Harriet. But Dave was resistant to a cultural explanation: "[The boy] is not getting into anyone's face because of cultural reasons, he's getting in people's face[s] to make them feel uncomfortable. No question in my mind." Katie pushed back, suggesting that culture could be at least part of the explanation: "That would be good to at least call [the agency that does cultural evaluations]. I do think understanding the cultural is a piece that's important . . . The more we can become educated." Finally, Carla, another coworker, appealed to Dave on a personal level: "[Dave], the second you got this case you said, 'I know the cultural aspect of this is going to be tremendous, I want to take it as a learning experience.' You could be right, [the boy] could just be trying to get into somebody's face to piss them off. . . . But, in terms of learning more—maybe there's something else there. That it comes from the cultural. Why not, if we can, why not explore? Maybe it will uncover some of those questions." After a pause, Dave concurred: "I agree," he said.

This discussion illustrates a work group wrestling with the role of culture in its work with families. Standing very close to someone could be a sign of hostility, a reaction to trauma, or a cultural norm. In fact, it could be all three. How can they know? The team ultimately recognized the limits of its knowledge and decided to pursue a cultural evaluation to enhance its understanding rather than settle for a simplistic explanation that either anointed culture as the only explanation or fully rejected it. The team's conversation, though, didn't reference only the family's culture. When Katie and Harriet praised his work with the boy, Dave thought his own "very open, animated" way of interacting rooted in his "Italian family" might have played a role. Although brief, the comment illustrates his awareness that he, like his client, is also informed by culture.

This conversation stands out because this work group was able to grapple with the often-challenging topic of culture, something that most workplaces largely avoid. Indeed, as we document in this book, even in the context of a child welfare agency that extolled cultural competence, explicit discussions related to culture were quite rare—and conversations referencing race rarer still. Ample research suggests that most of us shy away from exchanges related to race or culture, particularly in diverse groups, even if we think such topics are important.[2] We feel caught in a *color bind*. This team did not feel those constraints, however. This book explores how its story, and the story of other teams in the same agency, can help us break free of the color bind.

Although our study is based in child protection, analogous conversations might happen in other work contexts in which participants must grapple with the role and weight of race and culture. Policymakers investigate how a proposed public housing regulation preventing convicted felons from living there will have different impacts on black and white tenants because African Americans are so disproportionately ensnared in the criminal justice system. The vice president of human resources and the lead corporate counsel at a large manufacturer wrestle with a recent allegation of racial discrimination. A doctor, nurse, and social worker explore how best to approach a distraught patient in the emergency room, recently emigrated from Indonesia. A professor and her teaching assistants discuss how to teach the achievement gap in education without putting students of color on the defensive. A racially diverse team of field researchers studying a Mexican community checks in every evening to compare notes, including reflections on how their differing backgrounds may shape the way they understand an interaction they observed. Members of corporate teams, brought together from four continents to design and market a new product for a global audience, must learn together how cultural differences can affect how consumers will react.

As the child welfare workers grappled with how to work with the West African family, they reflected—knowingly or not—a larger societal debate about whether, how, and when race, ethnicity, and culture matter. Two basic models of diversity and inclusion contend for influence in the American arena. One is the color-blind approach that emphasizes similarity and assimilation, the dominant model in the United States since the 1960s. Color blindness, informed by a universalistic ideology that presumes a set of broad similarities among all people, argues that race and culture are largely irrelevant and that people should be understood as individuals, not identity-group members.[3] It downplays the existence of current discrimination and racism, seeing them as vestiges of the past. Color blindness is a step in the right direction when compared with slavery, genocide, and outright segregation. Scholars from many fields, however, including sociology, psychology, and education, have delineated how it contributes to searing inequities.[4] Whether driven by a well-meaning desire to do right, an anxious need to evade charged issues, or a hostile animus toward people of color, color blindness ultimately reinforces the current racial hierarchy.[5] Therefore, many call instead for color cognizance, drawing from a culturally particularistic perspective, which combines an awareness of the profound impact of race and ethnicity on individuals and communities, a belief in the richness of racial and cultural heritage, and an acknowledgment of prejudice and discrimination.[6]

Much of this literature aptly addresses the broad currents and institutions in American life that shape these discourses. On the ground, however, these models are enacted by people interacting with other people. Little research examines what enables color cognizance to flourish or even gain a foothold at the micro level—for diverse groups of people to actually engage in color-conscious behavior that includes discussing racial and ethnic differences as a point of strength and addresses these differences in real time.

In fact, in work groups, color cognizance is *hard:* it requires breaking with established ways of thinking; it challenges those who benefit from the status quo, usually those of European descent; and it means talking about things, like race and culture, that are hard to talk about. Above all, perhaps, it demands being willing to make mistakes. Therefore, many of us who believe these issues matter and think they should be addressed are reluctant to do so. In fact, research suggests that members of all racial groups can be apprehensive about such conversations, though for different reasons. Whites are likely to fear that they will say something racist or offensive or will be perceived as doing so, and people of color are worried that they will be the targets of such statements.[7] Because both sets of concerns are credible, we remain caught in the color bind.

This book, based on an intensive investigation of teams in a child welfare agency, builds theory on how we can transcend the color bind, creating work groups that can discuss racial and cultural issues in ways that advance the work and create trusting relationships.

We suggest that several elements are critical, including the team members' individual racial-cultural practices as well as characteristics of the team and its context. That is, we suggest a multilevel model.

Certainly the inclinations of individual team members toward color cognizance are very important. Our findings suggest that not everyone has to agree, but that there must be several members who model what it looks like to enact a color-cognizant practice. Further, it may be particularly helpful to have people of different racial groups acting as models, forming a kind of cross-racial partnership or commitment to color consciousness.

However, those individual predispositions don't exist in a vacuum. They are influenced by the work context in which they are embedded. Work group members exist in a set of nested contexts, including their profession, organization, office, and team. All these are important, but those most proximate to the individuals—the team and the office in which they are located—may hold particular sway. They make up the everyday interactional milieu in which the workers carry out their responsibilities, the location of countless, often mundane encounters that send implicit but decipherable cues about what kinds of thinking and behavior are appropriate and welcome.

Our study suggests that two kinds of environmental messages are especially important. First is the safety of the environment—that is, the extent to which individuals feel they can say what they think and be who they are without risk or sanction. This safety can include a broad sense of "psychological safety"[8] as well as a more particular sense of "identity safety"[9] that makes us feel that our own racial or ethnic identity is welcome in that environment. Second, and possible only in a safe environment, is the extent to which members engage in learning behaviors that voice and integrate disparate points of view, allowing the group to move forward, often in new directions.[10] If group members are able to bridge differences related to fundamental group tasks such as setting direction and specifying roles and responsibilities, they may be more likely to undertake the often more difficult task of exploring how race and culture are implicated in their day-to-day work.

Together, the presence or absence of safety and learning behaviors—in both the team and the office—are the foundational features of an *intergroup incubator,* a kind of hatchery. By *intergroup* we refer to the relationships between different racial and ethnic groups. Instead of brooding eggs, therefore, this incubator acts on the team members' individual racial-cultural practices, ultimately determining whether color-conscious leanings are cultivated into a fuller color-cognizant team practice or suppressed, creating a group-level color-blind approach.

Therefore, fundamentally, whether a group delves into race and ethnicity depends as much on its broader dynamics as it does on aspects that could be seen as more obviously race- or culture-related. A team's racial-cultural practice is fully bound up with its larger way of acting in the world.

These micro-level dynamics can get lost in the broader struggle for a more just and equitable society, but they are essential cornerstones of that campaign. As we know, "wicked problems" demand working across a variety of disciplinary, organizational, and sectoral boundaries.[11] But they also require the acumen and expertise of people from a variety of racial and ethnic backgrounds.[12] Whether we make policy, advocate for social change, create useful products, conduct research, or provide frontline care to people and their communities, we have to not only call for an approach that takes race and ethnicity into account, but be able to enact that every day with our coworkers, clients, and customers. That enactment can't happen unless we talk about the impact of race on our work and our collegial relationships—and those conversations can't happen without an environment that members of all groups find safe and open to learning.

Our Own Talking and Learning: The Authors as an Interracial Team

As an interracial team of scholars—Erica is white, Tamara is African American—we live much of what we write about in this book. Just as these child welfare workers had to make sense of the role of race and ethnicity in their work, just as they had to decide whether and when to raise issues, just as they had to negotiate relationships with colleagues from backgrounds different from their own, we have to as well.

In many ways, we've broken out of the color bind. We are both committed to color cognizance and to talking about race; indeed, teaching and writing about race are not only a professional responsibility, but a reflection of our personal identity. Yet we had to work through a variety of race-related challenges and dilemmas, including those when we had to overcome a desire to suppress, rather than engage, conflict. We have chosen to write about our practice, briefly here and at greater length in chapter 8, to show that we are subject to the same dynamics we see in others and to attempt the openness that we believe is so critical for learning.

One central dilemma dogged us in our writing, though it took us two book-length drafts before we were able to name and face it. This is odd, because it is fundamentally about our own learning orientation as we wrote this book. We think of this as the dilemma of probity versus generosity.

This dilemma faces many scholars in different forms, but for us it began with color blindness. How should we deal with color blindness? Inspired by probity and rectitude, we would condemn it by pointing out that color blindness, at best, overlooks the impact, value, and richness of race and ethnicity and, at worst, provides a seemingly neutral cover for racism. Motivated by empathy and generosity, we would seek to understand color blindness by exploring the anxieties and confusions that animate the lived experience of race. In fact, we, Tamara and Erica, oscillated between these poles as we wrote this book and even changed roles multiple times, one of us holding probity while the other affirmed empathy and then reversing our positions. As we equivocated, we sometimes criticized ourselves or each other for, on the one hand, not being righteous or scrupulous enough or, on the other, being too severe and judgmental.

It wasn't until we explicitly surfaced the dilemma for ourselves, as we began the third draft, that we saw how we were standing in the way of our learning. Holding, or living with, the tension—rather than judging ourselves for being unable to resolve it—allowed us to see the critical distinction between motivation and consequences or intent and impact.[13] Whatever the motivation for color blindness, however well-intentioned, its consequences are troubling, often devastating. That means we need probity: without the integrity of honest naming, we obscure the impact of color blindness—which prevents awareness and learning. But condemning people who hold color-blind views—whether out of racism, anxiety, confusion, or, most likely, some combination—provides no inducement to growth and development. And, honestly, we are not always righteous ourselves. That's where empathy and generosity come in.

Therefore we have done our best to live with the dilemma as we write about the social workers in this study. We have relatively little data about their intentions, so we try to make generous inferences and give them the benefit of the doubt. Also, because we explore the effects of context at length, we make the point over and over that beliefs and actions are not solely individual creations, but strongly shaped by their environment as well. At the same time, we do not shy away from naming the impact of the workers' beliefs and actions on their team and its work together. We also don't hold ourselves above scrutiny: in chapter 8, we explore times in the writing when we fell short of our ideals and the consequences of those choices.

The Structure of Our Argument

The following chapters bring our study to life, by embedding it in current debates in sociology, psychology, and other fields, by presenting more details about the professional and organizational context of the research as well as our methods, and then by providing extensive, qualitative data from the team members, their superiors, and their meetings about their approach to race and ethnicity.

The next chapter, chapter 2, connects our study with several related cross-disciplinary conversations and describes our research context and methods. We begin with a review of prior research on the models or discourses of color blindness and color cognizance.[14] Work in psychology and sociology names these as the two dominant approaches in the United States today and delves into their impact on individuals, groups, and society as a whole. Perhaps counterintuitively, given the broad dissemination and appeal of color blindness, work across disciplines suggests that color cognizance brings with it a variety of positive consequences, and that color blindness has much more troublesome implications. However, we also know from significant streams of research that a color-cognizant approach is very difficult for a work group to actually manifest. It's unclear what it would actually look like because there are few models; it undermines those in a more dominant position because it brings attention to the very existence of a racial hierarchy, and it requires conversations about the largely taboo topics of race, ethnicity, and culture. Extensive research on diverse teams, however, found in the psychology, organizations, and management literatures, suggests two primary elements that might enable its enactment: safety—or the degree to which members feel safe, comfortable, and welcome—and learning behaviors—the extent to which they are capable of both offering diverse perspectives and knitting them together to form a more complex and elaborated understanding.

The chapter continues with a picture of the professional and organizational contexts of the study. We review the debates within social work and child welfare about the role of race and culture. We then portray the child welfare agency in which the research took place, describing its commissioner and his priorities, change efforts going on at the time, and its particular emphasis on cultural competence. We describe the agency's experiment, involving seven teams, with using a team approach to engaging with families. We end with a summary of our research methodology, designed to build theory on how work groups can overcome the color bind. Data collection included team interviews (interviewing the team as a whole) at three points over about two and a half years as well as interviews with team supervisors and stakeholders.

For four of the seven teams, dubbed in-depth teams, it also included three rounds of individual interviews with all team members and observation of team meetings about every other month. As an intensive, qualitative, longitudinal investigation of seven teams, it explores and documents the complexity of how color blindness and color cognizance are actually lived on the ground rather than simply captured in one-time interviews, surveys, or lab studies. Moreover, these teams embody a broad range of approaches to racial-cultural practice, from color cognizance to virtual silence to a real hostility toward organizational policies that promoted racial and cultural awareness. Therefore, they have a larger story to tell.

Chapters 3 through 7 present the empirical findings of the study. Chapter 3 targets the individual level, providing an in-depth and layered illustration of how color blindness and color cognizance are actually performed day-to-day in the context of one particular profession. It draws on data from participants in all seven teams to illustrate how they individually conceptualized whether and how to use a racial and cultural lens in their work. Three questions guide the discussion: whether workers should engage with families differently based on their race or ethnicity, whether workers should draw on their own racial or cultural backgrounds, and whether workers and clients should be matched by race or ethnicity. We document the variety of their sensemaking, including whether workers see race and culture as constraints or taints to expunge or sources of insight and expertise. We also make a distinction between cultural cognizance, which attends to cultural differences only when working with recent immigrant families, and full color cognizance, which attends to the impact of race and ethnicity more broadly, including African American and white families who have been in the United States for generations. Finally, we draw attention to a phenomenon we call color minimization, a way to characterize the contradictions we often saw participants express. Color minimization constitutes a nod to the importance of race and culture, accompanied by a de-emphasis of them.

We move to the team level in chapters 4, 5, 6, and 7, focusing on three of the four in-depth teams as exemplars of different approaches to addressing race and ethnicity at work. In each chapter, we provide a detailed portrait of one of the three teams. We begin by describing the team's racial-cultural practice, drawn from observing its meetings. This data allowed us to determine how often and how intensively its members discussed issues related to race and ethnicity regarding their cases, their team dynamics, and their office context. Then each chapter investigates multilevel explanations for their particular practice.

This begins with descriptions of individual team members and their singular approaches, including the extent to which they acknowledged the impact of their racial or cultural heritage on their work and the degree to which they adapted their professional approach to work with families from varied backgrounds. This data comes largely from individual interviews. Each chapter continues by describing key features of the team context, drawing on individual and team interviews as well as team-meeting observations. It illustrates the team's learning behaviors, including whether it was able to constructively engage conflict, experiment, and reflect on its work. We then look at whether members felt generally safe and welcome on their team, including whether they felt their racial or cultural identity put them at risk or disadvantage. We also introduce relevant data from their office, including the degree of conflict, especially cross-racial conflict. Altogether, we conceptualize the team and office context as an incubator that, acting on individual leanings, ultimately results in teams taking up or avoiding racial and cultural issues.

In chapter 4, we paint a picture of Team North, the only color-cognizant team, which used a racial and cultural lens as a diagnostic tool to help them understand the challenges facing their cases and themselves as a group. We begin by describing the team's racial-cultural practice. We continue by suggesting the characteristics that enabled its color cognizance: the color-conscious approaches of individual members of the team as well as the learning orientation and relatively safe climate that defined the intergroup incubator.

A portrayal of Team East makes up chapter 5. We characterize Team East's racial-cultural practice as *color evasive* because though most individual members manifested not only interest but significant knowledge and skill in addressing race and ethnicity, the team as a whole largely evaded any such discussions.[15] Given the individual expertise on the team, the toxic team and office context seems to be the primary culprit in explaining why the team suppressed conversations related to race and culture.

The third team, Team South, was *color hostile,* as we describe in chapter 6. Its members mostly avoided discussions of race and ethnicity, but the conversations they did have sometimes revealed an animus to affirmative action and the agency's internal caucus for people of color. Its individual members described their practice as color blind, in contrast to the members of Teams North and East, which likely provides part of the explanation for their practice. But features of their incubator—a contradictory one that was learning-oriented in some ways but not in others and safe for many team members but not all—are also implicated.

Chapter 7 provides a schematic, multilevel model, induced from the team-based analyses, which brings together the elements and their interrelationships that can cultivate color-cognizant practice within work groups. The model suggests that the intergroup incubator acts on individual members' racial-cultural practices to produce different configurations of roles and relationships on the team, which then lead to the team's racial-cultural practice. We look at the roles of the team leaders as well as specific team members who seemed to have outsized influence on whether and how the team discusses race and ethnicity. Regarding relationships, we characterize the overall cohesion, or lack of it, within each team.

Chapter 8 explores the role of ambivalence and inconsistency in racial-cultural practice. Despite clear differences among the teams that enabled us to characterize them as more or less color cognizant, contradictions were rife among study participants. To deepen our examination, we discuss inconsistencies found in two of the teams. Team North delved further into race than any other team, but its members sometimes made insensitive comments and appeared to engage in stereotypes. However, we suggest that flawless conversations about race are impossible and that often that very expectation shuts down discussion entirely. Instead we suggest that Team North is a model of the contradictions that inevitably animate how we grapple with these issues. Team South's hostility to bringing race and culture into its work was palpable. Yet its members were seen as a team that engaged in a strength-based practice dedicated to working with parents to keep their children in the home, removing them only when all other avenues had been explored. One case, which the team and two observers described at length, showed a determination to avoid automatically blaming parents. We suggest that this mindset could perhaps be an opening to reflection on the team's stance on racial and cultural differences.

With these examples in mind, we also discuss some of the conflicts and contradictions the two of us encountered while working as an interracial team to interpret the data and write this book. Although ultimately we came to agreement about the argument presented here, we often disagreed along the way, sometimes heatedly. We share some of those battles to showcase our flaws and inconsistencies. We also use them to illustrate some of the bumps we encountered in our color-cognizant practice and how we worked through them—acknowledging that some are not fully resolved.

Finally, chapter 9 summarizes how our work contributes to both research and practice. First, we add an exploration of team-level dynamics to the continuing scholarly discussion of color blindness and color cognizance in macro fields such as sociology and political science. These literatures often call for racial and cultural awareness, but they often overlook the micro-interactions that would enable this approach to gain a foothold in a given environment. Moreover, we note that this work has explored the impact of these discourses on schools, communities, and participants in lab experiments, but paid little attention to the workplace. Second, research in clinical fields could be enriched by our examination of small groups, given that their work on cultural competence has focused largely on the individual and the organizational context. Finally, we further the management and psychology literatures on diverse teams by undertaking a longitudinal, ethnographic exploration of their dynamics. The quantitative orientation of most team diversity research has enabled cross-study comparison and some accumulation of knowledge, but has its limitations. In particular, while we know that certain characteristics seem to have an impact, we know much less about what these elements actually look like in the day-to-day lives of team members, or about how these various characteristics intertwine and play out in relation to each other.

We also elaborate in chapter 9 the implications for how groups and organizations can cultivate color-cognizant practice. We encourage practitioners to work at multiple levels—individual, team, and organizational. We point to the importance of leadership in modeling how everyone can take race and culture into account. We also discuss approaches to training that we think could be more fruitful than standard diversity workshops found in many contexts. We end by suggesting that a trade-off between unity and diversity isn't needed; rather, it is possible to attain a unity through diversity, a cohesion that is all the stronger for having been forged from difference.

Color Cognizance as an Achievement: Overcoming the Odds

The fundamental premise of this book is that color-cognizant practice is an *achievement*.[16] The odds are stacked against a group of employees trying to create a way of working that recognizes and understands the complex, nuanced, sometimes obscure and murky but nonetheless vital role of race and ethnicity. Yet teams and organizations in myriad contexts face challenges that require such explorations. We offer this book as a way to both herald and understand that achievement.

~ Chapter 2 ~

Achieving Color Cognizance

"Some people say there is too much talk about race and racism in the United States. I say that there is not enough."

—Tatum 1997, 193.

In the spring of 2010, CNN's website showcased the headline "Kids' test answers on race brings mother to tears." An accompanying video shows a five-year-old white girl looking at five views of the same face in increasingly darker skin tones. She chooses a light-skinned face when asked who the smart child is. She selects a darker-skinned face to indicate the mean child. "As she answers, her mother watches, and gently weeps," the article went on to report.

The article accompanied the results of a study, reported by anchor Anderson Cooper, of racial attitudes among black and white schoolchildren living outside New York City and outside Atlanta. The study showed that white students were more likely than black students to select "lighter skin tones" when indicating "positive attitudes and beliefs, social preferences and color preferences." They were also more likely to select "darker skin tones" for the "dumb, mean, bad and ugly" child.[1] The study results are disturbing but not surprising: much research shows that even young children have absorbed racist attitudes.[2] For our purposes, what matters is that the mother said she had never discussed these issues with her daughter, though watching her child participate in the study did prompt her to do so. In fact, one study showed that almost half of all parents, across racial groups, never or almost never discuss race with their children, though parents of color were significantly more likely to do so.[3] Another study showed only 10 percent of white parents who explicitly agreed to speak to their child about race as part of a research project actually did so.[4]

Many Americans, particularly white Americans, are reluctant to talk about race and ethnicity. This example comes from a family but could just as easily come from a workplace, a community meeting, or a place of worship.

We are particularly hesitant to talk about race, though conversations about ethnicity can also be uncomfortable.[5] Further, we are especially frightened of talking about race and culture in demographically diverse groups. It is much easier to talk about race in same-race groups.[6] Moreover, we are referring to explicit conversations about race and ethnicity. In fact, Americans talk about race all the time but usually through code and allusion. Although the apparent topic may be an upcoming election, a colleague's work style, or a music video, race or culture is often an unspoken subtext. Some Americans of all racial groups, particularly people of color, are willing to engage in direct, frank conversations about race and ethnicity in diverse groups, but they are relatively few and such discussions are rare.[7]

This reluctance to talk about race is widespread despite many exhortations. In the wake of the verdict finding George Zimmerman innocent in the shooting death of young, black man Trayvon Martin, Barack Obama encouraged conversations about race, including informal discussions in "families and churches and workplaces." He's not alone. Eric Holder, the nation's first black attorney general, took us to task: "We, average Americans, simply do not talk to each other enough about race. . . . If we are to make progress in this area, we must feel comfortable enough with each other, and tolerant enough of each other, to have frank conversations about the racial matters that continue to divide us."[8] President Clinton launched an Initiative on Race in 1997, which included spurring community conversations on race; many colleges and universities have programs that bring together students from diverse backgrounds to talk about the issue;[9] a number of scholars have also called for interracial conversations about race.[10] Yet we Americans still largely avoid these conversations.

Talking about race and ethnicity is related to color blindness and color cognizance. Color blindness has two elements: a belief that "we're all the same under the skin" in the ubiquitous phrase and that therefore race and ethnicity are largely irrelevant, and another belief that racism and discrimination are uncommon vestiges of the past.[11] A corollary of both assumptions is that talking about race is unnecessary. Color cognizance, on the other hand, is a belief in the importance of racial and ethnic differences because of their profound impact on individuals, groups, communities, and societies, accompanied by an acknowledgement of widespread racism and discrimination.[12] Talking about race and ethnicity, therefore, is essential.[13] As noted, most of us—color blind or color conscious—regularly talk about race in code. To have explicit, productive conversations about race generally, however, requires color cognizance.

The causal arrow may go in the opposite direction as well. Not only would color-blind beliefs lead to less interest in talking about race, a fear of talking about race could also lead to a kind of default color blindness. Given that many Americans want to bypass such conversations altogether, color blindness provides a ready and convenient justification: race and ethnicity don't matter anyway.[14] For many, color blindness may simply seem like a way to keep us safe, protected from encountering or confronting a charged and contentious arena. Ultimately, it's not surprising that color blindness has such a hold on the American psyche: not only is it what many of us are taught, it helps us skirt difficult conversations. That's why color cognizance is such an achievement.

In this chapter, we explore both color cognizance and color blindness in greater depth. We begin, after a brief discussion of terminology, by establishing these approaches as the two competing models or ideologies regarding difference and inclusion present in the United States today, with color blindness as dominant. We then draw on a variety of literatures to show the detrimental consequences of color blindness, despite the appeal of its apparent neutrality. We also demonstrate the benefits of color cognizance. However, we then make the case that enacting color cognizance, particularly in work groups, could be tough. We use the extensive literature on diverse teams and intergroup relations to elaborate what we know about group dynamics and what might be required for teams to overcome the hurdles to addressing race and ethnicity in everyday conversations. We end the chapter with a description of our research context, a state child welfare agency, and how we collected and analyzed our data.

The illusion is that we should not see or discuss race because it is too dangerous: it invokes guilt, anger, shame, sorrow, and fear. Our response is that we must talk about race and that it is possible to do so readily and productively.

Definitions and Terminology

Any investigation of this territory requires attention to terminology. Four terms—*race, ethnicity, culture,* and *color*—are commonly used. Although these four concepts are analytically distinct and meaningful, in practice they are often used interchangeably. Here we note how we are defining each of the terms and the decisions we have made regarding our terminology.

We define race as "a human group defined by itself or others as distinct by virtue of perceived common physical characteristics that are held to be inherent."[15] The physical traits and characteristics that are often included when making racial distinctions include skin color, phenotype, and hair texture.[16]

Even though physiological features are used as the basis for making racial distinctions, those features do not reflect significant genetic differences.[17] Therefore, though race was once presumed to have a biological basis, it is now understood to be a value-laden social construction.[18] It is likely to remain an important concept in the United States because it has significant power as a social category, serving as "a basis of social action, a foundation of government policy, and often a justification for distinctive treatment of one group by another."[19]

For our present purposes, we include the following racial groups: white, black, Asian, Hispanic or Latino, and Native American. People who identify as Hispanic or Latino may be of any race. However, in the United States they are often treated as a racial group, because ethnic distinctions tend to be over-shadowed by race[20] and because language is sometimes used as a racial marker.[21] In fact, analyses of the 2000 census show that the large majority of those choosing "other" for their racial category chose Hispanic or Latino as their ethnic group.[22] Therefore we do treat Latinos as a racial group. Whenever possible, however, we include an ethnic distinction rather than simply designating a racial category.

The construct of ethnicity is explicitly linked to our forebears. We under-stand ethnicity as "the national, regional or tribal origins of one's oldest remembered ancestors and the customs, traditions and rituals handed down by those ancestors."[23] Ethnicity is not the same thing as culture, though they are often conflated.

Culture is made up of the traditions, ways of living, values, norms, and beliefs shared by a group of people.[24] Culture is often the enactment of race and ethnicity, though not always. A person may choose to adopt a set of traditions and values that are distinct from his or her racial and ethnic heritage. Moreover, a person's culture may also be influenced by other dimensions of identity, such as age or sexual orientation.

Color, or skin complexion, often defines how a person is categorized and treated,[25] particularly when ethnic distinctions are unclear. Several studies have suggested that bias is triggered more by skin color than other physi-ological features.[26] While color is a marker of race, members of the same racial group can vary in skin tone, and people from different racial groups can have the same shade of skin color. Therefore, color and race are analytically distinct.

We use the term *color* for the two basic competing models of diversity and inclusion because of the ubiquity of the term color blind. It is the inevitable starting point. We also use it because it captures race as well as ethnicity and culture, which allows us to make a distinction between cultural cognizance in which people attend to culture and ethnicity among recently arrived immi-grants and a full color cognizance that acknowledges the importance of race itself, which is often downplayed.

Terminology

We use a variety of approaches and terminology depending on the distinctions that are most relevant for a given context and argument. At times we note differ-ences among broadly defined groups; for example, we often make a fundamental distinction between whites and people of color, treating people of color as a single group.[27] While we recognize that differences among people of African, Asian, and Latino descent are manifold, members of all these groups are gener-ally at a structural disadvantage when compared with whites.

At other times, our language needs to be more specific. Where necessary, we use the appropriate term, for example, ethnicity as opposed to race. Wherever possible, we also state a particular country of origin, such as Polish or Mexican, rather than a broad ethnic or racial group, such as white or Latino. However, to camouflage the identities of client families, we sometimes avoid naming a particular ethnicity or country of origin. We use African American to describe only those Americans of African descent whose ancestors arrived generations ago, almost all as part of the slave trade. We use black to refer more broadly to people of African descent whose more immediate ancestors are from countries in Latin America or the Caribbean.

When we speak broadly regarding issues related to race, ethnicity, and culture and for those times when it is impossible to determine whether race, ethnicity, culture, or some combination is in play, we use the terms *racial-cultural* or *race and ethnicity* or *race and culture*. We describe how individuals and teams do or don't take up dynamics related to race, ethnicity, and culture as their *racial-cultural practice*.

We often struggle with where and how often to provide a specific individual's racial or cultural identity. The first time we introduce someone, we generally make his or her race known, but debate at other points whether to continue to do so. Always providing racial or cultural identifiers feels repetitive and heavy-handed; not doing so could suggest that race or ethnicity doesn't matter. Ultimately, we use the particular context to guide us, recognizing that others might make different choices.

Finally, we are also aware, as intersectionality scholars have made clear, that race and ethnicity are not stand-alone constructs that have influence independent of the many other elements by which individuals are shaped and constructed, such as gender, class, sexual orientation, and religion.[28] A more comprehensive approach would be to explore all of these elements and how they are intertwined. However, such an investigation is beyond the scope of this book, for two reasons.

First, we feel an emphasis on race and ethnicity is particularly important because they make up such a charged and difficult terrain in the United States. Race in particular is largely a taboo topic in workplaces.[29] For two decades now, work organizations have been using the term *diversity* and moving away from identifying race and ethnicity in particular. Positive reasons for this terminology aside—in particular, the wide variety of differences that influence organizational dynamics—it has also had the effect of downplaying and shifting attention away from the role and impact of race and ethnicity in the workplace. Second, race has the greatest impact on life chances and opportunities: it is often the best predictor of wealth, education, health, housing, employment, and other important measures of well-being. Therefore, we very deliberately spotlight race and ethnicity in response to this trend. However, at times issues related to gender, class, religion, and sexual orientation arose in the data and we do bring in those topics when they impinge on racial and cultural dynamics in the teams.

Color Blindness and Color Cognizance

An extensive body of research in sociology, political science, psychology, education, and other fields has sought to document and understand the different ways that Americans make sense of race and ethnicity by examining models, discourses, or ideologies related to cultural diversity.[30] The large majority of this work compares color blindness with some version of color awareness, also called multiculturalism.[31]

The Perils of Color Blindness

The scholarly literature largely asserts that color blindness is the dominant model in the United States today, though the reasons for the dominance are varied. Some point out that color blindness is critical to maintaining the racial hierarchy and therefore serves the interests of whites, as individuals and as a group, by protecting their privilege.[32] Others argue that color blindness arises from fear and anxiety about race and that it provides legitimacy and cover for avoidance.[33]

Regardless of its intent, much of this work also details the often destructive consequences of color blindness. Many begin by pointing out that color blindness is literally impossible—of course we see color.[34] In fact, Stephen Colbert, the political satirist who plays a right-wing ideologue on television, sets this up beautifully: when speaking with guests about issues related to race, he will often ask them what color they are since, as he says, he is color blind and therefore can't tell. Research using brain scans shows that we appear to automatically categorize by race.[35]

Beyond its unlikelihood, many have exposed how color blindness, despite its claims of neutrality, actually leads to a variety of adverse outcomes. "Color blindness, though widely touted as the solution, is actually the problem," writes Michelle Alexander in her devastating critique of the criminal justice system, *The New Jim Crow*.[36] Because color blindness provides a powerful rationale for ignoring race and ethnicity and, therefore, obscuring inequity, racism, and ethnocentrism, both individuals and collectivities suffer unfortunate consequences.

First, color blindness sends the message that facets of identity that may be crucial to one's sense of self are, in fact, unimportant. Because racial and ethnic identities are usually more central to people of color, this dismissal disproportionately affects them. Being forced to give up a valued social identity can be perceived as a threat.[37] In fact, lab studies show that color-blind whites were perceived by blacks as more prejudiced[38] and less friendly.[39] Second, by suggesting not only that race is unimportant but that it literally should not be seen or acknowledged, color blindness suggests that race is bad, it's a problem. Because whites are generally seen as race-less, the negativity of race becomes associated only with people of color. "'Color,' which here means nonwhiteness, is bad in and of itself."[40]

Third, color blindness has the effect of framing whites as the norm or standard and whiteness as neutral. Because whites are members of the dominant identity group in the United States, they are "less likely to be reminded of social and cultural differences on a day-to-day basis."[41] Therefore, they are less likely to view their race or ethnicity as salient or important, instead taking it for granted. With whiteness as the "normalized center,"[42] race is located purely in nonwhites, who are again stigmatized by being nonstandard—literally not normal.

Moreover, framing whites as the neutral standard requires everyone else to imitate them. The neutrality of whiteness makes it aspirational, serving as the "unnamed, universal moral referent" by which all others are evaluated and found wanting.[43] Despite the positive imagery of the melting pot, "little or nothing in the cultures of the groups being invited to join the American mainstream is presumed worthy of preserving."[44] Moreover, those who name this dynamic and call for equality are vilified and seen as divisive or politically correct.[45]

Finally, color blindness gives cover to outright bias and racism that preserves white racial advantage. It is in the self-interest of whites to de-emphasize race and emphasize similarity because doing so obscures differences related to our racial hierarchy.[46] Color blindness, as a "legitimizing ideology,"[47] helps reproduce the racial order. "Privilege has the semblance of naturalness that in itself defends it from scrutiny."[48]

Alexander applies this understanding to her critique of the criminal justice system. She notes that the ostensible color blindness of the system obscures the basic fact that roughly 90 percent of prisoners in the United States are black and Latino. Because, in theory, individuals are locked up not because of their race but because they have committed some kind of crime, the shocking disproportionality of the prison population is seen as justified. Alexander notes, provocatively but convincingly, that the relatively small white prison population (about 10 percent) is needed to support the contention that the system is color blind. If 100 percent of prisoners were African American or Latino, the situation would not be tolerated. So whites in the system are "collateral damage;" it is necessary to imprison some whites to ensure that the entire system stays in place. Alexander points out that we are not blind to race but instead to what she calls racial caste or a racial hierarchy.[49]

Another way that color blindness helps preserve racial caste is to enable whites' assertions that they are the victims of discrimination. If our national norms call for full neutrality, then whites could just as easily suffer racism as people of color. In fact, affirmative action, a form of color cognizance designed to repair the damage done by centuries of slavery and segregation, has itself been framed as a form of racism, often called reverse racism, out of tune with American ideals. These critics have been devastatingly effective. The beneficiaries of affirmative action have paid the price as it continues to lose legal and political favor.

Ultimately, then, color blindness preserves the status quo. By dismissing the importance of racial categories, it can be used—both deliberately and unconsciously—as a tool to maintain the current racial order. It benefits particular interests by justifying silence about race, by rationalizing "colormuteness."[50]

Because these processes are largely invisible, many who champion color blindness are unaware of the consequences of their stance. They claim to be color blind not because of an explicit allegiance to white supremacy but because they believe it leads to neutrality and nondiscrimination. They believe they are doing the right thing. Regardless of their motivation, however, the consequences for people of color are real and grim.

It's important to note, though, that color blindness damages not only individuals and communities of color. Yes, whites benefit from the racial hierarchy that color blindness helps maintain. Color blindness also makes it easier to avoid conversations that could be charged and bitter. Whites also incur losses, however. First, color blindness prevents learning and discovery across difference. It arrests the curiosity and wonder that can come from exploring what makes us human and what makes us unique. Second, color blindness inhibits the capacity of whites to truly understand who they are and the influences that shape them. Finally, it can impede their interactions with those from other backgrounds. Many whites say they try to be color blind in order to not offend people of color, but remain unaware of how they may be slighting others all the time—by their silence or by implicit assumptions that sting even if they go unstated. "In situations where race is potentially relevant, whites who think that avoiding race altogether will shield them from being perceived as biased should think again."[51] Ultimately, color blindness can forestall deep and authentic relationships between whites and people of color: "[Such a] connection depends on frankness, and a willingness to talk openly about issues of race."[52]

The alternative—for whites and people of color—is to very deliberately *see* race, to be color cognizant, which brings a variety of advantages for individuals and groups from all backgrounds.

The Benefits of Color Cognizance

As we note, although we all notice race and ethnicity, many of us deny their influence. Color cognizance explicitly recognizes the impact of race and culture as well as the presence and import of racism. It is marked by our self-awareness of our own racial and ethnic categorization and identification and their consequences, and is an acknowledgment of race as a defining element of American society. "Race is present in every institution, every relationship, every individual . . . we are compelled to think racially, to use the racial categories and meaning systems into which we have been socialized."[53]

At the broadest level, we have to acknowledge and discuss race and ethnicity because only then can we know the full extent of societal inequities fueled by these differences—and only then can we garner the insight and commitment to fight for a more just society.[54] Recognizing race also has a variety of more specific benefits, to individuals, groups, and organizations, as well.

Most fundamentally, it demonstrates that racial and ethnic group membership can be a source of strength and pride, rather than something to downplay or ignore. A recent meta-analysis found that strong ethnic identification was more strongly related to positive well-being than to compromised well-being. This relationship held true regardless of participants' race, gender, or socioeconomic status.[55] Other work on individual racial identity development shows that earlier stages of identity development, which minimize the importance of race—similar to a color-blind stance—have been linked to lower self-esteem and other measures of well-being, whereas later stages that recognize the importance of race predict higher psychological well-being[56] and pro-social attitudes,[57] and less bias[58] and less in-group favoritism.[59]

Similarly, research on groups and teams has found that color- or identity-conscious approaches generally have better outcomes than color- or identity-blind models.[60] This research has found that, under certain conditions, groups with pro-diversity beliefs outperform groups with pro-similarity beliefs[61] and tend to have higher group identification.[62]

Other research has gone beyond team-level findings to look at organizations more broadly. Both experimental and field studies have shown that workers of color experience greater comfort, trust, and engagement when their employer and their own work colleagues evidence a multicultural approach.[63] Companies with identity-conscious human resource management practices—such as deliberate recruiting of members of protected groups, interest groups for people of color, and diversity training—had higher percentages of people of color in management than companies with fewer of these practices.[64]

Finally, work in clinical fields—including social work, psychology, and medicine—argues for a color-cognizant approach, often under the rubric of cultural competence in clinical practice. This interest is rooted in a growing recognition of racial health disparities deriving in part from clinicians' biases or prejudices that result in suboptimum care for their clients or patients of color.[65] In one study, implicit bias predicted whether black patients received the appropriate standard of care compared with white patients with the same symptoms of a heart attack.[66] In psychiatry, evidence shows that Latinos sometimes receive older medications with simpler dosing regimens because they are seen as more resistant to taking medication,[67] and that black patients are more likely than whites to be misdiagnosed with a severe mental illness such as schizophrenia.[68] Child protection itself, the context of our study, has been a frequent target of criticism: disproportionality or the overrepresentation of children of color in the child welfare system and foster care has been well documented.[69]

In response, researchers in clinical fields have developed research-based approaches to culturally competent care. The field of counseling psychology has perhaps the most well-developed literature in this area: cultural competence is part of a broader multicultural movement often referred to as psychology's "fourth force."[70] This movement has taken an ecological approach that places racial, cultural, political, economic, and historical factors at the center of theory development, research, and clinical practice. A similar awareness has been growing in social work[71] and medicine.[72]

Several fields have developed lists of competencies associated with a practice that is attentive to race, ethnicity, and culture. They specify three broad areas of competence: providers' awareness of their assumptions, values, and biases; an understanding of their clients' race and culture, without resorting to stereotypes; and skill in determining and implementing appropriate interventions.[73] Given that deep knowledge of other cultures is rare, some work notes the particular importance of a self-awareness and even "cultural humility" that enables individuals to observe their responses and adopt an inquiring stance with clients.[74]

A growing body of research shows that these approaches improve clinical outcomes, primarily for persons of color. Therapists who broached racial topics, irrespective of their race, created a stronger therapeutic alliance and were rated by their clients of color as racially responsive and more credible, which could lengthen duration of treatment.[75] A study of outpatient substance abuse treatment programs found that clinicians' culturally sensitive beliefs led to better outcomes for their Latino and African American clients.[76]

Across fields, then, we see growing evidence for the benefits—in clinical practice, workplaces, and other settings—of a color-cognizant approach. However, these benefits may be obscured by incorrect assumptions regarding color cognizance. Therefore, we feel the need to dispel some of these commonly held beliefs.

What Color Cognizance Is Not

It is important to clarify what color cognizance is not. First, some assume that color cognizance means matching or concordance, whatever that means in a given context—pairing a clinician and client, or sales clerk and customer, or supervisor and supervisee on the basis of similar racial or ethnic backgrounds. Although matching may make sense in some circumstances, it should not be the default assumption. In fact, as others have pointed out, some patients in therapeutic settings would prefer working with someone from a different background than their own.[77] However, being sensitive to this preference is just as color cognizant as being sensitive to preferences for a same-race provider—in both cases, race or ethnicity is being taken into account, though they result in different client-provider dyads.

Second, some believe that color cognizance grows out of a reductionist approach that oversimplifies highly complex individuals. We have seen no one argue that race and ethnicity should always take precedence over other considerations when thinking through how to work with clients or customers or coworkers. Cultural dynamics will certainly at times seem less relevant or less important in understanding how to proceed in a given situation. We can't, however, even figure out whether attention to cultural issues is warranted if we start out with a color-blind perspective that presumes it is not. To discern whether race or ethnicity might be in play requires that one be attuned to them, to be open to that possibility. Only a color-cognizant perspective allows people to learn when race and culture matter more and when they matter less— or perhaps, in some instances, not at all.

Third, and building on this point, color cognizance is not the same thing as cultural competence. Recognizing the importance of race and ethnicity and trying to keep them in mind when working with others doesn't automatically mean doing so with full knowledge or skill. In fact, color cognizance can involve drawing on simplistic generalizations or stereotypes. However, motivated by color awareness, at least the issues can be raised and discussed. A coworker who disagrees with how a teammate has characterized a particular ethnic group can respond, potentially prompting a conversation from which both could learn. All of us draw on stereotypes of other groups as we go about our daily tasks, but since they rarely get aired or debated, they just further calcify.

Finally, some presume that attention to race and culture will be used to promote a cultural relativism—to explain away very real problems because they are simply a reflection of race or ethnicity and therefore can be disregarded. For example, in the child welfare context, a mother could claim that a disciplinary technique was widely accepted in her culture and therefore unproblematic. A color-cognizant approach, however, would neither dismiss the claim nor accept it at face value; it would simply motivate investigation. If a form of punishment does appear to have a cultural basis, that knowledge can help the provider talk with the client about other approaches that are more appropriate for the particular societal context.

Breaking the Silence About Race

With further clarity about what color cognizance is not, we turn back to its benefits. Taken altogether, the multidisciplinary body of work on multiculturalism and color cognizance suggests that—even if it were possible—it is not preferable to be color blind. Yet its grip on the American psyche remains fierce. This is not surprising. As we've documented here, color blindness is a valuable tool because it reinforces the current racial hierarchy by obscuring advantage and disadvantage. It also provides ample justification for avoiding the topic altogether.

That does not have to be the whole story, however. Numerous people of all backgrounds genuinely find difference compelling and want to draw on race, ethnicity, and culture as sources of insight and expertise. Many are stymied, though, because engaging difference is difficult. It's hard because it's new, so people don't have models for how to do it. It's hard because it's rare, so people think it must be wrong. It's hard because it involves change, which is always difficult, no matter what issues are involved. And it's hard because it involves talking about racial and cultural differences in cross-racial groups.[78] Indeed, proponents of color blindness have effectively made the case that any mention of race or culture is itself bigoted, that "every invocation of racial invocation . . . is suspect."[79] No wonder we keep quiet.

It may be particularly important to break the silence about race in the workplace. Workplaces are one location in which people of different racial and cultural backgrounds often encounter each other, because neighborhoods, schools, and places of worship remain largely segregated.[80] Moreover, an ample literature shows that workplaces are one of the greatest contributors to inequality.[81]

Talking about race at work may also be especially difficult. At the executive level, organizations can make pronouncements about valuing diversity, but actually doing that on a day-to-day basis is complicated. Employees have to actually coordinate their work with each other—they are interdependent. Working closely together, team members must manage their diversity as it relates to both their task, for example, how to define their services or sell a product, and their team process, or how the team deals with communication or conflict. Moreover, they must do this on a moment-to-moment basis, even if it is never explicitly discussed.

Fortunately, an extensive research literature—in management, organization studies, and psychology—on diverse groups can inform our understanding of how teams can enact a color-cognizant approach. This work does not look specifically at whether teams are able to explicitly engage race. Rather, its goal is to identify the characteristics that shape the dynamics and performance of heterogeneous teams. However, their findings are still relevant because a team's capacity to take on potentially charged issues like race is related to its larger dynamics.

As we note, one stream of research has shown that diverse teams with a color-cognizant perspective tend to have better processes and outcomes than those holding a color-blind perspective.[82] The literature also suggests, however, that several other elements are also crucial: their capacity for engaging in learning behaviors such as integrating different perspectives and self-reflection, their level of safety or trust, and their organizational context.[83] Given that color cognizance requires breaking with established ways of thinking and involves discussions on taboo topics such as race, teams with safer, more learning-oriented environments may be more likely to break out of the color bind and dig into race and ethnicity.[84]

Racially and Culturally Diverse Teams

Although research findings have been inconsistent, it's generally agreed that diverse teams hold the promise of outcome gains such as greater creativity and thoughtful problem-solving but often fail to realize this potential because of process losses due to problematic group dynamics.[85] This is particularly true of teams diverse by race and ethnicity, which generally have both poorer performance and weaker social cohesion.[86] However, the team diversity research also explores what enables diverse teams to work and learn together—that is, how to turn the possible potency of such teams into reality.

Amid a thicket of different findings, several promising directions of inquiry stand out. A growing body of work has shown that team learning behaviors generally lead to better performance.[87] For team learning to occur, members must proffer their unique expertise and ideas, which the group then discusses and integrates in a way that allows it to move forward.[88] Therefore, surfacing and intermixing various kinds of differences is at the heart of team learning. If a team has the capacity to learn more generally, it would seem to be more able to learn about race and ethnicity.[89] Although the participation of all team members is important, the team leader plays an outsized role in creating this climate.[90]

Three specific learning behaviors are most relevant for our study. The first is the capacity to engage in constructive conflict and debate, what some have called elaboration. Several studies show that this activity leads to better outcomes in diverse teams.[91] The ability to experiment with new approaches rather than getting stuck in ruts or routines is a second hallmark of learning.[92] Debate and discussion can be interesting—even compelling—but if they don't lead to new ways of acting, their point is lost.[93] Third is the capacity for self-reflection or reflexivity, which has also been shown to be particularly important for diverse teams.[94] Team members must be able to contemplate their team processes and dynamics as well as surface mistakes or things that went less well than expected if they are to learn how to improve.

Learning behaviors are not easy, however. They require curiosity and openness and, perhaps most important, the ability to make oneself vulnerable. Significant research shows that the level of safety or trust in a group strongly predicts its capacity for learning, which could be particularly true for learning about race and culture. One stream of research on psychological safety—a "shared belief that the team is safe for interpersonal risk-taking"[95]—shows that it leads to learning behaviors as well as to improved outcomes, including in diverse teams.[96] This could be especially meaningful for teams that wish to broach issues related to race, given the level of threat that many feel when embarking on such conversations. Again, the team leader is crucial to setting the tone for the team by modeling vulnerability and openness to feedback.

Team dynamics such as learning and safety are critical but are also strongly influenced by the organizational and office contexts in which they operate.[97]

Research on diversity climate is most relevant, as it probes contextual characteristics directly related to the impact of social identities such as race and ethnicity on employees' well-being and performance.[98] Such characteristics include the nature of relationships across racial or ethnic groups, the extent to which employees feel valued and respected, and whether workers feel fairly treated.

Finally, as noted, an emerging body of literature has examined the diversity perspectives[99] or diversity mind-sets[100] of team members. Given our emphasis on race and culture, we think of this as a racial-cultural perspective. Perspectives similar to what we call color cognizant tend to lead to more harmonious team processes as well as to better performance.[101] Although studies did not explore whether these groups engaged issues of race and ethnicity, members' individual beliefs would seem particularly relevant for our project. It seems likely that teams made up of individuals with color-conscious inclinations would be more likely to enact a team-level, color-cognizant practice. At the same time, significant evidence indicates that our thinking about race and ethnicity is often strikingly contradictory: many hold both color-blind and color-cognizant perspectives at the same time.[102] Although identifying a dominant point of view and tracing its impact is usually possible, investigating the inconsistencies can also be very fruitful.[103]

In sum, research on teams and groups directs us toward four key elements to understand whether and how work groups can openly explore the terrain of race and ethnicity: the individual color-blind or color-cognizant perspectives of team members, the degree to which team members engage in learning behaviors such as constructive conflict and self-reflection, the extent of psychological safety, and the impact of the broader context in which they are embedded. However, another literature on intergroup relations deepens our awareness of what to look for.

Intergroup Relations Theory

The basic precept of intergroup relations theory is that we interact with others not only as individuals but as members of groups.[104] "Every individual member [is] a group representative whenever he or she deals with members of other groups . . . every transaction among individuals [is], in part, an intergroup event."[105]

In the workplace, groups can be based on organizational characteristics such as department or profession or on social identity groups such as race or gender. But the impact of social identity groups is likely to be greater because they are imported from a larger society in which they are highly stratified: on the whole, whites have more power than people of color, men have more power than women, and so on.[106] The term *intergroup* can refer to different kinds of groups. We use it to refer to racial and ethnic groups.

Research on diverse groups and teams has tended to gloss over intergroup power dynamics.[107] In fact, little work elaborates, using ethnographic data, how members from varying racial and ethnic groups might experience their work groups differently, which would then shape larger group relationships, processes, and outcomes.[108] An intergroup lens helps us understand each of the four critical elements—racial-cultural perspective, learning behaviors, safety, and larger context—in a deeper way.

First, it is likely that team members of different races will differ in their color blindness or color cognizance. Significant research shows that whites are more likely to be color blind, and that people of color tend toward a multicultural perspective.[109] Further, people of color are more knowledgeable about and comfortable with using a racial or cultural lens to interpret themselves and the world around them.[110]

Second, intergroup relations could have a profound impact on the capacity for groups to engage in learning behaviors. Stuart Bunderson's and Ray Reagans' work on the general effects of power and status on learning suggests that social hierarchy can confound a team's capacity to agree on their goals, take risks, and share knowledge.[111] Robin Ely, Irene Padavic, and David Thomas look specifically at how racial power asymmetries can disrupt learning.[112] They argue that people of color will have greater concern about prejudice and stereotyping and therefore may be less willing than whites to voice opinions that differ from others in the group. Yet we know that learning cannot happen if group members withhold their opinions and expertise.

Similarly, racial and ethnic groups could vary on their feelings of safety in the group. A sense of psychological safety is important, but it may not be enough for team members of color who may suffer identity threat.[113] An individual experiencing identity threat believes he could be devalued, marginalized, or discriminated against[114] in a given setting because of race. Therefore, a sense of identity safety might also be key. Identity safety is an individual's belief that her race or ethnicity is truly welcome in a group.[115]

Most work suggests that identity safety will be especially important for people of color. When it comes to discussions of race and ethnicity, however, identity safety may be just as important for white group members.[116] A body of social-psychological research suggests that whites are very concerned that they will say, or be seen as saying, something racist or prejudiced, which can cause great inhibition.[117] Therefore identity safety for all team members could enhance their willingness to discuss issues related to race and culture. In fact, studies show that one way to help whites and people of color overcome their fears and discuss issues related to race is to encourage them to treat it as a learning experience,[118] testifying to the important role of learning behaviors.

Finally, the intergroup relations in the team's office or organizational environment could also have an impact on its ability to broach conversations about race and ethnicity. The group is not an island: its members are aware of office morale and conflict and they interact with their colleagues in other units. Thus, the relationships between individuals and, particularly, racial and ethnic groups in the office context can certainly seep into the team's dynamics.

Altogether, the intergroup relations literature suggests that members of different racial and cultural groups could have very different experiences and reactions to the team environment. Given these asymmetries, they may play different roles related to both the group's task and its internal processes.

Explaining the Achievement of Color Cognizance

How can work groups achieve color cognizance? This review suggests that one clearly race-related element may be necessary: the racial-cultural perspective of team members. This summary also suggests that features that are generally not seen as connected to race—learning orientation, safety, office environment—may also be critical. Ultimately, many things that may at first blush be seen as irrelevant to racial and cultural dynamics could be quite relevant in that they shape how people of different racial and cultural groups experience the workplace and interact with each other.

In the remaining chapters of this book, we put the flesh on these bones, drawing from an empirical study of racially diverse teams of child welfare workers and the degree to which they engaged race and ethnicity in their work. Given that these teams work in a field where the connections to race, ethnicity, and culture are both relevant and salient, it was remarkable how little they talked about these issues. Only one team regularly used a racial-cultural lens to understand their clients and, more rarely, themselves. By comparing this team with the others, we can offer an explanation for how work groups can achieve color cognizance.

We can't understand work teams, however, without understanding the larger environment in which they operate. In the following section, we describe the professional and organizational contexts for the study. We also present how we collected our data and the analytic tools we used to develop our argument.

Exploring Conversations About Race in Child Welfare

In this section, we describe the context and methods used in our qualitative, longitudinal study of seven teams of child welfare workers. A field investigation involving both interviews and observation, it not only documents how color blindness and color cognizance are enacted day-to-day, it also explores how those ideologies are woven into and emerge from team life. However, while these teams had particular challenges related to child protection work, they illustrate dynamics experienced by work groups across a multitude of organizational settings. Their conversations—and lack of conversation—reflect familiar patterns. For the purposes of this book, we chose three teams, which represent a range of racial-cultural practice and team dynamics, to spotlight.

A lengthy description and analysis of a fourth team is in appendix C, which can be found at https://www.russellsage.org/publications/color-bind. We begin by describing the professional and organizational environments. They are critical to understanding how these child welfare workers understand the role of race and ethnicity and they were also consistent across the teams, which is why we describe them here. We describe the office and team contexts in the chapters relating our findings, since they varied significantly across teams and therefore are essential elements of our understanding of what enables color-cognizant practice. We then summarize the data collection and data analysis procedures. Additional detail about methods and brief descriptions of the teams can be found in appendices A and B.

Racial-Cultural Practice in Social Work

Even amid the dramatic contraction of the role and size of the public sector in the United States, the government's charge to protect children at imminent risk of abuse or neglect remains largely undisputed. States and municipalities generally provide direct care and oversight of families; the federal government plays a role in setting standards and providing resources. Despite this consensus (and perhaps because of it), child welfare agencies are routinely denounced for their incompetence and buffeted by high-profile scandals involving the injury or death of children. More recently, the growing movement in education and social services toward accountability and documentation likely further underscores the stress and anxiety providers feel to get it right.

Ultimately, then, child welfare work is a tough job that often requires choosing among unpalatable options. These workers suffer high stress, anxiety, and even secondary trauma.[119] Their job is also inherently racialized with employees, usually white, routinely making judgments about the parenting practices of families who are disproportionately of color.[120]

Both color-blind and color-cognizant ideologies are alive in the field of social work, leading to a contradictory environment for its members. On the one hand, it has explicitly attended to race, ethnicity, and culture for many years. In 2001, the National Association of Social Workers put out extensive guidelines on cultural competence in social work.[121] The Council on Social Work Education has mandated cultural competence training in social work programs.[122] For years, the subfield of child welfare was influenced by the stance of the National Association of Black Social Workers against transracial adoption because they believed black children should be placed with black families. On the other hand, this stance drew significant criticism and the organization softened its position.[123] Moreover, the federal Multi-Ethnic Placement Act, adopted in 1994, now prohibits agencies from using race in decisions about placement in adoption and foster care.[124]

Given the influence of both models, debate in the field, including in the subfield of child welfare, is robust about the appropriate role and impact of race and ethnicity on social work practice. Some believe that cultural competence is central to effective casework.[125] Others believe that race has been overemphasized.[126] Further, research on cultural competence at the organizational and institutional levels indicates that agencies vary in their adoption of the field's standards of cultural awareness.[127] Meanwhile, research at the individual level suggests that many workers lack the specific attitudes, knowledge, and behaviors that make up culturally competent approaches.[128] In fact, studies show that families of color are often treated differently, and more punitively, than white families.[129] In our study, we show how this debate between color-blind and color-cognizant approaches plays out among child welfare workers grappling with the urgency and complexity of families in crisis.

A State Child Welfare Agency

Of course, different organizations respond differently to this professional context. Our research site was a state child welfare agency, the body responsible for investigating allegations of abuse and neglect and making decisions about whether children should be removed from the home. The agency itself provided something of a contradictory context regarding whether and how race and ethnicity should be taken into account.

About a year before the research began, a new commissioner arrived at the agency and began making a host of changes, beginning with representatives from across the agency identifying six core practice values, one of which was "committed to cultural diversity/cultural competence." Another was "strength-based," which signaled the organization's explicit commitment to identifying the strengths of a family, rather than using a punitive or forensic approach to its work with families. This required the workers to take a more clinical, rather than investigatory, approach and to try and keep children in their current home by highlighting what the parents brought to their child-rearing, including culturally informed practices, as opposed to what they lacked.

The commissioner also made other changes. He regularly attended meetings of Aware (a pseudonym), the agency's internal caucus for workers of color and bilingual workers. Aware addressed issues of discrimination related to internal processes like hiring and promotion and related to the families they worked with—for example, whether families of color tended to be treated more punitively. According to Aware's president, an African American woman, the commissioner's regular participation was a marked change from that of his predecessors.

Further, he convened a two-day retreat for the executive staff on cultural sensitivity, triggered by a senior member's comment that invoked a cultural stereotype. According to Aware's president, the conversations at the retreat were intense and personal. "What really impacted me was there were very few at this training who weren't impacted. And I think the most telling thing was the three boxes of tissue that somebody went and got and put in the middle of the floor, and they were used." She pointed to more privileged workers as one example: "They begin to think about not only about their privilege but even some of the things that they had to give up in terms of being able to maintain that privilege. . . . So for many in the room that was a revelation." Although these were relatively recent changes that had not percolated throughout the organization or even the full executive team, the commissioner and other agency leaders sought to send a message that awareness, knowledge, and skills related to race and ethnicity were critical to child welfare practice.

On the other hand, some workers of color felt that there was internal discrimination in the agency and that they were treated differently from white workers. According to the Aware president, people of color were less likely to apply for promotions because they felt they were unlikely to receive them. They also felt that workers of color were fired for infractions that whites would not be. One Latina worker gave an example of this in her unit. Her white team member had her driver's license suspended for six months because she had so many speeding tickets, but received relatively mild treatment from the agency. The Latina felt that a worker of color would have been dealt with more harshly. The Aware president also said that her supervisors of color felt that their subordinates were more likely to go around them if they disagreed with a decision than subordinates of white supervisors. Several bilingual workers reported some tension around the $1,000 bonus they received for providing translation services for other workers in their office. Although we cannot speak to the validity of these claims, that they appeared to be relatively widespread suggests that the agency faced challenges in creating a truly egalitarian and inclusive environment.

While bringing a new emphasis on cultural diversity, the new commissioner also launched a pilot teaming program, which experimented with using teams of social workers, rather than individual workers, to engage with its client families. The pilot program began with seven teams located around the state. The agency hoped that a team-based model could facilitate better outcomes for workers and clients by bringing together a broader set of perspectives and experiences in thinking about how to work with a given family as well as by providing more emotional support to individual workers. This move to collective responsibility for cases represented a significant shift in practice because this agency and child welfare more broadly has used a therapeutic model based on the relationship between an individual worker and a family. The change was so significant, in fact, that the agency recognized that some teams might fail to make it.

In the traditional set-up, each social worker was a member of a unit with a supervisor and four or five workers. Members of these units sat near each other, but each worker had his or her caseload, and was solely responsible for those cases. In the pilot, the structure was similar: each worker was a member of a team with a supervisor and four or five social workers. However, service delivery to individual families would be managed by multiple workers and all team members could be called on for advice and assistance. Further, all teams were expected to meet at least weekly to discuss its cases, processes, and administrative issues. Other than these stipulations, their teams developed ways of working together that ultimately differed significantly across the teams.

These team members were the agency's frontline workers. The agency had divided the sequence of working with a family into three functions: *investigation*, the task of following up on allegations of abuse or neglect and determining whether to take on the case; *assessment*, the job of doing a more extensive exploration of the family and creating a service plan for the family; and *ongoing*, the work of implementing the service plan and engaging with the family to ensure a safer environment for the child.

The teams worked in different offices around the state. The frontline employees in each team, called "workers" in the agency (derived from the term *social worker*), were under the supervision of a supervisor or team leader. The team leader reported to a manager, who oversaw four or five units altogether and who reported to the office director.

The agency put into place a number of resources for the seven pilot teams. First, it hired a coordinator to oversee the pilot as a whole. She worked with a small group of team development consultants, external to the agency, who provided advice and support for the pilot as a whole as well as individual consultations with the teams. The coordinator and the consultants oversaw the official launch of the program and occasional day-long reflection meetings that brought together all the team members from around the state for training and team-building activities. They also ran several cross-team learning groups, including a monthly meeting for the team leaders of all seven teams.

Data Collection and Analysis

In the spring of 2003, Erica gained research access to the agency and began documenting the process of creating and implementing the teaming pilot. She ultimately gathered data for about four years, through spring 2007. At the same time, she was working with Tamara on several projects, including a study of racially diverse bank branches and a theoretical paper related to learning in racially diverse teams.[130] As Erica designed and implemented the data collection process for the child welfare study, she occasionally turned to Tamara for advice, such as asking for feedback on interview protocols. As the partnership deepened, it became clear that our distinctive training and ways of thinking about the work were complementary, so we decided to collaborate on the analysis and writing phases of the research project.

The research was designed as comparative case study research with each team as a single case. Its purpose was to build theory about what enables and inhibits color-cognizant practice in work groups.

Data collection began with observation of organizational meetings planning for the pilot and other initiatives in the spring of 2003. About a year later, the summer of 2004, Erica enrolled all seven teams in the research just as they began their work as teams and followed them for about thirty months, until the spring of 2007.

The bulk of data collection was from the teams, though the four in-depth teams received more attention. Erica conducted group interviews, interviewing the team as a whole, of all seven teams at three points, each about a year apart. She also conducted interviews with four team stakeholders or observers for each of the seven teams. For additional data from the in-depth teams, she conducted individual interviews with each team member at the same three points as the team interviews. Erica also observed team meetings approximately every other month. The meetings lasted at least an hour and often longer. Three of the four in-depth teams, each representing a different kind of racial-cultural practice, are described and analyzed in detail in the narrative; the fourth in-depth team is described in appendix C (available at https://www.russellsage.org/publications/color-bind).

All told, the data collection from the teams and their stakeholders included twenty team interviews, fifty-four individual interviews with team members, fifteen interviews with team stakeholders, and observation of forty-seven meetings. All names of teams and individuals are pseudonyms.

Erica also collected data about the agency as a whole. She interviewed the agency's commissioner, who was the driving force behind the teaming program. She also observed twenty-four other meetings that in some way related to the program. Finally, she collected about 130 program-related documents.

Data collection focused on two broad areas of interest: first, how each team engaged with color blindness and color cognizance in its work, and, second, the team's broader dynamics and characteristics, including its office environment. Because we have both individual-level data from individual interviews and team-level data from team meeting observations and team interviews, we can distinguish between the approach of the team as a whole and the approach of individuals on the team. Moreover, we can situate both the individuals' and teams' approaches to race and culture in their broader team and office dynamics to better understand how issues related to conflict, safety, and learning may influence a team's capacity to dig into charged topics like race.

The Sample

Overall, the sample consisted of seventy-six participants, including team members and their supervisors and stakeholders, about three-quarters female. Because the participants were largely women, we will use *she* to refer to them generically throughout the book. The racial breakdown was 68 percent white, 9 percent black, 12 percent Latino/a, and 3 percent Asian. Five percent were biracial and two participants did not provide a racial category. All of the teams had some racial or ethnic diversity; all included at least one bilingual worker, and more often two, over the course of data collection; all teams had significant diversity in caseloads; and all the members of all the teams faced a significant likelihood that they would work with families with backgrounds different from their own.

Cross-Race Interviewing

Erica, a white management professor, conducted the data collection, which meant she regularly engaged in interviews with people of color and with racially diverse teams. In other words, she was having cross-race conversations about race and culture, which, as we have been exploring, can be complicated. Some scholars argue against the practice altogether,[131] though there are more who explore how to make the practice more valid by increasing sensitivity and avoiding pitfalls.[132]

As data collection began, Erica had been engaged in research and writing related to race for many years. She is aware of the importance of locating herself in the work as a white woman and considering how her social identities might affect others' reactions to her. In an earlier project including a mixed-race sample she used a variety of techniques to establish rapport. She also asked for feedback, by email, from the participants in the study about the interview process and received comments from people of all racial backgrounds. Although the comments were overall quite positive, she received some candid and enlightening remarks from respondents of color. Based on this material, as well as on self-reflection, Erica published an article about the experience of cross-race interviewing and what she had learned about herself, her racial background, and its impact on her research.[133]

The dynamics of cross-race interviewing are similar to broader questions about racial or ethnic matching between providers and clients. We explore this at length in chapter 3, when we look at how our respondents thought about matching families and social workers, including the concern that requiring racial or ethnic concordance reduces complex individuals to a single dimension. Research suggests that caregivers' (or researchers') awareness and sensitivity to race and culture is more important than their racial categorization.

We will never know how Erica's racial identity may have shaped data collection, though it must have. Any researcher's background would do so. For that reason, we regularly reflected on how her role may have influenced what people told her. Ultimately, though, we do believe the data have a valuable story to tell. At the same time, it was critical to bring in another perspective during the process of data analysis and writing, which Tamara brought to the table, as a professor of psychology, a practicing clinician, and an African American. Additionally, because she was not steeped, like Erica, in the teams and their dynamics, she brought a fresh perspective, one step removed from the countless particulars of the agency and its workers.

Data Analysis

Data analysis was guided by the precepts of case study research and was both deductive and inductive. As suggested earlier in this chapter, we were influenced by previous research on diversity discourses in the United States, with its focus on color blindness and color cognizance, and therefore looked for manifestations of these discourses in both speech and behavior. We were also influenced by previous research on diverse groups and teams and therefore investigated elements identified by previous work, such as conflict, cohesion, safety, learning behaviors, the team leader's work style, and office context. In that sense, our approach was deductive.

However, we were interested in how all these various elements actually played out in the day-to-day work of the teams and, in particular, in how they interacted and intertwined. We were especially interested in how the team's color blindness or cognizance appeared to be connected to its broader team dynamics. In that sense, our work was inductive since little previous work has provided in-depth, complex portraits of the ongoing dynamics of diverse teams and, in particular, how they think and act regarding race and ethnicity in their group task and dynamics. As a result, we can contribute to previous work on all these features by mapping how they manifest in the quotidian details of team life; we do not simply impose a previously developed template.

Like most ethnographic research, data analysis went through multiple, iterative rounds of developing insights. Our overall analytic strategy was, first, to disentangle each element and attempt to understand it in isolation and, second, to track connections among them and understand how they informed each other.

Early on, we created case descriptions of each team that summarized their purpose, membership, approach to teaming, and key events. These case descriptions were meant to capture basic background on each team as well as important changes over the two and a half years of data collection. They provided the scaffolding of each team's narrative.

Once the case descriptions were complete, we began systematic coding of the team meeting data from the four in-depth teams, using Atlas.ti as our qualitative analysis software. Members talked about a huge range of topics in their team meetings. We were particularly interested in any conversation in which race or ethnicity was raised. We also gleaned critical information about team dynamics, including conflict, learning behaviors, evidence of safety, and the like. We identified discussions that referenced race or ethnicity in any way, excerpted that material, and put it into a separate document. We then independently reviewed each of these instances and assessed both its depth and its substance. From this analysis, we developed our understanding of each team's racial-cultural practice—that is, if the teams talked about race and, if so, precisely what members talked about. We also identified other particularly telling moments in the team meetings, which could range from lively debates to bitter conflict to lack of engagement to uproarious laughter.

We then turned to the interview data (team interviews from all seven teams and individual interviews from the four in-depth teams). We coded by placing data into buckets for each of our primary constructs, such as racial-cultural perspective, learning behaviors, and psychological safety. We then reviewed the material in each bucket for each team as a whole as well as for every team member. We used this review to categorize each team and every team member on each construct; for example, regarding psychological safety, we identified the degree to which each team member felt safe and then categorized the team as a whole.

After reviewing this material, we used analytic memos to trace connections between the constructs. Ultimately, we induced a graphic model that suggests the elements required for color-cognizant practice and their interrelationships, which is described in chapter 7.

Further detail about our methods comes up at relevant points in the empirical chapters and can also be found in appendix A. Appendix B includes thumbnail sketches of the teams.

~ Chapter 3 ~

Race, Ethnicity, and Culture:
Reflection and Deflection

WKR: Being a white woman, I try to really build a relationship with people who aren't—I know what some people [of color] might think, having a white social worker come into their home. . . .

INT: What do you think they might be thinking?

WKR: Well, I have clients say things like, "You wouldn't understand. You're a white woman. How would you understand?" And helping them really understand that—you're right, I'm not going to understand until you explain to me what your experiences are. And that it's not always about me being a white woman, and just really work through that with them. [Team Member]

"You know, I have to say I was bold enough to, when I was a worker, to always say to the families who I was. 'This is my cultural background. This is who I am.' And whenever there were issues about race, because I had them, I would immediately go to the family, sit down, and talk about it. I don't know if overall staff in the whole office, or other offices, have that kind of—I would say, boldness—to bring it up." [Team Leader]

"It goes back to how you do treat those folks [clients] and that you treat them fairly . . . it didn't matter what color they were. You know, you don't change your rules either. It's kind of a straight and narrow." [Team Leader]

INT: So, is there any way that you work with families differently when their background is different from yours—an African American family, Hispanic family?

WKR: It just may take more of an explanation as far as how accepted, say, physical forms of discipline may be. It just may take more time to explain it. . . .

INT: So, any way in which you might try to get information about the cultural background of these folks, talk to people [from the same background as the family]?

WKR: No. It's all the same. [Team Member]

These quotes illustrate very different ways of thinking about the role of race and ethnicity in casework. The first two suggest that they matter and they require reflection and discussion. The second two imply that they are largely irrelevant and off the table; the speakers deflect race and culture. As we've seen, color blindness and color cognizance are two encompassing and conflicting models of how we treat race in American society. What they actually mean—and the impact they have—depends on how they are lived day to day in countless ambits across the country. In this chapter, drawing on data from all seven teams, we document how these child welfare workers did or didn't take race into account in their work, thereby—implicitly—enacting color blindness or color cognizance, or some mix of the two. For this chapter, to illustrate the broad range of personal reactions and approaches, we treat the workers simply as unidentified individuals. In chapters 4 through 7, so we can chart the impact of their individual racial-cultural practice on their team's larger practice, we group the workers by team.

We approached the data from two directions to provide two different and complementary portraits of the participants' sensemaking. First, we identified three different, though overlapping, concerns that arose: Should clients be treated differently, based on race or ethnicity? Should social workers draw on their own cultural background in their work? Should families be matched with social workers of the same racial or ethnic background? We go through these questions and describe how the workers in the study answered them, articulating color-blind and color-cognizant approaches to each.

Second, we approach the data using a different lens, one that illuminates contradiction and inconsistency. Individual comments were relatively easy to categorize as color blind or color cognizant, but it was not uncommon to find participants expressing both perspectives as they thought through the role of race and ethnicity in their work. We show how the social workers engaged in what we call color minimization, or the tendency to claim the importance of race and ethnicity even as they simultaneously undermined that claim.

As we wrote this chapter, we kept several points in mind. First, we are interested in how people think about these questions, how they make sense of the role of race and culture in their work. That is what we are documenting here. Sometimes workers made claims—that they were color blind, that they did not draw on their own heritage in their work—that we think are likely untrue. As we discussed in chapter 2, color blindness is actually impossible and we are all shaped in part by our background, even if that influence is invisible to us. Because people are influenced by their understandings, however, it is important to document them, which we do in this chapter. We are interested here in how the workers explain their work in order for us to better understand the obstacles and enablers of color-cognizant practice. Explicit speech gives us a critical window into their sensemaking. We sometimes go beyond documentation to interpretation to draw out subtle points or link comments to our broader argument.

Second, as noted in chapter 2, we recognize a distinction between color cognizance and cultural competence. We don't assess whether statements are culturally competent—that is, whether they portray appropriate knowledge of a client's racial or ethnic background. Ours is a lower bar: we are interested in whether the study's participants invoke a family's culture as a factor in their diagnosis and decision-making, not whether they do so fully correctly. This is because we are interested in how the broad discourses of color blindness and color cognizance play out on the ground. Another significant body of work, found largely in the clinical literature, focuses on discerning cultural competence.[1] However, in chapter 8, we do explore how color cognizance without full cultural competence—in these workers as well as in ourselves—can lead to invoking stereotypes or using simplistic generalizations.

Finally, though we feel it is critical to investigate the workers' sensemaking, we do not condemn it. With acute awareness of our limitations, we make generous inferences about their intentions. As we noted in chapter 1, however, sensemaking has consequences, regardless of motive. In the spirit of probity, therefore, we do document what these workers thought and suggest the implications. In later chapters, we position their thinking in the context of their team and office environment.

Should Clients Be Treated Differently Based on Race or Ethnicity?

A color-blind perspective generally dismisses the usefulness of a racial or cultural lens when working with families and therefore presumes clients should be treated as similarly as possible. A color-cognizant approach, on the other hand, recognizes that such a lens can illuminate why a family is acting in a particular way, as well as how to intervene, and therefore should be considered. Two tensions emerged related to this question. The first was approaching people as individuals devoid of race and culture versus approaching them as members of racial and ethnic groups. The second was treating people consistently versus treating them differently.

Treating People as Individuals Versus as Members of Cultural Groups

Generally, those expressing a color-blind view felt that people should be treated as individuals, not as members of a cultural group, as illustrated by this respondent: "I really think that you need to take each family individually, whether they don't speak English, or they're from a different religion. . . . Just because this Polish family works this way, I could meet another Polish family, and it might be totally different. And I'm sure it is because every family is totally different." A white man married to a Puerto Rican woman echoed this: "Well, I've been around Spanish people. I know what's going on. But, so, the approach is pretty much the same. You just try to meet people on their own terms. That's all, I guess." Meeting people on their own terms seems to mean viewing them as individuals because working with Latinos is pretty much the same as working with other clients.

This point of view often came up when respondents talked about issues related to substance abuse or child abuse. Some people saw these issues as clear-cut: either a client was abusing drugs or not, either a child was being battered or not. For example, this conversation took place in response to an interview question about how much this worker's team discussed race or ethnicity as part of its casework.

> WKR: I would say the majority of time, it's not really brought up because . . . we just haven't had the particular cases where the issues have been because of different cultures, [like when] what's accepted in one culture may not be accepted here. And how do we bridge that gap? I don't really think we've had families where that's the issue.
>
> INT: How would you know whether that was the issue or not?
>
> WKR: I mean if the issue was substance abuse . . . You know, you can't be using substances if you're going to take care of your children.

This way of thinking presumes that determining whether someone is abusing drugs or alcohol is straightforward and completely divorced from culture. The possibility of using culture as a lens to help diagnose whether abuse was happening or to determine how to address it did not seem to occur to him.

Others understood how cultural assumptions—either the worker's or the client's—could also be in play, however. A woman who had emigrated from Mexico as a child gave an example of how such determinations can be culturally informed. She felt that Latin Americans were more likely to be labeled as alcoholics when that was inappropriate.

> A lot of people that come from Latin America are from the ranch. They either make their own alcohol or they have to travel long ways to get

alcohol. . . . But when you come here, like, you have liquor stores everywhere. They are like next to your house. And they just get liquor happy . . . But people [agency workers] don't understand that now it is easier for them to get alcohol and . . . all they [the workers] have to do is [say] "you know what, you don't need all this alcohol. Moderation is good." And they [the clients] listen.

Instead, she said, the workers label the clients as alcoholics.

Other workers, taking a color-blind stance, used domestic violence as an example of something clear-cut and unaffected by racial or cultural background. One team member described how spousal abuse could be affected in immigrant families by documentation status: in one Latino family, the husband—who was the batterer and had documentation—was emboldened by the fact that his wife was undocumented. Knowing this could help the worker formulate a response to the situation that did not put the wife in danger of being deported.

These examples suggest that some of the respondents saw only two choices: either treat each family as unique, with no potential underlying similarities with others from a similar background, or see racial and cultural groups as fully homogeneous, with no significant intragroup differences. The possibility of a middle way that considers cultural factors as it attends to each family's unique dynamics seemed unimaginable. However, we have also provided illustrations of team members who were able to see their clients as individuals while also using knowledge of a family's racial or ethnic background to deepen their understanding. Such a stance synthesizes the two poles of the dichotomy: there doesn't have to be a choice between seeing individuals as unique (and therefore culture doesn't matter) or seeing cultures as homogeneous (and therefore individuals don't matter). Both individual and culture matter, which could mean a variety of working arrangements to adapt to these different circumstances. In fact, lab studies show that individuals holding a multicultural perspective similar to color cognizance made judgments based both on individual and group information, whereas color-blind participants focused only on individual information.[2]

Treating People Consistently Versus Differently

Informants operating from a color-blind perspective insisted that they treated clients from all racial backgrounds consistently. Those with a color-cognizant approach indicated that it seemed natural that different approaches might be appropriate for different families.

As a color-blind worker noted, "As far as ethnicity or anything like that, that's never been an issue, whether it's a Caucasian family, whether it's an African American family, there hasn't been any differences with us and the way we approach families, and work with families. I mean, we treat everyone the same." This insistence seemed to stem from a concern that treating people differently would be a form of discrimination. Another worker seemed to imply that her work with a Puerto Rican immigrant family had been just as conscientious as her work with any other family.

> INT: So, do you feel like you handled that case any differently than . . .
>
> WKR: No. We got all the services right in place really quickly. I don't think I've handled it any differently.

Although these workers felt that treating clients fairly required treating them consistently, fairness does not have to mean treating families precisely the same. In fact, fairness could require learning about a client's culture to assess its impact. Even that, though, seemed out of the question for color-blind workers, as illustrated earlier: the interviewer asked a worker whether he ever tried to get additional information about clients who came from backgrounds different than his and was told, "no, it's all the same." This worker seemed reluctant to seek any additional insights that might broaden his understanding.

But color-cognizant workers could cite multiple examples of how they had adapted their approach based on a family's background. Some spoke more generally, without referring to particular families. Multiple workers said that disciplinary techniques varied from culture to culture. One team member said he had learned to be careful assessing candor because of differences in interpersonal norms: in "some Southeast Asian countries, as a sign of respect, they don't look people in the eye. Where here we think they're not being truthful."

Other workers described particular cases. One worker referenced a Latino family in which the Latino parents did not want to put any of their seven children into day care, and instead relied on other relatives. Even though the agency didn't see this as "totally appropriate," she made an exception. "It works for them. And I think we need to say, you know, this is a family that has support through their extended family . . . and that's a cultural thing—I don't need to push this. So, if it works, it works."

Another worker described in detail a relationship she cultivated with a black mother who had said she didn't "allow white people in her home." The mother "really felt like I was going to judge her house, that I was going to see another—these were her words—'another dirty black woman's home.'" Because the woman's mentally ill son had already been removed from the home, the worker told the mother she did not need to come in the house at that point, though that would have been standard procedure. Instead, "we worked on how we were going to deal with what was in front of us together around placement of her child and understanding his mental health illness, and her goal was to get him home, and our goal was to get him home, and how were we going to do that together and what needed to happen." The worker recounted how she gave rides to the mother when she had to get to meetings held in a distant town, so that the mother didn't have to take a commuter train. The worker said that she "used those opportunities to be able to talk to her about stuff and allowed her to share what her concerns were and then we would address them." Finally, the child was deemed ready to come home, and at that point the worker had to see the house, which the mother allowed her to do. "And it hasn't been an issue since."

Holding a color-cognizant perspective by taking race and culture into account doesn't mean a cultural relativism that rationalizes away real concerns. A Latina working with a Haitian family described a mother who was breast-feeding her ten-year-old son and who said that this was normal in her culture. This seemed doubtful to the worker, but she asked Haitian colleagues, "'Is this your experience? Is this a cultural norm?' And they didn't concur that that was." So the worker did not let this go. Rather than simply presuming, however, the worker took the extra step of checking.

In sum, color-blind workers seemed caught in a perceived dichotomy: either treat people similarly or engage in discrimination that would harm some families. Such concerns may have been grounded in a common understanding that underlies color blindness more broadly: that making any distinction among people based on color or culture is inherently problematic or even racist. Given such worries, it is understandable that workers would say that race and culture do not matter. In fact, lab studies show that whites will go to great lengths to avoid mentioning race—even when it is obviously related to the task at hand—because of this belief.[3]

This color-blind stance has three unfortunate consequences however. First, it means that workers may miss important clues or dynamics regarding what is going on with a family. Second, for many families, racial or cultural background is a source of strength and resilience. Ignoring it could mean overlooking something of great value to the client. Further, color blindness cuts off access to approaches to working with the family that could be quite generative. Finally, though many individuals avow color blindness as a bulwark against discrimination, it could actually contribute to it; overlooking race can also deny racism. Many families of color are profoundly affected by racism and the structural inequalities that result from it, however. Ultimately, blindness to race, racism, ethnicity, and ethnocentrism could limit a worker's ability to design a successful intervention.

Color cognizance simply means that workers are open to insights that a racial or cultural lens provides but do not assume that they are definitive. Treating people differently, based on race and ethnicity, means creating an adaptive or tailored approach that integrates cultural awareness, as well as an acknowledgement of racism and discrimination, into the clinical knowledge base of the provider.

Should Social Workers Draw on Their Cultural Backgrounds?

Whether workers can describe how they draw on their race and ethnicity in thinking about their work emerged as a second key concern. In fact, this question is critical to whether practice is color blind or color cognizant. First, simple awareness that one has a culture stemming from one's race or ethnicity—that one is influenced by cultural norms, values, and perceptions—is foundational. If individuals do not understand that we are all affected by these cultural norms, then they are likely to see their attitudes, assumptions, and behaviors as natural, neutral, and fully aware, than as partial understandings that are inevitably limited and biased. Therefore, they are likely to see perspectives that differ from their own as incomplete and even prejudiced yet overlook their own bias. Second, if workers can articulate how they are influenced by culture, they can more likely understand that others may also be drawing on their culture when they engage in particular behavior.

Sensemaking regarding this question differed by racial group: for the most part, whites responded differently than people of color. Some informants, all white, took a color-blind approach by denying any impact of their own race or ethnicity on their life and work. Many could name an ethnic heritage but downplayed its influence. One team member said, "I have an Irish ethnicity. . . . I really don't identify with anything that would stand out culturally. . . . I don't really even know how to explain my culture. . . . As far as ethnicity, I'm not really connected." Another white respondent echoed, "I don't feel like that [my culture] was really, really prominent or evident or anything that stands out." A third, after describing her heritage as Scottish and Swedish, also discounted their impact: "I don't know that I would say my ethnic background—I draw on more . . . being raised in—you know, my dad was a teacher; my mom worked at night. Those are things that I draw on more than anything."

These informants seem to suggest that if they are not aware of any impact of their race or ethnicity, they are unaffected by them. However, being Irish or Scottish or Swedish, and therefore white, aligns them with the dominant racial group—in their office, organization, and larger society—and therefore its impact may be invisible to them. This is very common for whites. As we described in chapter 2, facets of ourselves that align with the dominant group are often invisible to us even though they can have a profound impact on our lives. Although understandable, this lack of awareness is also problematic. These workers may use a similar lens when working with clients of color by presuming that their race or ethnicity, including their experiences of racism and discrimination, have limited impact on their lives, leading to the workers' overlooking critical information that could inform their work.

In fact, some workers felt that their background should be basically off limits. One white worker described working with a mother from a country in West Africa "whose very first question" when the worker contacted her was "are you black?" This client said that she had suffered racism throughout the fifteen years she had lived in the United States. The worker noted that "race is definitely a matter for [the mother]" and "it is good to be aware of it and to acknowledge it" but that the focus was on protective work for the children in her caseload and "not my race or not my background or whatnot." Certainly the worker's primary job is to protect the well-being of the children in her care, but that task is not antithetical to self-awareness, and indeed can be informed by it. A consciousness of her racial background is not a distraction from her responsibility to care for children, but instead is integral to it. Cognizance about her race and racial attitudes could help the worker address this client's concerns about racism as part of doing the best job she can of enhancing the well-being of the client's children.

As a whole, white workers tended to downplay the influence of their racial and cultural backgrounds, but some color-cognizant white participants could articulate the impact on their work. In some cases, the workers seemed to see their background as largely detrimental, something that had to be guarded against, whereas others saw it as positive because it could be a source of insight and knowledge.

Several white team members from well-off families felt they had to guard against the consequences of their own privilege.

> INT: Do you think there's any way in which you draw on your background and how you think about your work?
>
> WKR: Well, I think everyone does it. . . .
>
> INT: So, what are some of the things that you draw on?
>
> WKR: Well, as a white Anglo-Saxon Protestant . . . I mean, I think that we try to overcome our prejudices, and sometimes it's difficult. I don't think we ever—we're not in a color-blind society. . . . We have to strive to overcome [our biases] our whole lives. . . . I try not to be [like] where I came from in [state], because I mean, I think there's a certain arrogance to growing up in white Anglo-Saxon [name] County. So, you tend to look down on certain people.

While the question had been about how the worker drew on his background, his response was about how he tried *not* to do so to avoid prejudice, which framed his background as purely a negative, as a taint to be expunged. Some white workers acknowledged their bias but could give examples of how they had overcome particular prejudices through learning. A manager described her response to *coining,* a practice in some Southeast Asian cultures of placing very hot coins on the skin that can leave marks that can appear as abuse, though the practice is not meant to harm. She initially assumed that those engaging in it didn't know any better: "I think there was a level of judgment that I had because they were doing this. I thought, 'they just don't know any better and I'll help them.'" Then she spoke to Southeast Asian social workers in her office who had experienced coining and believed in its value. She also spoke to another worker from Honduras who said her beliefs about voodoo influenced her work with families. That led the manager to look at herself "and really kind of mak[e] the shift that these are people who I see as professional, as being with it, as making good judgments, and being appropriate parents of their own children, talking about how some of this, some of their culture, is incorporated in their day-to-day living." It was, she explained, as if "I said, 'oh everything is going good today, knock on wood'—you know, I kind of put it in the same category." This woman started with a judgment of other cultures but, through interactions with others from different backgrounds, was able to recognize the impact of her background on those judgments. She then made the connection that cultural beliefs from her background were not that different from beliefs of other cultures. For her, culture was not something that only affected other people; she recognized how it also affected her beliefs and actions.

In addition to these workers on watch for any negative effects of their racial or ethnic background, a few white workers conceptualized their background as a positive good, a kind of resource. One felt her background, specifically Scots Irish and German, provided a foundation that affected her work. Not only did it make her more "open to other ideas," it also made her more aware of "people who you may say are more like the downtrodden, those who don't have as much." She continued:

WKR: And also being assertive in a positive and political way to get what you need for you and your family, because like my grand-father, when he was younger, was a member of the National Farmers Organization. And my dad . . . we lived in a small community, and you know, I mean, community service is part of my ethnicity, because he was a volunteer fire chief for many, many years. No pay, no nothing.

INT: And how did you connect that with his ethnicity?

WKR: I do think there is—you know, in that immigrant culture, that helping each other out is very important, and it's also a source of growth and, well, personal satisfaction. It's not like "what can I get for myself?" The focus is "what can I do for others?" And through that I will receive for myself.

INT: Does that affect how you approach the families you work with, or how you approach other agencies, or is there any way that it comes into play, do you think?

WKR: I think that the—it does affect that fact that I see families more as team players. Like we're trying to work on this as a team.

INT: What's the connection there for you with your ethnic heritage?

WKR: That within my ethnic heritage, neighbors helped each other out, and they worked as a team. And you know, they could depend on people to help, like if—and the sad thing for me, and what I have a hard time finding a balance, though, is that there's that almost expectation that if someone asks you to do something, you have to say yes, whether you can do it, or not. And I struggle with that, because that's not being fair to myself, and it's not being fair to the other person.

At another point in the interview, the worker noted that her family had been in the United States for multiple generations, but she still clearly felt a connection to her ethnic background and considered herself as coming from an immigrant sensibility. She largely viewed this inheritance positively—she connects it with honesty, openness to others including the poor, and to joining with communal efforts—though she also acknowledged that it can carry a burdensome sense of obligation.

This white worker was cognizant of how her cultural background affected her practice, an important cornerstone of a color-cognizant perspective. Few whites did so in any depth, however.

On the other hand, people of color were more capable of making that connection. Like some of the white workers, some workers of color were aware that their background could bring bias, especially when working with clients whose background was similar to their own. A Cape Verdean worker described her reaction to some Cape Verdean clients.

> WKR: I'm talking about the Cape Verde clients that I used to have. . . . Maybe I set the standards like too high like I said, "Gee, my mother came here as an immigrant. She worked in a factory really hard. Why can't you just get up?" Like I don't say these things to them. I'm thinking them, you know, which is clearly an effect, and I'm glad that I could realize that and sort of put that past me. Sometimes they'll make quick judgments like that: . . . "I'm an immigrant." "I have to put up with the public school system." [Then, as if she is talking to a client]: "I did it. Why can't you? Why do you have so many excuses?"
>
> INT: And how do you get over that? How do you not let that get in your way?
>
> WKR: Well, because they're not me. People are all different. And I can't use my personal experience and who I am. . . . That's not who they are. . . . Just because my mom did it doesn't mean that you're going to do it. You may have other issues. . . . I mean I understand. I make a point of not reading assessments when I get cases because I don't want to go in there with this prejudgment about the family or this is exactly what happened.

This worker was aware of her biases and took steps to manage them. She was therefore on the watch for potential limitations that came with her background. However, much more often, participants of color considered their background a source of insight and expertise.

A common theme was the ability of workers of color to connect with people from a similar racial or cultural group. When the interviewer asked, "does your background have an impact on how you do your work here?" one Spanish-speaking Latina replied, "Hmm. I think I would say that most when I'm working with my bilingual families. I see myself obviously able to understand their culture, you know, and speak to them in their language. And I think they can relate to me, seeing me as a Spanish worker." Others felt they could act both as a representative or advocate and as a role model for others from their background: "There wasn't a lot of advocacy for the families that I worked with, like the bilingual families. And I came to [this agency] thinking that I would play kind of like an advocate to the minority families, to the Hispanic population. And I thought that I would better advocate in schools and things like that. And become a good role model kind of for them."

An African American worker also said "it's like a modeling thing" but explained the response at greater length.

> WKR: I think the families that we work with need to be represented, not just as the families that we work with but also as social workers and also having some power to make decisions and power to help. Not always being seen as the victim or the problem, so I definitely think it helps with some of the families. You know, that is one of the reasons that I came into this field in the first place.
>
> INT: How do you think it helps?
>
> WKR: I think it helps some families to see people who—even something as simple as someone who looks like them, someone who can talk to them. . . . So I think it definitely helps and I think it's like a modeling thing. It's not always someone else coming in to help but actually we're helping each other.

Many workers of color also felt they had specific cultural knowledge from their backgrounds that could be helpful both in deciphering how best to work with families and with their coworkers. Several people mentioned different kinds of disciplinary techniques; for example, several Latinos mentioned that corporal punishment was more common in the Latino community. A number of other examples were also cited. A Puerto Rican worker mentioned one way in which she was able to lend insight to her fellow team members. "Like in the Hispanic culture . . . you take a picture of your baby naked, like at a year old and two years old, and [others ask] 'why do they do that?' I don't know but it's there and it doesn't imply any kind of sexual—and so I've been able to use that. . . . It's something that's normal. That doesn't mean that they're being sexually abusive or you shouldn't be so negative about it or think about removing the kid from the home because of a picture. Like give me a break."

Other workers gave examples of generalizing from their experience to other cultures. Another worker felt his Dominican background helped him connect with people of all backgrounds, not just his own.

> INT: I'm curious if there's ways that your [Dominican] background influences your work more generally with all the people, or any of the people that you work with?
>
> WKR: I think just having hope for the people . . . And I think that has to do maybe with the way I grew up and just in general. My mother first didn't have a great educational background and I've seen her go to school. My stepfather . . . he ended up going to school, even later in his life, like in his thirties and stuff like that. And then they put education in me, so I've kind of seen where you can still have hope; it doesn't matter what age range you're at. For me it's easier when I walk into a family, I can see it as something that they could change. I think that's something that helps me in doing my work.

Overall, workers of color were more likely to consider their racial or ethnic background as a source of strength and insight, though several also mentioned cultural influences that they needed to watch for. Many white workers, influenced by color blindness, denied any impact of their racial or ethnic background, though there were also those who recognized its effects, both positive and negative.

Should Families Be Matched with Social Workers?

Whether to match workers and families—that is, have employees work with families of their own racial or ethnic background—was the third consistent debate that arose in the interviews. A color-blind approach basically rejects the notion that matching could be important, based on the same logic that individual differences override cultural ones. A color-cognizant perspective, however, doesn't insist on matching; instead it acknowledges both its strengths and limitations. Moreover, it looks more deeply into what matching is intended to achieve and identifies other ways of reaching those goals.

Color-blind arguments against matching were relatively simple and straightforward: "I just don't think that because two people are from the same place that you're going to work better with them, or you're going to work worse with them. I don't think it has anything to do with that. It's not about where the family is from," said a white worker. Another white worker agreed and connected her perspective with her understanding of basic American values. She criticized a decision in which a black family was assigned "to the black supervisor and the black worker and the black [manager]." She didn't agree with the thinking that black staff "could relate better." She continued, "I don't think that was a good forum. It might be a comfort level for some people, but it may not. You don't know. It's not giving people the opportunity to grow within themselves to learn about different cultures. It's not giving the family the benefit of the doubt that they can relate to other cultures, so that is a downside. . . . You can't just . . . that is not what our nation is about. . . . You can't just stick to your own—"

Although it was more common to hear this from white workers, some workers of color made similar statements. An African American worker felt that it came down to how the worker interacted with the family, not whether there was a concordance based on race or ethnicity: "I've gone into white homes and it didn't matter that I was black. I've gone into black homes and it didn't matter to them that I was black. Maybe I could relate, maybe I couldn't. But I think once you get in there, it's how they're treated by whomever is in there that makes a difference."

This reluctance to consider race could extend to situations in which a family, usually of color, asked for a worker from a similar background. Some felt this was usually a red herring: if a family didn't like what it was being asked to do, "sometimes that triggers them to say, 'well, I can't work with you because I need somebody of my own race.' . . . I've seen that more often than not." A team leader said that in these circumstances a client generally wanted "someone who is going to do what I [the client] want them to," and for that reason she rarely granted these requests.

However, those taking a color-cognizant approach didn't presume matching. They saw such a practice as potentially helpful, especially under certain circumstances. However, they also, drawing on the assumption that race and culture do matter, made the case that matching can have significant downsides as well.

Arguments for matching relied on several rationales. First, families might be more likely to feel comfortable with someone from the same background. "I think it [matching] makes some people more comfortable," said one worker. A team manager noted that families "brighten up" when they see they'll be working with a worker from their background. Others made the point that employees who have their own lived experience of a given culture can have useful insights that other workers could lack, that "people can be experts on their own experience," in the words of one respondent who referenced a Puerto Rican team member as an example. Several informants used the example of coining or cupping in some Southeast Asian cultures. Workers who may have experienced the procedure themselves or knew it as a common practice would know that it is meant to heal, not to harm.

Others felt that matching would help families feel represented in the larger system. Matching is important, said one respondent, because "it's always good to be able to kind of mirror the clients or the population that you're working with. . . . It gives them a sense of . . . it has something to connect to in society, I think in general. It definitely helps." Another noted, "I think it's important for people of color or families of color to see other people of color in some sort of position of . . . not necessarily power—but they need to see people of color helping people of color. And they need to know that it's not just, you know, white people who are, kind of, coming in and helping them." Finally, some argued that it was easier for workers to work with families from the same background, since they did have cultural insight. Mismatching workers and families created not only a "burden for that family," one worker said, but also "a burden for the worker."

For these reasons, some felt that workers and families should be matched if possible. One worker said, "I think, whenever possible, if you can match it you should. . . . And I think definitely families do feel more comfortable when you're with a worker who has some sort of similarities even if it's only visual."

Most respondents, however, believed that matching was complicated: it was one solution but not always the best solution. These respondents agreed with the positives of matching already stated but also felt there were downsides. First, an emphasis on matching could mean some workers had a homogeneous caseload—generally those workers who came from underrepresented groups, such as African Americans or Latinos. That homogeneity was a problem, for several reasons. To begin with, there was a general feeling that workers should connect with a variety of families for their own learning. Additionally, though, bilingual workers often faced additional work, both because they were asked to take on additional cases because no one else spoke the language, and because much of what they did had to be written in both English and the second language. As one team leader, whose team had only one Spanish-speaking worker at the time of the interview, noted, "My concern is that, boy, my [Spanish-speaking] worker is going to burn out. And I don't want her to get an experience of only Spanish-speaking families, because I want her to enrich herself with other families."

Second, matching was often predicated on simplistic assumptions about very complex beings: that similarity on cultural background would inevitably lead to a good relationship and that race or ethnicity would trump any other characteristics when it came to whether two people would connect. As a Cape Verdean worker noted, "I can tell you that when I had a lot of Cape Verdean cases, I had some families—I didn't like working with them. I don't care if we were from the same [background]." An African American worker noted, "I've had African American families that just did not want to see me coming. No matter how hard I tried, that just did not work for me. Whereas [white team member] came into that exact same lady and talked with her and she was very accepting. And he gave me cues, like 'try this, try that.' It just didn't work for me and her but it worked for him." A team leader recounted how assigning a Latino worker to a Latino family had seemed the best option but in fact had led to a difficult relationship; she learned that she couldn't pigeonhole people.

Third, some workers had learned that families sometimes expressly preferred to work with someone of a different cultural group, for a variety of reasons. In some cases, the concern was that, because their communities were small, word could spread, making their circumstances public. One white worker noted, "I've worked with a couple of different families with a Haitian background. . . . Actually, this other worker [of Haitian background] was able to tell me that other Haitian families tend to not really want to have a Haitian worker. Which I found very interesting, because I thought, well, the language barrier, I mean, it would be so much easier to speak with someone in your own language. But for them, it's about being ashamed. And shaming your family and shaming your country." In a case from another team, a black mother, who was mentally ill, found that black women workers reminded her of her mother and she requested a white man. These kinds of situations were sometimes brandished by color-blind workers to show that race and culture didn't really matter. Deciding not to match by race based on a family's preference is also an example of color-cognizant practice, however. Doing so takes race into account by listening and responding to a family's concerns and finding a worker of a different racial or ethnic background.

Fourth, a couple of workers pointed out that, when there was a match, it could be assumed that the worker would share experiences or opinions with the family that she, in fact, did not. Mismatching by race or culture meant that issues might be more likely to be explicitly brought to light because there was no assumption of shared understanding.

> I'm a strong believer that just because a family is black doesn't mean they should have a black worker because a black worker would necessarily understand better. And I'm a strong believer that sometimes they might understand *less* because there's an implied understanding that won't then be discussed. Where with me, my clients who are from a different racial group than me, often feel they need to describe what their experience has been in relationship to their race, or the fact that they grew up in an urban environment. And therefore they educate me and share their experience. So, sometimes I think that people need to be reminded of that because I think, we get really caught up in [the notion that] clearly by face value we would understand people and that implied understanding can be very dangerous.

Finally, everyone acknowledged that even if matching was preferable, it was often impossible because the agency was disproportionately white compared with its client population. As one worker pointed out, "You culturally match as best you can. It is not going to work out that way" because "you are never going to have a staff that matches the culture of the community."

Given the benefits and detriments of both matching and not matching, some respondents used a color-cognizant approach to resolve the dilemma, rather than a color-blind perspective that would dismiss it. Informants mentioned several strategies, which could all work together. One was to identify circumstances in which matching was particularly important. Most said that language was critical: although workers could get translators, it was better for everyone when the worker could speak directly with the family members. Other considerations also came into play. A number of people said it was important to take direction from the family, who "will downright tell you" that they want a match, in the words of one team member. "I mean if it [a mismatch] is a huge problem for the family, and it's becoming a burden that the worker is not working with the family, because the family sees it as so much of a problem, then, we should at least try to, you know, help the family out by trying to match them up with somebody that they feel most comfortable with in order to have a working relationship." Another said that if a family was nontrusting, it could be better to try and match. Finally, one worker said she felt matching was most important for families of color: "I might say that I feel it's more important for persons of color than I do for white families." When asked why, she said, "They [the families] can be more honest and a little bit of that judgment is being knocked off. Do you know what I mean? Like, I just think it's not so many barriers that they have to go through."

A second approach was to work on building empathic and respectful relationships with clients across different backgrounds, but it had to be done with a sensitivity to race, not a denial of it. One team leader noted that workers have to "get a sense of how important is their [the family's] culture, their race or ethnicity to them, and then you try and do your work based on that." Another made an explicit (and rare) connection with power inequities: "I have a client who has made the comment 'white people just don't understand me.' She's African American. I've had conversations with clients about . . . power and control and predominantly a lot of social workers are white and going into the homes, and we've had that whole conversation." He felt his ability to have those discussions enabled him to create closer relationships with his clients.

This approach also emphasized that workers had to be alert to what they could learn from families. Some, though, were concerned that families shouldn't have to play a teaching role. An African American worker said, "I think if you were to get, you know, a white worker fresh out of college who's like twenty-two and put her with an African American family who's been involved with the department for years—depending on her feeling and their feeling—I don't think that's fair to the family to have to always be a learning experience for someone else."

Therefore, a third strategy was to build a diverse and representative employee population not to match as much as possible, but to learn from each other, whatever the background of the families they were working with. As one worker put it, the benefit of employee diversity was, "The ability or the opportunity, I should say, to share all the differences and learn from each other." After being asked whether there were benefits to diversity, a different participant responded, "Oh, absolutely. I have gained so much knowledge, firsthand, from workers." She used the particular example of learning about the Cambodian culture and experience from workers in her office: "You can read about it, but to fully sit down with them, and talk with them about their experience, is so rich, I think, and you gain so much from them." She also acknowledged that it could be difficult for these workers to provide this source of learning rather than assuming, as some informants on other teams did, that there was no cost to them: "For them [Cambodian workers] to be willing to share—that was also really huge. To talk about that's why—you know, these are some of the cultural struggles that the Cambodian people have now. I wouldn't have known that." An office director also made the point that people with knowledge of other cultures made a particular contribution: "I really see our bilingual, bicultural workers training all of us . . . the understanding that they bring . . . sometimes it cuts through things that the rest of us can't cut through."

Another respondent thought in terms of office cultural competence, not just individual awareness. "When . . . the competency in terms of cultural diversity in an office is very solid and strong—the stronger it is, the more you are able to say [to another worker], 'I don't really know this, can you tell me about it' and not be afraid to say that 'I don't know.'" She then connected that with their work with their clients: "Then we mirror that again with our families when we say, 'You know what? Tell me about that because I don't know about that.'" The director makes the point that being able to say "I don't know" to a fellow worker could make it easier to say "I don't know" to a family.

In sum, those with a color-cognizant approach to matching acknowledged and wrestled with the complex issues it raises. To them, seeing matching as the only solution was a kind of simplistic racial determinism that discounted the ability to connect across differences. Denying its importance, though, dismissed the fundamental role of race and ethnicity in making us who we are. Ultimately, color cognizance meant encouraging cross-fertilization: engaging with others by going through difference rather than around it, by exploration and learning rather than suppression.

Color Minimization

Whereas lab and survey studies tend to differentiate between two clearly defined perspectives—termed color blindness versus multiculturalism[4] or pro-similarity versus pro-diversity[5]—we found these respondents' sensemaking to be much more layered, fragmented, and even contradictory. Most of the social workers clearly leaned toward either a color-blind or color-cognizant approach, but many revealed some ambivalence or inconsistency. As we noted in chapter 2, this is not uncommon: other studies have found similar patterns.[6] In this section, we enter the data from a different angle, to showcase how workers blended color blindness and color cognizance. We illustrate a phenomenon we call color minimization, a perspective that initially acknowledges the importance of race and culture, and then downplays them in some way.[7]

Color minimization manifested in several ways. In one, race and culture were cited as important factors to be aware of but then were seen as largely divorced from the core work of child protection. Some workers would characteristically say that race and ethnicity mattered but then add that something else mattered more—the parent's drug abuse or mental illness—without exploring whether that could be connected with culture. In fact, race and ethnicity were also seen as entirely separate from a child's best interests, the concern that they had to keep in the forefront of their minds. "We're sensitive to their culture but we also have to be even more sensitive to the child's well-being," said one worker. Another said that as a team they need to be "looking at all the kid's needs and discussing that, and then being culturally sensitive." From this point of view, race and culture seem to be tangents or luxuries that could be taken into account if there were the time and space to do so, as opposed to being fundamental elements of clients' backgrounds that would permeate their life experiences.

In a second manifestation of color minimization, it was common for workers to focus on the cultures of the families they worked with, but to avoid reflecting on the impact of their own racial or ethnic background. This is another kind of color minimization—one that minimizes attention to one's color or culture and how it contributes to casework.

A third indication of color minimization was revealed in the examples informants of all backgrounds used to think aloud about the role of culture, which usually referenced ethnicity rather than race. We think of this as cultural cognizance, rather than a full color cognizance. "With just ethnicity, I would say it's vitally important," said one team member, responding to a question about when matching worker and client might be more important. "You can't have five white workers in the Cambodian unit," said another worker, implying that it was particularly important to have ethnic matching with that population.

Respondents also made a distinction between recent immigrant families and native-born families or families who had been in the United States for a number of years. This was clear implicitly because, when giving examples of when it was important to attend to race or ethnicity, informants were much more likely to describe families who had been in the United States for a short period. It came up explicitly as well, however. For example, when asked if the team worked differently with families in which "race or ethnicity plays a role," one respondent said, "I think it is individual to the case. If you have a family that has just recently been here . . . their level of acculturation is certainly different . . . than somebody who has been here six years, fifteen years." When asked whether the team discussed issues of race and culture in their team meetings, another participant said it was rare. "Because most of them have been families that even though their diversity is different, they're like living in the United States for a long period of time, so there's really not questions that I have about, you know, what their lifestyle is like, I guess." Others also made a distinction between recent immigrants and those families who had been Americanized: "If they are first immigrating, I think it would be a benefit to the family to have a social worker of similar background just so they can—they have that connection and they can connect within the community with someone with a similar background and I am sure again language might be a barrier. If they are Americanized why wouldn't I be able to connect and learn about their culture from them and books and so forth?" Another informant made a distinction between African immigrant families and African Americans who had long lived in the United States: "I think if it's a family from Africa, like that they've migrated from there . . . because I think those cultures are so different. Should there be someone that may be more familiar with that culture? I think it would be helpful to the family. But in terms of a black family, I don't know if that's politically correct, but I don't really think that matters."

Other workers did believe that race, and not just culture, was worth attending to, however. A white woman worker, after being asked whether matching a worker and family by race or ethnicity was particularly important, noted, "I think that maybe families—it's more desirable sometimes for families. And I think especially for—like African American families kind of comes to mind. I feel like a lot of—and I don't know how many even—a lot of African American families or my perception is that they would probably prefer to have an African American worker." She stood out as the only white member of the sample to mention race in response to this question. Another worker said he believed that black families were sometimes treated more harshly than white families by the agency. These are examples of a fuller color cognizance that recognizes race, and not just ethnicity, as a critical factor in casework.

The Range of Individual Sensemaking

Our intent in this chapter was to showcase grounded conceptions of color blindness and color cognizance by illustrating how individual workers both reflected on and deflected issues related to race and culture in their work. We began by documenting the range of individual approaches to thinking about three questions related to the role of race at work. Regarding the first—whether social workers should treat families differently, based on race and culture—we noted that color-blind workers tended to get caught in two dichotomies. First, they seemed to think they could either treat families as fully unique, with no cultural influences, or as fully culturally defined, with no individual differences. Second, they appeared to believe that they must treat their clients completely consistently given that any deviation would suggest discrimination. Color-cognizant workers avoided this dichotomous framing. While they understood that every family is different, they were able to factor in race and ethnicity when they seemed relevant. They also tried to culturally tailor their approach if they felt it was necessary, aware that doing so would not automatically mean bias.

The second question posed whether social workers should draw on their heritage when carrying out their work. Color-blind workers, all white, claimed that they did not do so at all. Color-cognizant workers recognized the impact of their background, though in different ways. Some, mostly white, saw it as a blemish or defect that had to be erased, but others, largely people of color, saw them as sources of knowledge and expertise.

Question three related to whether social workers and clients should be matched. A color-blind approach implied no, because race and ethnicity didn't matter in the first place. Those holding a color-cognizant approach did not automatically assume that matching was either appropriate or preferable. They recognized both its upsides and downsides as well and considered how to reap its benefits without falling prey to its defects.

We ended the chapter with a different angle on the data that highlighted contradiction. We noted several common kinds of inconsistencies that exemplify what we call color minimization—a cognitive style that highlights but then diminishes race and culture.

Individual beliefs matter, but our primary interest is in how the teams did or didn't engage race and culture. In the next several chapters, we move from looking at individual participants to looking at their work groups. To do so, we focus on three of the in-depth teams that exemplify a range of approaches to racial-cultural practice. We begin with the only color-cognizant team, Team North.

~ Chapter 4 ~

Color-Cognizant Practice:
Team North

Teresa, a member of Team North and a bilingual Latina, was filling in her team members on some of her cases. She told the team that the local Catholic social welfare provider had just closed, which meant that its bilingual parent aide was no longer available to them. (The child protection agency sometimes hired parent aides to work with particular families on things like budgeting, disciplinary techniques, and the like.) "Completely gone," she said, "All of my families that had this service . . . She was the only Spanish-speaking—no services anymore." The full team, in dismay, reacted with "ooooohs" and "oh nos!" Antonia, the other Latina on the team and also bilingual, noted they had recently lost another Spanish-speaking support person; they were "losing all of these parent aides!" she said. A couple of minutes later, she turned to Teresa: "When's [Aware meeting] again? We need to go to that. The 27th?" Aware was the agency's internal caucus for employees from racial and ethnic minorities, as the agency called them, as well as bilingual workers. "We need to go to that [meeting]. We need to protest," she suggested. Teresa noted that she had it on her calendar. Antonia concluded, "I think we need to do something about that."

In this and the next two chapters, we spotlight teams rather than individuals by drawing in-depth portraits of three exemplar teams. Team North was the only team with a color-cognizant practice: it regularly discussed culture and, though less often, race and did so in-depth. The opening vignette gives an example of the group concern about the lack of bilingual resources as well as its intention to advocate at a higher level to change agency practices. The other teams we profile took very different approaches. We call Team East's practice, explored in chapter 5, *color evasive* because it discussed these issues infrequently and, when it did, only briefly. We explore *color hostile* practice in chapter 6 when describing Team South: it also spoke rarely about race and ethnicity but twice criticized the agency's color-conscious practices.

We use our observation of team meetings to determine the racial-cultural practice of the team as a whole. All of the teams met at least weekly. These meetings were the primary place in which the team discussed its cases and processes. If team members were thinking as a group about whether race or culture was related to a case or to team dynamics, this would be the place where they would have those discussions.

This source of data does raise several larger questions related to all three teams that require explanation before we delve into Team North.

One concern is whether the cases from the three teams were truly parallel and, therefore, comparable. Perhaps Team North brought up race and culture more often because its cases called for it. Maybe it had more cases in which the background of the worker did not match the background of the client. Perhaps the substance of its cases happened to differ and race or ethnicity appeared more relevant. We cannot know for sure, but we believe our comparisons and conclusions are plausible, for several reasons.

First, all the workers in all three teams could give numerous examples of instances in which they worked with families whose background differed from their own. This did not occur just with Team North. This was a common occurrence for all the members we spoke with. Second, the differences between Team North and Teams East and South were dramatic. If we were comparing relatively minor differences, then looking at explanations in terms of caseload differences between the teams might be fruitful. Team North regularly and fluidly discussed these issues. Team East and Team South did not.

Finally, and most important, the question of whether race or ethnicity might be relevant in a case is not an objective status but a subjective determination. It is influenced as much or more by the perceptions and assumptions of the perceiver than by the empirical characteristics of the case. Color-blind workers are much less likely to see race and culture as relevant; color-cognizant workers are more likely to explore whether they could be revealing or explanatory. Team North was simply more likely to hold the possibility that race and culture should be explored. For example, its members sometimes brought up questions about culture even when the worker was of the same background as her client. As we more fully describe later in the chapter, a Latina member brought up a particular disciplinary technique—kneeling in the corner—common among Latino families and asked whether it could be considered abusive. The worker was bringing to the group a question about her culture and its impact. This suggests that culture or race can arise in all manner of different situations; the question is whether the workers themselves perceive its possible relevance.

A second issue about our data relates to our focus on explicit conversations about race, ethnicity, or culture. We are aware that race is often discussed in code: that conversations that may appear to be about other things—differences in work style, issues related to poor families—may in fact implicitly draw on assumptions or stereotypes that are deeply influenced by racial politics and dynamics. Those conversations are important for understanding how race influences group interaction and decision-making.

However, we are interested in explicit conversations because they are explicit—because it was in these discussions that team members chose to make their thinking visible to others, chose to name race or culture and, sometimes, to explore their implications. Such conversations are quite rare in most workplaces; we have the opportunity to look at how people explicitly talk about race in a setting where such conversations were somewhat more common (though still infrequent overall). Moreover, our interest is in how diverse teams can learn together about the role of race in their work, and having explicit conversations is critical to group learning—whatever the differences in play, whether they are differences of opinion, professional background, organizational unit, or race and culture. It is through explicit conversations that much of the learning occurs. Conversations that operate through code, innuendo, or the presumption of shared assumptions (that may not actually be shared) often lead to confusion or inaction.

However, though we focus on explicit conversations when describing the team's racial-cultural practice, at other points in this and the following chapters we do explore implicit assumptions that may underlie participants' stated words. Further, we explore silence as well as voice: we look at what conversations are not happening as well as those that are, and at silences within conversations—for example, when a comment elicits no reaction from team members. Overall, therefore, our analysis relies on words spoken and unspoken, both of which are critical to understanding racial dynamics.

Finally, a third concern regarding the data relates to whether these explicit conversations were actually sensitive and insightful. Talking about race doesn't necessarily mean doing so productively or skillfully. However, we do not evaluate the individual judgments that team members make about whether and how race and culture are relevant in their work. That is, as we noted earlier, we do not assess teams on cultural competence. We are interested in whether teams operate in a largely color-cognizant way that is open to the role of race and culture (whatever the team ultimately decides) or in a generally color-blind way that presumes that neither is particularly important and therefore largely avoids them. Therefore, here we describe all the instances in which these topics are raised. We do take up concerns about stereotyping in chapter 8.

We begin the chapter on each team by filling in some background on the focal group. Then we describe its team-level racial-cultural practice. Following that, we explain each team's practice by delving into two areas in depth. First, drawing on data from individual interviews, we depict the team members' individual practice regarding color blindness or color cognizance. Second, based on data from individual and team interviews as well as team meeting observation, we portray the team and office context in which these individuals were embedded. We call this larger context the "intergroup incubator."

The Backdrop

Team North served a small racially and culturally diverse working-class city. The city had a large white population, a significant Latino population, a smaller black community, and a concentration of people from Southeast Asia. The caseload of Office North was roughly half white and a quarter Latino, the last quarter roughly split between blacks and Asians.

Team North was created out of an existing unit, though by the time the team formally got off the ground, it had already lost and gained two members. Significant turnover continued during data collection. However, it was always majority white and also had a white supervisor, a white manager, and a white male director. Two Latinas were on the team, one for the entire period of data collection, and another for about a year. The team also included one man for the first two years or so; by the end of data collection, two other men had joined the team. All the men were white.

Team North met once a week for a couple of hours, usually including only the team members and the team leader. Occasionally it had a consulting psychologist come in, and several times it worked with the teaming consultant to discuss items such as its goals and operating procedures. Discussions of cases dominated the time together, though members did discuss team processes and dynamics a number of times. The team also spent time giving quick updates, dealing with scheduling issues, or asking others to cover a meeting or supervised visit with a family. Additionally, members spent a lot of time talking, joking, and filling others in on developments in their personal lives.

Team Racial-Cultural Practice

Team North regularly discussed ethnicity, culture, and race in team meetings, the only team to do so, which is why we call Team North's a color-cognizant practice (though as we explain later in this chapter, the team talked much more about culture and ethnicity than about race). Not only did members discuss these topics often, but overall conversations were much lengthier and more in-depth than those of any of the other teams. Members were much more likely to use ethnicity, race, and culture diagnostically, that is, to help them understand what was happening with a family or to help them discern how to work with them. Further, multiple team members were usually involved, and a majority of the white workers, as well as the two Latinas, raised issues related to race. Team North was also the only team to discuss how differences in race and culture affected team dynamics. Therefore, not only were these topics discussed more often, they were more fully engaged on this team than on any other. In fact, Team North seemed quite comfortable in this territory in a way that set it apart from the other teams.

Case discussions involved culture, ethnicity, and race in a wide variety of ways. Roughly half these conversations were about individual cases and how a racial-cultural lens could help them comprehend family dynamics or suggest ways to work with the client. In one instance, team members explored why their perception of a dark-skinned mother—they were not sure whether she identified as black, biracial, or Latina—differed from the perceptions of the staff at her residential drug abuse program. The team members believed the client was doing a very good job with a very difficult child, but the program staff had concerns about her parenting. The team wondered whether the all-white environment of the program might be related to these differing assessments of the client. "We need to put that into consideration. She's going to address her kids differently [because of her background]," said one worker.

In another discussion, Antonia, of Mexican descent, asked the group whether a particular disciplinary technique—having a child kneel in the corner, which she said was common in Latin American culture—might be considered abusive in a U.S. context. They talked about how duration would matter—was it ten minutes or three hours? The consulting psychologist, a white man, thought about how to work with the mother: "When you deal with these cultural things, you need someone who will talk to her about alternatives . . . in terms of what is acceptable. . . . What's a better way of doing it [disciplining child]?" He also pointed to the limitations of the family's living situation: "Not much alternative if you're in a studio apartment. Can't send her to her room—she doesn't have a room. Corner's all you got."

Whether "hearing voices" could be culturally influenced, and therefore not a worrisome sign of mental illness, was the subject of a discussion about a young Dominican child. The team also made plans to find out whether the psychological evaluation of the child had been done in English or Spanish, given that both mother and son spoke little English. In another conversation, the team discussed an "African" father who was raising his children solo. Eliza, the lead worker, who was white, noted, "Culturally, he has major issues with the fact that he's raising these kids alone. . . . But he did it. He totally stepped up to the plate." As the team made empathetic comments, Eliza said, in a low tone so as not to be overheard by other staff, that she was keeping the case open because it was the only way that the father could keep the subsidized day-care slots that enabled him to stay in college without needing full-time work.

In several discussions, the team used immigration status to better comprehend family dynamics. In one case, Teresa used lack of documentation to understand why a family was sometimes out of compliance with their service plan. "They're from Mexico. They're illegal. They are petrified, absolutely petrified, of everything and everyone. A lot of what they do that they're not supposed to, or don't—it's more out of fear, not because they're being defiant in any way. They're a loving family, very close." The team also explored how differences in documentation status could aggravate domestic violence in a discussion about one couple in which the husband was documented and the wife was not. This may have added to his power given that she might be less likely to seek help or inform the authorities. In chapter 3, we discussed how some workers approached issues like substance abuse or domestic violence as straightforward and clear-cut with little connection to culture. This example shows how concerns related to culture and immigration can enhance understanding of abuse dynamics and enable more thoughtful intervention.

In their longest culture-related conversation, about forty-five minutes, team members discussed the extremely complex case of the family who had escaped from a civil war in their West African country, the case we described briefly in chapter 1. As we noted there, the team wondered whether the teenage boy was "getting in people's faces" because of aggression or because of a cultural norm. Arlo was concerned that his diagnosis of PTSD was "attached to every kid that comes from Africa." The team also determined it should get a cultural evaluation of the family from an outside agency to guide decision-making. In other parts of the conversation, team members brought up other culture-related issues. They discussed how difficult it was to find translators and therapists who spoke the particular dialect used by the family. They also decided that the male caseworker assigned to the case should no longer work with a female family member in her twenties, feeling that it might be more culturally sensitive to assign a woman caseworker for her.

The team also went beyond talking about race or culture as it affected particular cases to think about it more generally. At several points, the team deplored the lack of bilingual resources available to their Spanish-speaking families. In one of those conversations, quoted at the beginning of this chapter, one Latina member turned to the other and suggested they go to the next Aware meeting to protest the situation. At another point, they applauded when they learned that a bilingual worker had been hired as a substance abuse specialist for their region.

Team North was also the only team to have a conversation about how its demographic make-up affected team dynamics. In this instance, Katie, the team leader, noted that she and other team leaders would be meeting with the commissioner and, in preparation, had been prompted to ask their members about potential topics to raise with him. A white member of the team brought up the fact that Antonia was, at that time, the team's lone Latina and its only Spanish-speaking member (Teresa joined the team several months later) and wondered whether this could lead to an imbalance, given that Antonia could help others with their cases but that they could support her only to a limited extent. "Good question," said Katie. "How do you feel like we support you?" she asked Antonia, who responded that she did feel supported. She told her team that they were all "pretty much in touch with different cultural differences that are out in the community" and also knew when and how to ask for help when necessary.

Finally, we also include here one example from a team interview because it says so much about the team's comfort with and even eagerness to discuss these issues. In the first team interview, the team responded to a question about whether the agency should be racially and ethnically diverse with an animated debate among themselves about whether race itself was the critical factor as opposed to power dynamics that came from racial and class differences. Several workers, both white and of color, said they often had more difficulty working with white families because whites were more resistant to working with the agency. One said she felt that immigrant families "have more fear of those authority figures and have more respect toward authoritative figures." Another agreed: "Caucasian families have definitely been at least more vocal about being absolutely disgusted that they are involved with [the agency]. . . . I think that the other populations feel the same way . . . but they are not—the power thing and the authority and the respect for authority is taken differently." A third wondered whether the issue was more about socioeconomic status or class than about race: the wealthier the family, regardless of race, the more it would confront the agency's involvement. This exchange, which went far beyond simply answering the interviewer's question, not only demonstrated an interest in race and class dynamics, but also raised issues of power inequities that were virtually absent from the discussions of other teams.

In sum, as noted earlier, Team North attended to these issues in its casework and in its team processes, and also seized an opportunity in a team interview to explore the role of power in racial and ethnic dynamics. Overall, the members had a comfort level with these conversations that differed significantly from that of the other teams.

Team North did have patterns that revealed member assumptions about when race and ethnicity matter. Most of the discussions in team meetings were about immigrant families and therefore focused more on ethnicity and culture than on race. The team only twice discussed issues related specifically to race in the meetings we observed, once quite briefly. As we illustrate in the next section, white members of Team North, when asked in individual interviews to give examples of their thinking and practice, did discuss the challenges facing African American families. Additionally, one Latina worker described some inhibitions she had in working with a white family. Thus at least some members of the group showed racial awareness. As a team, however, its practice appears to be more culturally cognizant than color cognizant, though it was both. Again, this is likely as much or more a matter of the workers' perspectives than of the characteristics of the cases they worked with.

Team North was certainly much further along the path of color cognizance than the other three teams, however. Team North talked about these issues regularly and frequently and the other teams rarely did. This drove our analysis: what was it about Team North that enabled its color-cognizant stance?

Individual Racial-Cultural Practice

In this section, we begin the exploration of why Team North was able to create a color-cognizant practice—as a first step in understanding how the teams' racial-cultural practices varied so greatly—by focusing on individual-level practice. Certainly, the team members' beliefs and behaviors should have a significant impact on how the team worked as a whole. Therefore, as in chapter 3, we investigate individual thoughts and behaviors, but unlike that chapter, we organize them by team in order to assess their collective implications.

We look at two key dimensions of racial-cultural practice: whether a worker sees her background as having an impact on her work and whether she uses a racial or cultural lens to better understand the families she works with. Again, we are looking for color cognizance, not cultural competence. We are interested in when and how the workers invoked race or culture, not whether they did so with full skill and knowledge.

To inform this analysis, we draw largely on data from individual interviews. In those interviews, we asked a number of questions designed to elicit the respondents' espoused theories about whether and how race and ethnicity matter in casework. Then, to discern whether informants' practices actually aligned with their intentions, we asked them to talk about cases in which race or ethnicity had been an issue or had played some kind of role. If they said they had had no such cases, we asked whether they had a case in which they worked with a family whose background was different from their own. All said they had had at least one such case, which they then described.

As we describe individual practice, we make distinctions between team members and the team leader because the team leader has greater influence than team members and therefore requires closer attention. Where relevant, we weave in consideration of the team leader's racial or ethnic background.

We also make distinctions between the members of color and the white members because who says what matters. Because it is more common for whites to learn about race from people of color than vice versa, it is worth a special note when a worker of color describes learning about race from a white person. Because whites tend to be less aware of the impact of their background, they stand out more when they do. Moreover, the weight or meaning of a particular belief or action can differ profoundly depending on the race or culture of the actor. We all know that certain words can be said by a member of a racial-ethnic group but not by those from other groups. A person of color advocating color blindness has a different resonance than a white person doing so. A white person calling attention to discrimination against a person of color can—however unfairly—lend credibility compared with a person of color doing the same. Given who says what matters, after a brief introduction, we organize our discussion by looking at the two groups separately and then bring them together.

Team North's members were largely color cognizant. They agreed, at a basic level, that race and ethnicity matter and that the agency needed to be culturally diverse. Going beyond rhetoric, most of the team members, both white and of color, were able to provide numerous examples of how they manifested this color cognizance in their practice. As whites comprised the majority on the team, we begin with them and follow by exploring the practice of the two Latinas. Then we discuss Katie, the team leader, in more depth. We end by bringing all these threads together as we explore the individual contributions to the team's racial-cultural practice as a whole.

White Members

The white members were nearly unanimous in their belief that racial and cultural diversity was positive: "I can see different cultures and learn, and maybe be reflective about what other groups have to offer, or what other groups know," said Eliza. Workers spoke to the importance of reflecting the client population, but employee diversity also enabled cross-cultural learning among staff, as Dave suggested: "The more we have a staff that can suit the population of the community, the better. Not just for the workers to work with the client, but for the workers to learn with each other here." In other words, employee diversity meant that everyone had a chance to learn from each other and apply that to their own work with clients, whether their backgrounds matched or not.

A number of the white members, however, went beyond espousing the importance of diversity. They stood out among the white workers in the entire data set in their reflection on both key dimensions of a color-cognizant practice. First, they reflected on the consequences of their backgrounds, including an awareness of their prejudice, which was virtually unknown among white workers on other teams. Second, they were also able to provide specific examples of how they had used race and culture to better understand how to work with a family.

In reflecting about the impact of their heritage, several voiced concern about the possibility of bias that came as a result of their racial privilege, often intertwined with their privileged class background as well. Chris, as described more fully in chapter 3, said he had to be concerned about his Anglo-Saxon Protestant background, especially given that he had grown up in a wealthy community. "We have to strive to overcome [our biases] our whole lives," he said. His teammate Eliza acknowledged a similar dynamic but said that it was possible to turn preconceptions into a positive.

> INT: Do you think you draw on your background in any way, when you think about your work?
>
> ELIZA: I do. I do. I certainly have ideas about the way things should be. . . . We [agency employees] all say if a family has a decent

house, and a car, and they work, we tend to say, well . . . they're probably okay; whereas, a similar situation with a family that's in a Section 8 rundown apartment, and mom's home all day with welfare, we probably say we need to stay involved for a little longer, maybe. . . .

INT: Is that a problem?

ELIZA: I think that's definitely a problem. I think I've gotten better and try to say everybody doesn't have to have what I had to be safe, and everybody's happiness, even, is different, too. I tended to probably more, in the beginning, feel bad for people that didn't have what I had, or kind of pitied people, maybe, a little bit, which isn't fair. . . . So, I do think we draw on that, and sometimes we can use it positively, if we can turn it around like that, and say—

INT: How can it be a positive? And what's "it" exactly?

ELIZA: I guess those stereotypes that we have, because I guess, you know, at first glance, it's probably negative to have certain stereotypes about a family that's poor, but if we can say "what do they have, or what are their strengths, or what's positive for them?" then we can reflect about that, and not only what it means to me, but what it means to them, or what it means to the community, then that's what's important, I guess.

In this excerpt, Eliza made a critical point by not just acknowledging her stereotypes but mulling over how to challenge them to learn from clients about her work. For example, she noted that workers can ask "what are the strengths of this family?" rather than looking only at what could be perceived as weaknesses. She further pointed out that they can then reflect on the lessons from that exercise, not only as they pertain to that particular family but to the community as a whole.

Other white members were aware that their racial or ethnic background could be a resource and not just a wellspring of prejudice. Dave described how he drew on his Italian background in carrying out his work, seeing both its strengths and liabilities. He felt his "personality is somewhat reflective of that [being Italian]. . . . I know my weaknesses and I know my personality, and I know the way I present myself." He described his Italian-influenced personality as "open, honest, rigid." He felt, overall, that these characteristics were positives in working with clients, but he also recognized they could hamper his work as well: "I recognize what problems could come by addressing things in certain ways and acting a certain way." He added, "I don't think it matters where that personality or where those convictions came from, as long as I'm open to changing them if needed."

Dave not only could trace some of his personality to his Italian roots, he also understood that that didn't make his qualities immutable. Once aware of the influence, he could assess whether change might be needed. Most important, he, like several of his white team members, was able to articulate how his cultural background affected his work practices—an important cornerstone of a color-cognizant perspective.

Many of the white team members went beyond reflecting on their background to give numerous examples of how they had attended to others' race or culture in their casework with families. They provided many more of these instances than members of the other teams. In just one example, Chris mentioned learning that Khmer students in school were, with the best of intentions, being assigned to a Vietnamese counselor. Given the history of animosity between the two cultures, however, he knew this could actually create more problems than assigning them to someone who was not from Southeast Asia.

Moreover, several of the white workers on the team were not only culturally cognizant, but fully color cognizant in that they understood that awareness could also be critical with black families who had been in the United States for many generations. In fact, Team North was the only team in which multiple white workers acknowledged this. Eliza is the white woman described in chapter 3 who, in response to a question about whether to match workers and families by background, mentioned that it could be especially important for African American families. Arlo described facing an information gap when working with a black teenager. As part of his casework, Arlo had to determine how much the boy needed to cover his expenses but he was aware that his experience would not necessarily be helpful. "There are certain things that I don't know about," like hair care, he explained. So he turned to African American workers in his office and asked, "I prefer to go to a barber shop, because I just like that whole idea, but I can go to Great Cuts and pay $11 and get my hair cut. Is that realistic [for this teenager], you know? I clearly think that he needs to go to a barber shop. . . . How much is a haircut? I don't know." With the information in hand about this and other expenses, Arlo was then able to estimate how much pocket money the teen would need.

Another example involved Chris, who wondered why the agency had opened a new case, just added to his caseload, involving a black father. The case was brought to the organization because the father, who had been an agency employee in the past and was a consultant to the agency at the time of the allegations, had hit his son. Chris acknowledged to the interviewer that it was a "bad beating," but added that the abuse was not an ongoing issue and that he felt the mother could handle the situation. He didn't think the agency needed to be involved. Therefore, he disagreed with the agency's decision to open the case for assessment, in part because he felt that a wealthy white man would have been treated differently: "I've just seen cases like that go away, when there's a white person involved." He wondered whether the investigator had supported the allegations because of pique, perhaps influenced by a traditional white requirement that African Americans should act subserviently:

"I got the feeling that [the father] wouldn't act contrite. And I think we backed him into a corner where he felt like he couldn't say the words we wanted him to say." Chris, because of his understanding, was able to work with the man: "You know, he got around to saying he shouldn't have done it, but I didn't stick him in the corner saying, 'I want your apology now.'"

In sum, the white members of Team North stood out for their self-knowledge and reflection, as well as the ways in which they used their clients' race and culture to inform their work with them, including recognition of discrimination. Other teams each had one white member who had significant sensitivity, as we describe in later chapters, but no other team had such a concentration. We believe this was critical to the team's color-cognizant practice, but so were the contributions of the Latina members.

Latina Members

Two Latinas were on the team during the period of data collection. Antonia, who came to the United States from Mexico when she was five, was on the team for the entire two-and-a-half years of data collection and in fact had been on the unit, before it became a team, for about two years; the other, Teresa, of Spanish and Latin American descent, identified racially as white, was born in the United States, and was on the team for more than a year. Both women contributed to the team's color cognizance. Because of Antonia's longevity on the team, as well as her strong feelings about the importance of attending to race and culture, she had more of an impact.

Both Antonia and Teresa agreed with the white team members that it was important for the agency to be racially and ethnically diverse. Whereas Teresa felt that it was particularly important to have bilingual workers for those families who did not speak English, Antonia felt that a variety of issues related to race and culture could arise and that a diverse employee population would catalyze broader awareness. For examples, she cited such issues as when it was appropriate to use the terms Hispanic, Latino, and Spanish or on understanding the difference between economic and political migration.

Like several of the white workers, both Latinas were clear about how they were influenced by their backgrounds. Both described how they had to watch for bias given that they had grown up in middle-class families. Teresa explained, "We treat them [the families like ourselves] better. We give them more leeway. . . . And I don't think that's okay. Yes, it's actually kind of striking." Teresa described how the team had discussed this recently and that Antonia had personally owned up it: "I know Antonia responded. She acknowledged it. Like, 'yes, it's just hard because they're just like us, and it's just a normal family.'"

In fact, Antonia referred several times to a specific incident where she felt biases arising from her background had led her astray. Soon after coming to work with Katie, the team leader, she had a case with a Dominican family.

Antonia's immediate reaction to the family had been harsh: "I just couldn't accept like . . . they just didn't know how to parent the children, lack of advocacy with the schools or with the courts the children were involved with. I just wanted the children to be removed [from the home]. Because I just didn't agree with the way that they were being raised." But Katie helped her see the situation differently: "I can't push my values on them," she said. She couldn't remove children unless they were truly abused or neglected. She described this experience in a team meeting, willing to air it in front of others.

Therefore, both Teresa and Antonia, it appears, understood that they were raised to see certain things as normal and were working to counter those embedded assumptions, though Antonia was more willing to call out her mistakes. However, though they acknowledged their bias they more strongly emphasized the value of their cultural heritage as they conducted their work.

> INT: Are there ways that you draw on your cultural background in thinking about your work?
>
> TERESA: Yes, definitely. I think a lot of it, too, for me is I grew up in [city], which is primarily Hispanic. And I sort of lived both lives. I could be Hispanic. I could be white. And I very much was able to see how it was for both. . . . In a lot of ways I do walk into some of my families' homes, and I feel right at home. I had more than they had. I never really wanted for anything. But I sort of know where they came from.

Antonia's motivation for entering the child welfare field was to be "an advocate to the minority families, to the Hispanic population." She also believed that families were more likely "to open up to you if you know where it is that they're coming from. And you do have some sort of awareness about their background. Culture. Traditions. And the way that they do things."

Teresa and Antonia both had examples of how they had drawn on their cultural knowledge when working with families, though again Antonia went on at greater length.

Teresa said that she and Antonia always took culture into consideration, using domestic violence as an example: "Say the family is from Guatemala or Nicaragua or wherever from, that's a conversation that you have with this family." She noted that the women would often say "'This is what I know; this is how it was for my mom; this is how it will be for my daughter.' You can't tell them it's necessarily wrong, because that's their culture, you know?" When the interviewer asked, "What do you say?" she responded, "That I understand that that's the culture, and I just explain that it is different here. . . . So, somebody can be dominant, but it doesn't mean that they need to use their fists to show you their dominance."

Given her cultural background, Antonia felt strongly that she had expertise to share, especially about the local community and its Latino population:

> There's the Dominicans and then you have your Puerto Ricans and then you have your other array of Hispanic-speaking clients that we have here. And they have different traditions; they sometimes talk in different tongues; you have to have an understanding of that. And I grew up here and I grew up working for this community. I grew up working up for the Boys and Girls Club. I understand how my community functions. I understand how the public schools function. I understand how it all runs and how it all is put together.

She gave a number of examples of how this expertise had influenced her work with clients. One stood out, however, because it shows how she was able to connect with Latino clients while continuing to learn about cultures that differed from her own Mexican background. In this instance, a Dominican mother, whose children had recently been removed and placed in a foster home, called in to report on a Dominican foster parent who she felt was acting in an irresponsible way. Even though the individual was not hosting her children, the Dominican client felt she needed to notify the agency because, as Antonia put it, "I just wanted to report [because] I wouldn't want my kid to be treated this way in foster care." When Antonia recounted this incident to her teammates, they asked her how the client knew about the foster parent. Because Antonia went to a Dominican hairdresser, she had learned that the Dominican community was very connected: "Like everybody knows each other's business. . . . They all know about you from bottom to like the top." She continued, "Even though we service a large Dominican population in the city, they just all have the same traditions. . . . They all go to the same little market to get the spices. . . . they all go to the same church on Sunday. . . . And they're all there [at the hairdresser's] and they're all talking about each other's business." Therefore, Antonia was able to explain something about the Dominican community to her teammates.

Antonia's reliance on her cultural knowledge did not prevent her from learning about race or culture from her teammates. We've already described how she learned about her bias from Katie, the white team leader. She also gave another example when describing a wealthy white client family. "I do have a family that is Caucasian, well-off. . . . I'm like this kind of Spanish girl walking—you know, going into a very wealthy [town name] community— so it's more intimidating for me than it is for them." She said she was "very professional . . . play by the book, make sure that you're doing everything systematically." She also got some help from Arlo, her white colleague from a middle-class background. "I just think Arlo was able to kind of build a better rapport with them. And, yes, Caucasian, that had a lot to do with it. But I think his style . . . I think that he was able to give me a lot of feedback in regards to the makeup of the family and how they worked." Things changed over time:

"I've warmed up to them. . . . They see Antonia; they don't see Antonia the Spanish-speaking. . . . And now they're to a point where they're actually engaging with [agency] and they're using us as resources." This is the only example in the entire dataset of a person of color's learning from a white colleague about race or culture. Learning about race is often presumed as whites' learning from people of color; this shows Antonia's openness to the reverse.

Antonia herself was a catalyst for learning, as attested by multiple teammates. One team member noted, "her [Antonia's] Latino culture—she expresses kind of all the time, and talks about it, which is great, and I learn a lot about that, which I think is really, really helpful." Her colleagues also pointed out that Antonia, recently divorced, was a single mother raising two children while working full time. One suggested that, given her background, Antonia "has a different take on that [single parenting] than other people would." Her teammates also believed she could be a role model for the families she worked with: "She can kind of hold her families, and other families, to kind of a higher level, and say you can do this. There's a way to do this."

Antonia believed that she did play a special role in the team. "I feel like I am unique. I am a minority but I have also gone through a divorce within the life of the team. I am a single parent to two kids. I am involved in the community. And I will continue to be involved with the community. And I have strong views on the diversity of the community," she said. She was also largely positive about the team's sensitivity to these issues. Early on, she said she believed her team members were interested in what she brought to the team: "They're empathetic. They're willing to accept my contributions. So they're really open to diversity with different ethnic families." At another point, about a year later, she said, her team members were "definitely very open to listening to what it was like for me growing up and just my values." She also felt they brought their own insights to the table.

In sum, both Latinas contributed to the team. Teresa had cultural expertise regarding Latino families and provided this perspective numerous times. Antonia went beyond this to be a persistent voice on the team for attending more broadly to race and ethnicity. The combination of Antonia, Teresa, and their racially and culturally aware white colleagues created a strong source of support for color-cognizant practice. The role of the team leader, though, was also important.

Team Leader

Katie, the white team leader, did bring a consciousness of the importance of race and ethnicity to her work. Although she did not place the same emphasis on it that Antonia or some of the other white workers did, she showed some interest and self-awareness and never obstructed others' attempts to raise the issue. However, she never suggested that she might harbor bias, nor did she seem to recognize the racism and discrimination that often challenge people of color.

Like other white team members, Katie understood that she had been influenced by her cultural background, though she had less of the self-reflective capacity that Antonia and several of the white members of the team showed. She did articulate some of the assumptions she had that she felt came from her cultural and family background. Her great-grandparents had come from Sweden but had "become American": "So through my whole life, that was definitely engrained: you come to America, you learn English, you adopt American traditions and values. And so a part of me very much still believes in that—I don't understand in many aspects, why some—mainly Hispanic families—don't adopt that same practice." Katie seemed unaware that becoming American can take many different forms, depending on the individual or the cultural group. She also overlooked how being seen as American can be much more difficult for people of color than for white ethnic immigrant groups, such as her Swedish ancestors.

She went on to say that she had also learned that her family "never took money from the government, because you don't do that, you know? My grandfather used to send back his social security checks. That was very much, I think, engrained in me as a kid, too, from him." When asked how these "engrained" values affected how she did her work, she referred to things like picking which of the team's clients could get a turkey basket at Thanksgiving or Christmas: "I make choices all the time about what families get certain things, and I may pick a family, if the mom's working hard, is like the working poor, for lack of a better word—I will pick that person over a mom who may just sit at home, and could work, or doesn't do anything." When asked whether she had any concerns about that, she said, "It's probably not right," but did not indicate any real regret or any indication that that should change. Therefore, though she showed self-awareness of some of her embedded assumptions, she did not acknowledge, as Dave did, that such presumptions are mutable; nor was there self-reflection about whether those should be modified.

She was able to provide a number of examples of how she had taken race and culture into account when working with families. She mentioned getting a case of a Khmer-speaking family that had been transferred from a worker in another unit in which the father had been "labeled as resistant, combative." She and the worker assigned to the case met with the mother and tried to get some information about the father. "And one of my first things was 'which does he feel more comfortable speaking with? Would he feel more comfortable with English or Khmer? What do you think, Mom?' And she was like, 'Nobody has ever asked me that before. The other social worker never asked me. Do you have somebody who speaks Khmer?'" When told they did, the mother felt this would help. Katie recounted that Dave and a worker from the Southeast Asian unit went to meet with him "and he is fine. But I think it was understandable where he was—we are the government. We are a government agency. [Agency] has traditionally treated his wife like garbage. The old social worker was terribly mean to her. Horrible. Horrible. So why should he trust [agency]?"

Antonia had interesting insights into her supervisor, Katie. She believed that Katie "is sensitive, as far as having good cultural awareness about what goes on with the families," but she also thought the story was more complex and had seen her relationship with Katie change over time. "I think in the beginning we kind of bumped heads a little bit. . . . I think at first [it was] hard for her to adapt to me because I think that she already had a bias." Relatively quickly, however, they forged a close and respectful partnership. At the time of the interview, Antonia did not call Katie biased, but came close: "I think that she has had a very Americanized kind of . . . I am not going to say bias, because she has worked with a lot of families and a lot of different types of families." But she also felt she had learned a tremendous amount from Katie: "I had a different perception of how to be a social worker and I think . . . she has a lot to do with the fact that I am very family centered and I am talent driven and strength based. I think she has had a very great impact on that."

Overall, Katie brought empathy, some cultural sensitivity, and some self-awareness to the team. Antonia clearly gave Katie credit for her personal development. Antonia and several other white members, however, brought a capacity for greater self-reflection—including the willingness to identify their bias—to the table in a way that Katie did not. Moreover, Katie seemed particularly attuned to issues facing recent immigrants, a cultural cognizance, rather than those facing African Americans or other long-standing populations, a fuller color cognizance.

Individual Contributions

Team practice begins with individual practice. The racial-cultural practices of the individuals who made up Team North stand out in a number of ways. First, in Antonia the team had a clear leader, what some term a cultural broker.[1] She was an enthusiastic advocate not only for the groups she felt a personal connection with, but also for the broader importance of cultural awareness. Going beyond rhetoric, she demonstrated knowledge of a variety of Latino ethnic groups, based on her experience and long-time participation in her community. Not surprisingly, Antonia raised these issues several times in their team meetings and actively participated when others brought up the topic.

Antonia was not on her own in this territory. Teresa contributed her cultural knowledge as a Latina to the team; she also initiated race-related discussions several times. Further, the white members stand out in the entire sample for their self-reflection and sensitivity. They did not leave these issues up to Antonia and Teresa. Several described their concern with their own bias, based on their racial and class backgrounds. Most gave multiple concrete examples of how they put cultural awareness into practice, including times they were fully color cognizant and not just culturally cognizant. The team leader, Katie, though less knowledgeable and aware than some of her teammates, did show an openness and a capacity to learn. Therefore it is not surprising that we saw white members bring up racial and cultural issues about as much as Antonia and Teresa did.

In fact, learning was a continual thread through their discussions of their individual racial-cultural practices. Workers had multiple examples of learning from other workers in the office as well as from team members: Arlo spoke of reaching out to black workers to gain information about the cost of hair care; a number of workers testified to learning from Antonia; Antonia described learning from Katie about strength-based practice and from Arlo in ways that helped her connect with a white client family. Moreover, Antonia openly shared learning experiences that did not show her in her best light. Her airing of these prejudices may have been particularly influential since being open about her limitations may have helped the white team members feel safer about acknowledging and discussing their own. This learning theme is reflected in their meetings, as described earlier, where they dug into and tried to assess the role of race and ethnicity in their cases as well as in their team dynamics.

However, no one individual or even set of individuals can fully explain team practice. We flesh out the story of Team North in the next section when we look at their incubator: their broader team and office dynamics.

Intergroup Incubator

The intergroup incubator is the team and office environment, including the team and office leadership, in which the team members operate. We use the term *intergroup* to refer specifically to racial and ethnic groups. We chose it to highlight those aspects of the context that appear to have the greatest impact on relationships within the team and, therefore, the degree to which they are able to talk about race and ethnicity. In using the word *incubator*, we mean to bring home the potent role of the context. Just like other incubators, this incubator hatches or causes something "to develop or take form,"[2] but rather than chicks or embryos, it hatches a team's racial-cultural practice.

We investigate two primary dimensions of the context. First, we dig into learning behaviors. As noted in chapter 2, the literature highlights three particular behaviors: how a team resolves conflict (or doesn't); whether the team experiments with new ways of doing things; and its capacity for self-reflection, including the willingness to raise ineffective processes or even mistakes and errors.[3] Second, we look at the degree of safety that team members feel, that is, the extent to which they feel comfortable and welcomed within the group setting. We call this the *safety climate*. Research suggests that safety—a sense of assurance and protection from harm—is a precursor to learning behaviors.[4] Our inquiry explores both their psychological safety or general sense that they can take risks without disapproval,[5] as well as their identity safety,[6] the belief that they are accepted in spite of—or even because of—their racial or ethnic background.

For both these dimensions, we assess the impact of both team dynamics and the larger office context. We also weave in as relevant the influence of key leaders—including the team leader, team manager, and the office director. To do this analysis, we rely on data from several sources: individual interviews in which team members, including the team leader, could talk candidly about team and interpersonal interactions; interviews with the team's superiors, including the team manager and the office director, who were asked to assess the team on a number of dimensions; team interviews, in which the team as a whole discussed their practice and in which we could observe group dynamics; and their team meetings, at which we could observe both the content of their discussions as well as how they interacted as a group.

Team North was excited about being part of the teaming pilot: its members felt they had had a teaming ethos even when they worked as a traditional unit, and they were eager to move into this approach more formally. At the first training for all the members of all the groups, the team had a comfortable rapport with each other that stood out from the others.

The team had initially proposed, as part of its application for the teaming pilot, that it take on cases beginning with the investigation phase and follow the cases through to closure. Aside from a couple of cases, this shift did not occur, which was disappointing. The team's pleasure at participating in the pilot was still palpable well into the experiment, however. They felt that partnering on cases enhanced their connection with families. They particularly enjoyed their team meetings, which were animated and spirited. This seemed to be due, at least in part, to the team's larger dynamics. It showed a remarkable degree of learning-oriented behavior as well as a relatively high degree of safety, particularly identity safety.

The team's office may have played a role. Office North was generally seen as a well-run office, committed to the strength-based approach to working with families, and was often used as a site to run pilot projects to experiment with new ways of working. Team members generally reported office morale as positive and showed relatively little intergroup conflict. The office director stood out among the other directors as self-reflective and open to rethinking past behaviors.

Learning Behaviors

Team North demonstrated all three of the key learning behaviors: productively resolving conflict, experimentation, and self-reflection.

From the start, the team's dynamics related to conflict and difference were in strong contrast to the other teams. Team North was a lively, talkative group whose members loved to discuss and dig into issues. Far from being apprehensive about conflict, its members enjoyed throwing different opinions and approaches into the mix and seeing where they ended up. This was vividly apparent in team meetings and team interviews, in which we could watch their unruly dynamics firsthand, as well as from how they described the team and each other in their individual interviews.

We witnessed several examples of the team debating different aspects of its work in team meetings.

One intense debate concerned the boundaries of what its work entailed, triggered by an office memo that referenced two incidents, one involving Team North. In the first instance, two Team North members took a child in their custody into the office bathroom and cleaned out lice and nits (lice eggs) from her hair so that she could be transferred to a foster home. In the second, a worker in another unit cleaned a family's home to prevent the children from being removed. The union raised these issues with management to clarify whether workers were obligated to engage in these kinds of activities. Management had responded by saying it felt that these were personal style questions, up to individual workers, rather than ones suitable for collective bargaining. This set the stage for a very lively discussion by team members.

Teresa and Katie, the two workers who had cleaned the girl's hair, felt what they had done was completely appropriate. They pointed out they had repeatedly asked the parents to do it as well as approached the school nurse but had gotten nowhere. No foster home would take the girl unless she was lice-free. Other team members suggested that using the office bathroom might have been unwise, but Katie said they had fully cleaned and bleached the bathroom after they were done. "The bathroom was the cleanest it's been in a long time," said Katie, to laughter. Antonia agreed that sometimes social work meant providing this kind of hands-on support to families. "We've bought cleaning supplies for several of our families. To keep kids home? I would definitely clean [or] help them [the family] clean. Some people are depressed." Dave disagreed, "I think that's more of a role of a parent aide. We can teach, talk, have conversations—as far as getting down on our hands and knees and helping, that's their responsibility." Arlo agreed with Dave, "Putting on knee pads and getting down and scrubbing the floor for somebody is a little different than, 'Alright, I'm here, I've got some cleaning stuff, I'm going to talk you through it because this is what we expect.' That way you're able to clinically say, 'I've worked through this kind of thing with them.'" The team manager, Harriet, said, "You seize opportunities when they present themselves to really engage the client, get them to work with you." Dave said that he worked with clients on their finances: "How you're spending your money, stuff like that. I will sit down with a piece of paper, say 'this is all your money. This is what you're spending for this.'" This seemed different to him than cleaning, but Harriet disagreed: "It's the same, Dave. It's just that it feels more comfortable to you and that's all right." That seemed to capture the general feeling among the team— that there were differences in their approaches and that was fine, even good.[7]

The belief that productive conflict made them stronger was even more apparent when they discussed team dynamics, topics that most workgroups avoid. Team North members were so comfortable with conflict that they aired ongoing issues in the team interviews, meaning they were discussing internal tensions with an outsider present. For example, in their second team interview, Antonia described how she had made an error—one so serious that she had to speak with the team's manager and the office director. (She did not describe her error, but the other workers knew what it was.) She ascribed her behavior to the fact that Katie and Eliza—team members with whom she had had a longer relationship—were not in the office and therefore she couldn't consult with them. If she had spoken with them, she felt she wouldn't have done what she did.

Teresa, a newer team member, pointed out that she and two other more recent members were in the office but that Antonia had not asked them for advice. Antonia acknowledged this, saying that she was more comfortable with Eliza and Katie because she had worked with them longer. She explained, "You guys are kind of like newer and you're warming up what your roles are going to be on the team." Teresa empathized with Antonia: "I completely understand that you would prefer to speak to other people that you know better, especially because in a sense it was a little bit more personal, too, for you." Antonia agreed. Katie, the team leader, recognized another dynamic: "If Eliza was there, she would have said [to Antonia], 'Sit down and shut up and calm down and take five minutes.' Whereas you guys [Teresa and the two other newer workers] don't know her as well and couldn't [say that]." Antonia continued to reflect: "I'm like this person, [I] keep going and going and going. Just there's times where I just have to stop, reflect, and look. And I'm working on it." However, Teresa also pushed the team to consider the ramifications of the incident, using the discussion as an opportunity for learning: "That's interesting to look at [that Antonia did not come to her or the other newer team members], because we are all part of the team." And another member chimed in, "I also feel like maybe . . . ideally every team member would feel comfortable talking to whoever, the team members in the unit, on something like that."

This conversation stands out as an example of productively addressing something that could have blown up into a conflict. Rather than squelch the issue, the team chose to discuss it, regardless of the outsider in the room. Team members actually used the team interview as a chance to discuss tensions among themselves, rather than simply respond to interview questions. Further, team members attempted to empathize and understand the motivations of those with whom they disagreed. Teresa understood why Antonia chose not to go to the newer team members—because the issue wasn't a straightforward work decision but something more personal. Katie, the team leader and very close to Antonia, tried to see the perspective of the newer team members; she recognized that it could have been difficult for the newer team members to intervene because they didn't have the same kind of relationship with Antonia that Eliza had.

In fact, the team had ongoing and productive conversations about differences in work style—a type of conflict that can be particularly destructive—and in members' beliefs about how they should work together. In general, team members made an effort to reach across and understand a different approach, rather than to simply say it is wrong because it is different.

The biggest source of difference, everyone agreed, was between Dave, the lone male for the early period of data collection, and most of the other workers. First, he was less interested in the discussions about personal life that the group engaged in; second, he felt that sometimes the group "processed" cases too much, having long discussions that meandered and lacked focus. He would sometimes challenge the team to streamline its conversations. He also described himself as more self-reliant, but this he named as a problem: he was too independent and needed to learn to ask for help and work with others. This was one reason he was excited to be on the team.

In both team and individual interviews, team members surfaced the conflict with Dave and agreed with him that he needed to work on being more interdependent, but also said they could learn from his approach. Eliza noted in a team interview, "Everybody brings strengths to the table. Dave, you do have good advice about things. And so then I think we could all grow on that. And I think you could grow from saying 'I need help' a little bit more." Others' simultaneous recognition of his strengths and areas for growth may have contributed to his sense of feeling safe and open to learning. In an individual interview, Dave felt his team members were open to the different approach he brought: "They're open to learning and doing things differently, and they do utilize me in that way, and they do see that as positive." He was also open to feedback from others. He described a time when one of his teammates told him that he was more sensitive with families than with his coworkers, which he had found quite helpful.

The members' ability to learn from work-style differences is noteworthy, but for our purposes, another aspect of the debate is even more important. Dave believed, and several others agreed, that the contrast in work style was driven by gender, that he had a different way of approaching the work because he was a man. "It is definitely interesting being the only male in the group. I think it brings a perspective that they'd never had before and that will also cause them to disagree with some of the ways I view things." Others agreed: "I think Dave sees, because he is a man, he does see things differently but he will present his concern and we will take it and we will work with it because we have to utilize his feedback, too."

Dave also felt it was difficult to be the only man, that it added additional pressure to an already stressful job.

> INT: Are there particular dimensions of diversity that stand out for you on the team, that are salient for you on the team?
>
> DAVE: Gender. I don't have another male to bounce things off of. I'm the male opinion in the unit. They like that and appreciate that and validate that. But it is hard for me to be the only male perspective.

INT: What's hard about it?

DAVE: That I don't know everything . . . or my perspective might not always be right. I don't have another male social worker to say to, "You're a male, you work with fathers, or you work with a female client as a male, how do I work with a woman who's been the victim of domestic violence?" That's a whole different dynamic, that they can't help me with, the female social workers.

Dave's ability to reflect on gender dynamics, including how they contributed to a sense of insecurity, is noteworthy. It suggests both a high level of self-awareness and a relative comfort with making himself vulnerable. Indeed, Dave's experience of being the "only" could resonate with some workers of color when they are in the minority and called on to speak on behalf of their group. He did not make the connection, but it might have influenced his openness toward issues related to race and culture.

The team as a whole also stands out for engaging quite openly in this discussion. Although gender may not hold quite as potent a charge as race, it can be difficult for mixed-sex groups to discuss. No other team had these kinds of conversations. Team North did. Its members' ability to discuss issues related to a core identity like gender could be a sign of a larger curiosity and willingness to take on other primary differences, including race and ethnicity. That is, the team's comfort with difference and conflict, including gender-based conflict, could be a foundation of its color-cognizant practice. At bottom, color blindness is about similarity; it's about insisting that whatever racial or cultural differences exist are unimportant because fundamentally we are all alike. Color cognizance is about acknowledging and thriving on difference—something that is easy to claim and very difficult to enact. But difference was not threatening to Team North—it was intriguing, even exhilarating at times. Team members felt that it made the team stronger, not weaker.

Learning from difference is one critical learning behavior, especially when thinking about how to break the color bind, but there are others as well, in which Team North also engaged. Experimentation with new ways of working is a crucial activity, because it suggests the team is constantly searching for new and better approaches. Team North tried a variety of new things. For example, it instituted a formal check-in and check-out during team meetings when members could discuss how they were feeling. A whiteboard was used for important updates that everyone needed to know. Team members created business cards with all their names and telephone numbers on them so if the client couldn't reach the designated caseworker, he or she could call someone else on the team. Whenever possible, the caseworker introduced the client to all the team members (for example, when the client came to the office) so he or she would feel more of a relationship with others on the team.

The third learning behavior—perhaps the most difficult and most important—is the capacity to review prior work, identify errors or things that should have gone better, and then discuss what the team could do differently in the future. The team had a long conversation about its work with fathers, in response to a memo from higher-ups concerned that the agency's traditional emphasis on the mother had been eclipsing the role of fathers. "I think we haven't, in our practice, incorporated the fathers as much," said Antonia. Katie criticized the agency's "historical disregard and indifference for fathers." Teresa pointed out, "I think we should at least take the steps to find out what role the father thinks he wants to play. A lot of times we don't make contact. We don't know." "How do you think we can change our practice within the unit?" asked Katie. Antonia said they should apply the core practice values of the agency, which focused on being strength-based rather than punitive, to their work with fathers. They discussed whether they were too likely to suggest restraining orders to the mother before they knew whether they were necessary, "just to cover our own butts," as Eliza remarked. They ended when someone interrupted the conversation to tell Katie that she needed to come to another meeting.

As another example, several team members referred to a time relatively early on when the team had three removals (an agency decision to remove children from the home because of immediate concerns about abuse or neglect) in quick succession. Katie explained: "There was that week when we had those three removals. And afterward, as a team, we talked about it, like, 'we did the first one beautifully. What happened that by the third one we fell apart?'" They decided in the future to have a brief meeting with whoever was in the unit to identify who could help and assign roles.

Understanding a team's capacity for learning is incomplete without looking at its leadership. Team North's learning orientation may, in part, have been influenced by its superiors. Katie had the capacity to reflect on her behavior, as she showed several times in interviews and meetings. In one meeting, the team was recounting the story of a particularly difficult client, a "mom who could easily suck you dry," in Katie's words. This client left daily answering machine messages so long that they would fill up the entire repository for messages. "I realized that this mom just really grates on my last nerve," she said. "She's very draining," empathized Antonia. Katie continued, "Definitely transference issues. Her dad taught high school, my dad taught high school—you know. I was like, 'I'm having transference issues.'" By *transference*, she was likely referring to *countertransference*, a common clinical term meaning that she was having strong reactions disproportionate to the actual case, because the client's circumstances triggered emotions from her personal life. Katie was ready to send the case out of the unit when the lead worker left the team, but relented when the other team members convinced her that the case needed continuity. Recognizing and managing her reactions, and sharing that with the team, shows a capacity for self-reflection and making herself vulnerable.

Katie's supervisor, Harriet, was also self-reflective and open to learning. She is the participant in chapter 3 who described learning from workers from other backgrounds that coining and voodoo were not that different from her own culturally influenced beliefs, such as knocking on wood. The office director was also remarkably forthright and reflective about his style and decisions, which may have helped create a climate of openness and safety in the office as a whole. Unprompted, in two interviews, he raised things that perhaps he should have done differently.

In sum, Team North was a learning team. Like its comfort with conflict and difference, the team's ability to experiment with new ways of working and to review past actions could also be related to its color-cognizant practice. Being color cognizant means entering new territory: it requires trying to set aside one's culturally based tendencies and assumptions and being open to other ways of doing things. It means navigating among a variety of options and, sometimes, choosing one that is unfamiliar. It also means being able to admit when one is wrong and to regroup and try a different approach. The team's experimentation and learning from previous errors may have made it more natural for team members to experiment and learn in the racial and cultural realms as well. These skills, along with members' capacity for constructive conflict, mark their learning approach. This approach was only possible, however, because of the safety climate that the team had established for all its members.

Safety Climate

Research suggests that safety—a sense of assurance and protection from harm—is a precursor to learning. Adopting a learning orientation can be risky—it involves addressing conflict head-on, reviewing mistakes or areas in which the team feels it is lacking, and trying out new approaches rather than sticking with the old. It is not surprising that safety would be a prerequisite. As noted earlier, both psychological safety and identity safety are important, and Team North had relatively high levels of both.

Regarding the broader sense of psychological safety, team members generally felt they were accepted for who they were and what they brought to the team, as revealed in this example:

INT: Do you feel accepted on the team? Do you feel like you can be who you are?

ARLO: Yes.

INT: A hundred percent?

ARLO: Yes. I definitely speak my mind or kind of act like a clown, and own it, and people seem to be cool with it.

Carla, who joined the team about a year after the launch of the teaming pilot and had no previous experience at the agency, felt that her contributions were appreciated, even though she was new to the organization. When asked, "Do you feel like you can have an impact on what happens in the team?

Are your ideas taken seriously?" she responded, "I do. I think I have a lot of ideas about the team probably from a different perspective." She proceeded to give an example of a recent discussion in which she questioned the basic premise of the conversation. Instead of being defensive, the team picked up on her point and decided to institute her suggestion moving forward.

Another indication of psychological safety is the willingness to make oneself vulnerable, including admitting that one is stuck or asking for help. Harriet, Team North's manager, saw changes in this respect soon after team members began working together. "I really see a shift that they're more willing to ask for help of their peers," she said, adding that the requests had started to shift from simply asking someone to cover for them when they were in a time crunch to "I'm a little uncomfortable about this doing it alone or I don't feel like that's my best skill." Katie also felt that the team had gotten to a place where members went beyond sharing work to sharing the more personal burdens of doing very difficult work day in and day out and explicitly connected that with safety: "These are major life decisions that we are making and I think as a group you are able to share that and you are able to really look at the good and the bad and the hardness of it and wrestle in a safe place because it [the team] is such a safe place. . . . I know I can go in there and say 'this is what is happening to me' and they are going to support me."

Several people noticed a particular change with Dave, who had said from the beginning of his participation with the team that he needed to be less independent and more interdependent. Katie said that she had seen a big adjustment: "Actually, Dave has been so much better . . . really a huge sort of [change]—him just saying 'okay, guys, I need your help with this' has been really nice to see."

Another indication of safety is the degree to which members feel they can criticize their superiors. While it's not uncommon for individuals to say they can do that, it's very rare to get an example of it. Dave felt that Katie had created an environment in which it was okay to raise a concern with her and gave an illustration.

> INT: If you thought that Katie had overlooked something or made a decision that you really didn't agree with, or made a mistake, would you feel comfortable pointing it out to her?
>
> DAVE: Yes. And that's her strength. That I could point it out to her. . . . She's very open not only to discuss decision-making and client stuff, but personality stuff as well. She's very open to growing, very open to change. And that's rare.
>
> INT: Can you think of anything that you've ever pointed out to her, that you've raised with her?
>
> DAVE: I've actually talked with her in the past month, that she gets very emotionally wrapped up in things. . . . And she knows that.

She said, "Yes, you know what, I am. [The director] talked to me about it, too." And like I said, Katie is one of the best supervisors I've ever seen at [agency]. . . . And that [being open to talking about her weaknesses] is also one of the things that makes her a good supervisor.

This is another example of holding the complexity, both a person's strengths and areas for development, which can make it more palatable for the receiver to hear the overall message. There was also evidence of identity safety, not just psychological safety. No team members explicitly referenced a particular social identity when describing feeling safe on the team, so we had to look for implicit evidence. Dave said he found being the only man on the team difficult in some respects, but his willingness to raise those issues with his teammates suggests a measure of gender-identity safety. Antonia's comments, detailed earlier, that she believed her teammates valued not only her cultural knowledge connected with her Latina heritage, but also her leadership on these issues suggests that she felt identity safety as well. Perhaps more important, no Team North member suggested that they felt any level of identity threat. We show in a later chapter some individuals on another team named a particular social identity, such as their racial group, as putting them at some risk.

A workgroup's larger environment will also affect whether its members feel safe. Team North's office context may well have contributed to its sense of safety. Higher-ups in the central headquarters praised Office North for its commitment to the strength-based approach to working with families, effective administration, and relatively strong morale. In fact, Dave felt the office was a place where issues related to identity could be explicitly discussed.

I think we can openly all talk about this in this office. You're more than likely to see a male work with a batterer and a female work with a victim, for example. I think we all kind of know that. That could be looked at as sexist. But I think we all kind of understand that . . . might be what's in the best interest of the client. So we have to look at that. To have an African American worker work with an African American family, or vice versa. . . . And it's great to have that diversity so we can learn from each other. And again, that sounds cliché. But I see it in practice every day. And I would think everyone in this office appreciates that and sees it as a great strength.

Dave is suggesting some level of identity cognizance and even color cognizance in the office as a whole, not just the team. A couple of team members did note that individuals from different ethnic or racial groups tended to spend more time together and that occasionally Latino workers would speak Spanish to each other in front of non-Spanish-speaking workers, but these were seen as largely low-level issues and to be expected in a diverse office.

Overall, then, Team North was a relatively safe team. For the most part, its members felt that their contributions were valued and that they were accepted for who they were; they also made themselves vulnerable to others by asking for help and admitting what they did not know, and at least one member felt that he could raise concerns he had about the team leader with her directly. There were indications, as well, of identity safety. Safety is likely also critical to engaging in color cognizance. First, it is an important contributor to learning behaviors, like self-reflection and constructive conflict, which are likely connected to color cognizance. Safety may also have its own direct effect: issues related to race and ethnicity can be fraught and difficult; they can raise hackles and cause discomfort. To be able to take on the tensions related to such conversations, members have to feel that they can take a risk, which is fundamentally what psychological safety is about.

It's important to note that the team was by no means a nirvana. In fact, its largely functional conflict turned, toward the end of data collection, into more problematic contention. As new team members arrived, they questioned things that the older team members took for granted. They didn't feel that they worked that differently from how they had worked in their previous units. They wondered whether their long weekly meetings were that productive. However, though psychological safety diminished somewhat, identity safety remained strong. Even as team dynamics became more conflictual, Team North continued to engage in thoughtful case conversations, including ones that involved discussion of how race and ethnicity might affect the family. Color cognizance seemed wired into the team.

Explaining this cognizance requires attention to both individual practice and the intergroup incubator. Team North's members, both white and Latina, and including the team leader, had largely color-cognizant leanings. Several recognized the importance of race, not just culture and ethnicity. The team atmosphere was productive. Members raised all kinds of potentially contentious issues and tackled them, often with zest. They experimented with new ways of thinking about their work. They had a habit of returning to previous work that they felt didn't go as well as it should have and think about how to improve in the future. Team members felt comfortable and safe enough to admit when they felt they had erred or to ask for help or to raise and discuss issues related to culture and gender on the team. Their leaders, including the team leader, manager, and director, all had a similar interest in learning and reflection. Office North had a reputation for good work, being open to experimentation, and positive intergroup relations.

As we show in chapters 5 and 6, Team East and Team South diverged considerably from Team North, though in very different ways. Each profile illuminates different and pivotal individual, team, and office dynamics. In chapter 7, we synthesize the stories of all three teams to describe a model, in both graphic and narrative form, that brings together all these elements and their relationships to each other.

~ Chapter 5 ~

Color-Evasive Practice: Team East

On a cool fall morning, Team East's leader welcomed a visitor to the team's meeting, a representative from Aware. She had come in hopes of recruiting members for the organization. Aware was twenty years old, the representative recounted, initially formed in response to concerns about the "disproportionate number of minority kids in the system." It had tackled a variety of issues over the years, but its members sensed a new opportunity, as the Aware rep noted: "The commissioner is trying to enforce and bring [Aware] to the forefront, trying to make it bigger." She encouraged team members to come to the caucus's annual meeting to be held the following month and noted longer-term needs. "The organization is always looking for members, to sit on different committees, help with some grievances. . . . Most of all we want you to join and participate," she said. The members sat silent. Finally one asked about the time commitment, which the representative downplayed: just a monthly meeting held not far from the office's location, she said. After another silence, the team leader thanked the representative for coming and moved on to discussion of a member's case.

In this vignette, the team's actions literally speak louder than its words: the members' reticence is conspicuous. Majority of color, its members individually attended to issues of race and culture and were color cognizant in their own practice. Yet as a group, the topics were barely mentioned and never explored. Therefore, Team East presents a puzzle. To solve it, we begin with some background on the team and then describe its racial-cultural practice as observed in its team meetings.

The Backdrop

Team East was located in the heart of a large and diverse community of color in a big city, and the majority of office employees were of color, a much higher representation than in most other parts of the agency. The office caseload was roughly half black, a third Latino, and the remainder whites and Asians. Team East was a new unit, unlike the other two teams, which had been formed from existing units.

Staff from Office East and its regional office had decided to create a team whose caseload would be made up of families with children who had mental health diagnoses. Most of its members had previous experience with the agency and two knew each other as coworkers, but none had worked together before they joined the team. The team leader was hired from outside the agency, though many years before she had worked for the agency in another office and capacity.

Although the membership changed somewhat over the period of data collection, it was always majority people of color, including African Americans, Latinos, and a Cape Verdean worker, along with white workers. Its team leader was a Puerto Rican woman who identified racially as black. Its manager was a white woman and its office director was Latina. It had one male worker, of Dominican descent, who was present during most of the period of data collection.

Team East usually met twice a week for roughly two hours at a time. Meetings included the team leader and members and the team's manager (the direct supervisor of the team leader). Occasionally, one or two psychologists who could provide advice and consultation about mental health issues also sat in, given the team's focus on families with mentally ill children. Because of this focus, the team leader and several of the team members brought more clinical training and experience. Case discussions therefore tended to be more clinical than those of the other teams, about mental health diagnosis, treatments to date and other options, medications, and attempts to understand the deeper psychological motivations of the parents and children they worked with. This meant that the team tended to have very long discussions about an individual case—often thirty or even forty-five minutes. In addition, it spent time on logistical issues—clarifying agency guidelines, scheduling meetings, and so on. It also had a number of conversations about team structure and process, often facilitated by the teaming consultant.

Team Racial-Cultural Practice

In their team meetings, the team—which was about two-thirds people of color and one-third white—rarely discussed the role of race and culture in their work and when it did, the conversations were quite brief. Given this, we have named the team's practice *color evasive.*

Over the course of data collection, we observed only a handful of conversations that in some way related to race, ethnicity, and culture. One was the Aware recruitment attempt we describe at the beginning of the chapter. The others came in the context of case discussions. All were quite brief, a few turns at most. (Research using conversation analysis sometimes refers to turn-taking or the back-and-forth participation by multiple people in a discussion.[1]) There was no pattern in terms of who raised the issue; both whites and people of color brought up the topic and no one did so more than anyone else.

In one case, the group spent a moment trying to identify the racial or cultural background of a family, but with no success. The presenting caseworker remembered that "a long time ago" she thought the mother had said the family was Italian, but other team members theorized the family could be African American or "a little bit of everything." Without additional comment, the team moved on. In another, a white worker working with a black family noted that the mother did not want to let the worker into her house: "She has a million reasons against anyone coming in. One is racial—doesn't trust white workers, [she thinks] that I would judge the look of her home, but she's also had nonwhite providers and she's refused to work with them because they're ignorant, in her words." The worker said nothing more and no one else responded.

Although none of the conversations were in-depth in that they used a racial or cultural lens to really dig into what was going on with a given family, on a few occasions workers made empathic comments informed by cultural sensitivity. One long discussion concerned a Latina mother dealing with both domestic violence and three mentally ill sons, all diagnosed as bipolar and in foster care. As the lead caseworker noted, "She [the mother] is being thrown too much—even with just the domestic violence history and meetings and her kids. In another language, in another culture, that would overwhelm me. And she's homeless." A consulting psychologist responded, "How terrible for the mom to be separated from her kids, trying to work." These workers try to identify with the mother and avoid blame or judgment, but neither they nor anyone else went the extra step of, for example, using a cultural lens to potentially help understand why all three children had been diagnosed as bipolar. This contrasts sharply with Team North, whose members—taking just two examples—used both cultural and mental health expertise to comprehend why the boy from West Africa stood so close to others or why the young Dominican child might be hearing voices.

At the end of a discussion about a Dominican grandmother and the two grandchildren she was raising, the worker noted that the risk of abuse or neglect was low: "There are parenting concerns, not major concerns, but the way she parents, one, it's cultural and, two, she has some resentment to her own kids [the parents of the children in her care] and that plays out in parenting." She did not elaborate. In this case, the worker did suggest that culture may underlie some concerns she had about the grandmother's parenting, but she did not explain her reasoning and no one else asked her to clarify or said anything further.

Overall, and in noteworthy contrast to Team North, Team East discussed race and ethnicity rarely and, when it did, did so very briefly. When a white member dismissed a black mother's concerns about working with a white caseworker, no one else on the team said anything. Several workers made empathic comments regarding immigrant parents or grandparents who were struggling with difficult issues, but none ever used race or ethnicity as diagnostic tools that could guide their intervention with the family. This is why we call this practice color evasive.

Individual Racial-Cultural Practice

Like Team North's, most of Team East's members individually engaged in color-cognizant practice, both regarding their awareness of their backgrounds and how they took others' into account. Here we investigate how their individual approaches may have influenced their team practice. Because members of color were more numerous than whites, we begin with their practice and then show how that of the white members aligned or differed.

Members of Color

The team's members of color held a color-cognizant perspective. When asked whether it was important for the agency to be racially and ethnically diverse, all nodded. Some agreed with Team North's members that it was important to reflect the community as well as provide the opportunity for workers to learn from others. Others provided different rationales: "I think it is important . . . for the staff to represent the people that we are serving . . . but I also feel that it is important for the families we work with to know that people of their same background are also helping and can also be on both sides. . . . That it is not just people of another background helping or fixing. That we can also help and fix each other," said Esme, an African American.

As with Team North, these workers went beyond espoused views to give a number of concrete examples of how they took race and ethnicity into account, in terms of both the impact of their background, including watching for bias, and using a racial-cultural lens in their work with families. Several described how they could draw from their life experience. In some cases this was particularly relevant for people from the same background as theirs. For example, two members of the team felt that their Cape Verdean teammate had good success working with families from that country.

Team members also felt their expertise was more broadly relevant. Jasper, a man from the Dominican Republic, described how he could help team members understand corporal punishment in some Latino families: "I'm not saying all Hispanic cultures but sometimes they . . . spank a kid on the butt or something like that. You have to kind of see how far is it? Is it abuse or was it within their cultural norms? This is important." Jasper is also the worker in chapter 3 who described how his background gave him "hope for the people" and a belief that people can change.

Isabelle, the Puerto Rican worker who grew up in a poor New York neighborhood, also felt her heritage had broader resonance: "I think that [being Puerto Rican] brings a spin on it, the way I speak. Sometimes I use, like, slang." She also felt that her background made her sensitive and elaborated, "I think I give the clients the benefit of the doubt, where my supervisors old and new have been like, 'get outta here, like once a drug addict, always a drug addict,' and I'm like 'no, maybe this time they're going to change.' So I kind of tend to be a little bit more sensitive in that area." At another point, she provided a specific example related to sleeping arrangements. Team members were concerned that children of seven or eight were still sleeping with their parents "and there was such a huge issue and I was like, 'I slept with my mother until I was like thirteen.' . . . I don't think it's such a big deal. I mean, if we can help them get a bed, that's great. Maybe they can't afford a bed; that's why I was sleeping with my mother 'til I was thirteen, because we couldn't afford a bed.' "

Overall, Team East's workers generally believed that their background was a resource for them as they grappled with tough problems, but two workers described dynamics in which their background made their work more challenging. Dolores mentioned two instances, in both cases echoing Antonia's experience on Team North, in which she felt she had to more carefully manage her identity. The first, described in more detail in chapter 3, was that the success of her immigrant family made it harder for her to work with some Cape Verdean families that were struggling: "Maybe I set the standards like too high, like I said, 'Gee, my mother came here as an immigrant. She worked in a factory really hard. Why can't you just get up?' " This recognition led to greater awareness as she worked with cases more broadly: "I make a point of not reading assessments when I get cases because I don't want to go in there with this prejudgment about the family or this is exactly what happened."

Second, also similar to Antonia, Dolores felt her background could put her at a disadvantage when working with well-off white families, because she felt intimidated by them, though she could turn the situation around.

> INT: Are there ways in which [your cultural background] makes
>   it more difficult for you to do your job in any way?
>
> DOLORES: Yes, sometimes. I'm often intimidated . . . working with
>   new Caucasian clients. Like I remember I had a case
>   where the family lived in [wealthy community]. . . . The
>   class was different. The race was different. The culture
>   was different. So, I was intimidated, and I had to sort
>   of learn more to get past that. . . . Automatically you
>   assume, well, they really shouldn't be involved with [this
>   agency]. . . . You think . . . they know more than you;
>   they know the law better than you . . . and you're kind of

like, "oh, my God, what's going to happen when I walk into this family's home?"

INT: How did you manage them?

DOLORES: Well, I met with the family, and I talked to them. That changed everything . . . Just getting to know them. It was hard meeting with them, you know, because "who are you? This is what you have to do before you can come into my home." . . . And finally like setting my foot down and saying, "Well, I have to meet with you." And going in there and sitting down with them and sharing my knowledge and my information of what I know. "This is what's presented to us. Why don't you tell me what's right and what's wrong"—just having a conversation.

This example, along with the similar story from Antonia in Team North, shows how the power dynamics of race and class have impact, even when workers have clear legal authority. Even though Dolores and Antonia had formal jurisdiction, and even though both were seasoned social workers, they were intimidated by working with wealthy white families. Both squared their shoulders and overcame the challenge, but their stories show how broader inequities can worm their way into day-to-day professional relationships.

Isabelle also felt her background occasionally posed a challenge. She believed that her low-income Puerto Rican origins often helped her connect with clients but found that she had occasional difficulties with African American clients:

I would hope to be able to develop relationships with my clients because I'm similar, you know, to most of my clients. It works, but at the same time, I have African American clients that would prefer a white worker versus a Hispanic worker and [they are] very rude when they contact me and that's kind of hard. And I found it difficult to work with impoverished, excuse me for saying, ghetto, very poor African Americans. . . . I don't know why but sometimes it is and they're not very receptive and I've had to really work hard at forming relationships.

Overall, these workers were quite clear about the impact of race and ethnicity, often flavored with class, in their work with clients. For the most part, this impact was positive in that they felt they had knowledge, empathy, and expertise from their own heritage, though two also mentioned concerns related to identity that they had to manage. One member of color, however, put particular emphasis on the role of race and ethnicity in her work. Esme, the only African American, felt that workers and families should be matched whenever possible because workers of the same race were likely to have greater empathy and understanding and could act as advocates. She also felt that the team did not pay enough attention to these issues. She brought up a case in which she felt that the mother had not been treated fairly because of her race but that the other team members did not agree with her. She also felt that the team did not talk about race and ethnicity enough, especially when workers were working with a family different from their own: "Just to say you're working with another culture" does not "erase the issue," she said. "I think it needs to be a conversation about what's that like and what kind of biases you may have. And that's for everyone." She went on: "That's how you learn and grow. Just to say that we're social workers and by definition social workers are these unbiased people who love everyone and want the well-being of all people—[that] is not necessarily true." Esme's attention to racial issues stood out among her colleagues of color.

So, like the two Latinas on Team North, the members of color on Team East were color cognizant. The white members of the two teams were not aligned the same way, however.

White Members

The two white members of Team East each had a different approach. One, Libby, was clearly color conscious. She believed the agency needed to be culturally diverse so that workers could learn from each other when they worked with clients whose backgrounds differed from their own.

The other, Grace, seemed much more ambivalent, a stance we identified in chapter 3 as color minimization: she stated the importance of race and culture but would then deny that assertion. For example, when asked whether she felt the agency should be racially and ethnically diverse, she said yes but then noted, "It doesn't matter really the color, it's just the person is what's different," making it sound as if everything came down to individual rather than racial or ethnic group differences. She used exactly the same pattern when she discussed the friendship she had with Isabelle, the Puerto Rican worker. She seemed to value the friendship in part because she had never had a Puerto Rican friend before: "I've never been friends with anyone Puerto Rican, you know?" She was able to identify specific things she had learned from her friend, such as how different cultures may value material goods differently. Immediately after expressing her appreciation for knowing someone with a Puerto Rican background, however, she said, "to me, it [cultural background] doesn't matter and I don't think it mattered to her." Grace seemed caught in a dichotomy we raised in chapter 3: she felt she had to choose between a perspective that sees individuals as unique or one that suggests color or culture trump everything. She had not yet found a way to resolve the dilemma, so she went back and forth.

Both Grace and Libby could connect their background with their work, though Libby went on at greater length. Grace, having grown up in a Polish family, felt "that my perspective of something is going to be different than someone who's Puerto Rican, because of the way we're raised, which totally makes sense to me." She did feel connected to her Polish background in part because she was close with her grandparents, who were immigrants. She felt her family had been able to escape the cycle of poverty and encouraged her clients to believe they could as well. But she also felt that she had to distance herself from one aspect of her background: "in terms of like how my grandfather was . . . Because he was just very prejudiced, and judgmental. . . . I loved him—so much! . . . but I learned that you can't work with people that way." While Grace's repudiation of her grandfather's racism is commendable, she never acknowledged the possibility of her own bias, nor was she able to consistently see race and ethnicity as potential sources of strength and insight.

In contrast, Libby emphasized the enriching aspects of her upbringing. Unlike several of the white members of Team North, she never raised the possibility of her own racial or cultural bias. Instead, she talked at length about the strengths of her background, having grown up in a small college town in a rural area:

> I grew up in a community that's a little bit different than most traditional communities . . . [my community] is primarily a white community, and those people who are of color . . . are actually some of the most wealthiest people in town . . . They're the professors in the college in my hometown. . . . So, my experience is really different than the mainstream, around what it means for me to be a white woman . . . and so . . . my experiences have been really positive, where I think [for] other white women, that's not necessarily true. And I think that really does impact how I look at families and work with families.

As an example, she described a previous work experience "being the only white, English-speaking worker in an all-Latino organization":

LIBBY: So, I think that also has impacted me around my job to understand and work with cultures that are different than mine.

INT: What kind of skills has it given you that you rely on?

LIBBY: I think a cultural sensitivity; the ability to feel comfortable in asking questions that can often be difficult, about race and about other things—other cultural differences . . . And have an understanding of what it means to be different. And being able to sit with that.

Libby could have used her class background to deny white privilege, but instead it seemed to have added complexity to her understanding of race and culture and her comfort with confronting issues of difference. Rather than having the need to erase difference and emphasize homogeneity that comes from a color-blind perspective, she was "able to sit with" and explore difference. Because of this sensitivity, Libby felt she had been able to build relationships even under challenging circumstances. It was Libby who, as we described in chapter 3, was able to cultivate a relationship with a black mother who had said she didn't "allow white people in her home." Libby described how, over time, she gained this mother's trust and, eventually, entrance into the woman's house.

At the same time, Libby also felt that issues of race and ethnicity could be overplayed, compared with other kinds of identities or facets of difference, such as sexual orientation, immigrant status, and religion. She mentioned these in an individual interview. Esme also recalled that Libby had made this point at an all-staff meeting: [Libby] "made a comment that one of her pet peeves is that 'we're always talking about families of color and it's not just families of color. There are immigrants. There are, you know, gay, lesbian, bisexual families who also face these as barriers, so we shouldn't always limit it to families of color.'" Libby seemed to be somewhat irritated with what she perceived as too great a focus on race and ethnicity.

In sum, Grace appeared to be grappling with what weight to give to race and ethnicity, both naming their importance and then denying it. She seemed to focus more on avoidance of prejudice than the richness of cultural background. In contrast, Libby was color cognizant: she had been thinking about the role of her background in her work for years and had examples of how she had been able to manage significant racial differences with her clients in part by learning from them. However, she was unlikely to champion these issues, given some equivocation on her part regarding their importance. Neither took these issues as seriously as the white workers on Team North, who never, for example, suggested that race and ethnicity were overplayed. This helps us understand why the team failed to create a team-level color-cognizant practice. Understanding the role of the team leader and her superior will help fill out the picture.

Team Leader and Team Manager

The manager for Team East (the team leader's supervisor) sat in the same area as the members of Team East and regularly attended their team meetings. Therefore, she had much more of an impact on her team than Team North's manager did on Team North. For that reason, we include her in our description of those who made up the team.

Pilar, the team leader, had a long history of clinical work with mentally ill children and adolescents. She was born in Puerto Rico and identified racially as black. She described herself as "very big on knowing the race, ethnic backgrounds of families." She recounted how she had worked with families when she was a frontline worker: "I always made sure to tell the families who I was. And say, 'Look, I don't know what your thinking is, but we can work together. I can work with you, tell you more about my culture. You can tell me more [about yours].' And I think in many families, especially adolescents, that was a way to let me in their lives, and I'm very grateful for that."

She also thought about issues related to race and culture in her role as a supervisor of other workers. She felt that workers' practice was improved overall when they worked with families different from their own, but she also recognized this could bring challenges. In her interviews, she brought up two cases in which she felt her workers seemed intimidated by the difficulties of working cross-racially, which worried her. In one case, "they [the family] prefer to have an African American worker, and my staff [on the case] is Latina. So she feels that she needs to, every time she goes over there, she has to find somebody who looks like them." In another case, a black mother told her white caseworker, "You don't know what it's like to be black. I don't work with white workers,' and so on and so forth." Pilar asked the worker how that felt, but, according to Pilar, the worker didn't directly respond: she "went around it." As the casework progressed, Pilar felt she was "carrying the case" for the worker; the worker, who Pilar felt usually did excellent work, seemed to be abdicating responsibility for the case. "I always will wonder if this worker did not carry on the more case management duties because of that barrier." This shows how Pilar used race and culture to diagnose what might be happening not only with families but also with her own staff. Overall, she was far more familiar and comfortable with these issues than Katie, the leader of Team North.

Debbie, Pilar's white supervisor, did not foreground race and culture as Pilar did, but did affirm the importance of racial and ethnic differences. When asked whether she saw any benefits in working with an ethnically diverse team, she responded, "Oh, I see a lot of benefits. . . . The ability or the opportunity, I should say, to share all the differences and learn from each other." Also, though she did not reference the possibility of her own bias, she did acknowledge some effect of her Jewish background. "Well, maybe just that I can appreciate family, and so when I know that I'm working toward reunifying a family or creating a situation that kids are really going to benefit from being in a safe, supportive, nurturing environment . . . maybe it does come from that [being Jewish]."

In sum, both Debbie and Pilar brought cognizance to their work, though Pilar championed it to a much greater extent.

Individual Contributions

Given that Team East rarely and only superficially discussed race and ethnicity, the team shows that even if most team members engage individually in color-cognizant practice, the team as a whole will not necessarily do so. It also demonstrates that advocacy, even strong advocacy, by the team leader is not enough. This helps us see how difficult it is for color-cognizant practice to gain a foothold, even when the territory would seem friendly. The intergroup incubator is a critical contributor, as we describe in the next section, but the roles of individuals on the team are also telling.

Most important, Team East had no equivalent of Team North's Antonia—no one who both took leadership on these issues and was acknowledged as someone to learn from by others. One would think Pilar would have played this role, and indeed she tried to. She emphasized the importance of race and culture with the team and in fact instructed the team members to include this information when presenting a case either orally or in writing. However, she said, the team resisted. "I have to say, I am struck that the workers don't do that [note race or ethnicity] at all. They present the case as if there was no race or no ethnicity. And I brought up clearly in the beginning how important this was. And I have to say it does not happen." Pilar said that she used to ask about cultural background when her team members presented cases, but she had stopped: "At this point I'm like, you know, 'do I always have to be the one bringing up this matter?'" As we discuss in the next section, there was bitter conflict between Pilar and most of the team members regarding a variety of issues, including her management style. Because she had so many struggles with them about other things, she felt she had to "choose [her] battles," and emphasizing race and culture was one she had largely given up. Because team members were harshly critical of her, not only were they unlikely to follow her lead in this area, it may also have become one of the ways that the workers resisted her authority. Therefore, though she tried to play a leadership role like Antonia did, others did not allow her to do so.

Esme, who also felt very strongly about these issues, might also have played a role similar to Antonia's, but did not. Unlike Antonia, she did not continually champion these issues, nor did other workers see her as a leader. She said that she had spoken up in a couple of case discussions based on her sensitivity to racial issues but the other team members had not agreed with her. Moreover, no one said anything about learning about race or ethnicity from her. It's noteworthy, in fact, that when team members referred to others having some kind of cultural expertise, they referred to those from immigrant backgrounds—Puerto Rican, Dominican, or Cape Verdean. Esme's strong awareness and knowledge from growing up African American was never mentioned. Although she might have been able to create a united front with Pilar on these issues, the two of them had an acrimonious relationship, as we explore further.

Libby brought significant awareness and even ease with race and ethnicity to the team, something that can be very difficult for white workers. As noted earlier, however, she did not turn her gaze on herself as the white members of Team North did. Although she spoke about her racial background, she never suggested that it could bring bias, nor did she ever explore how it might have influenced her practice. Moreover, as we described earlier, she seemed annoyed with the attention that race and ethnicity received in her office. Therefore, Libby also did not champion these issues as Antonia did. It is also true that white workers were a minority on the team and, despite her seeming confidence on this terrain, Libby may not have felt fully comfortable or safe raising or exploring these issues with her teammates.

Not only did the team lack an authorized leader on these issues, the lack of learning among teammates was striking, particularly compared with Team

North. Dolores described two dynamics that were quite similar to dynamics that Antonia described. In the first instance, she described the intimidation she felt when working with a wealthy white family. Unlike Antonia, however, she never mentioned speaking with any of her white teammates to gain insight about how to work with them. She also described having to manage her bias when working with some Cape Verdean families, just as Antonia did with some Latino families. This came up only in an individual interview, however; we did not see her mention this in a group setting so that her teammates could learn from her experience. Isabelle described difficulties she had with some African American families, but never spoke of reaching out to Esme to garner greater understanding. These could be matters of circumstance or individual differences, but they could also suggest larger team dynamics. In fact, given the individual potential on this team, their rare and largely superficial conversations about race also point to the intergroup incubator as a player. To explore the incubator, we drew on team and individual interviews as well as team meeting observation.

Intergroup Incubator

Team East confronted significant problems from the start. First, its focus on families with mentally ill children, with no reduction in number of cases, proved to be overwhelming; after about a year, this focus was dropped. Second, it was created specifically for the pilot initiative; most of the others were existing units that chose this new way to practice, though because all the teams had significant turnover, they often welcomed new members. Creating the team from scratch, though, meant that Team East's members were also meeting and working together for the first time. Although this didn't necessarily bode ill, it did add another layer of complexity and uncertainty.

Third, the team received inconsistent messages about how much ownership and autonomy it had. Members were told they would play a greater role in defining their work compared with workers in traditional units. However, this wasn't reflected in practice. New members were added to the unit without consulting even the team leader, much less its members. Further, though the team was told to come up with ways of structuring members' work together, the team superiors vetoed members' ideas without making any attempt at discussion or negotiation. In part because of these mixed messages, the team never figured out a way to formally share responsibility for cases and worked much as a traditional unit would, except that it met weekly to discuss cases and team members found it easier to ask other team members for help. The group was disbanded after about two years because of its inability to come together as a true team.

Finally, and crucially given our topic, Office East, in which the team was located, had recently undergone a tumultuous period that continued to reverberate. The office director at the time, who was white, was perceived by some as favoring white employees in hiring and promotion. Further, several interviewees, both white and of color, recounted a racial incident in which, as one described, a black doll, "gagged and bound and a Tootsie Roll up the butt," had been placed on the desk of a Latina worker "who was very vocal." After this incident, the agency hired a consultant to work with the office on race relations. At around the same time, higher-ups merged Office East with a neighboring office, resulting in "complete crisis," according to Debbie, Team East's manager. The leadership from the neighboring office largely supplanted the leadership from Office East, including its director, which created resentment. All of these issues continued to simmer at the time that the teaming pilot began, providing a sharp contrast to Office North's environment, which was largely seen as constructive and functional.

This larger history and context set the stage for a very dysfunctional set of team dynamics. An exploration of the team's learning behaviors and safety climate sheds light on how the team foundered so substantially and helps explain why the team largely evaded discussions of race and culture.

Learning Behaviors

In strong contrast to Team North, Team East evidenced a lack of capacity to engage in any of the three key learning behaviors: productively resolving conflict, experimentation, and self-reflection. Like Team North, it had a lot of conflict, but Team East's was almost entirely dysfunctional. Rather than experiencing differences as a springboard for seeing things in a new way, the team remained stuck in intractable divisions, the most severe between the team members and the team leader.

The polarization began early on: within six months, team members were openly challenging the team leader's authority in team meetings. From then on, serious dissension in team meetings was typical and frequent. In their individual interviews, the team members, the team leader, and her superior described animosity. Team members had many criticisms of Pilar, the team leader. First, because Pilar was hired from the outside and had not worked for the agency for many years, the team members believed she lacked knowledge about basic questions of paperwork, agency rules, and the like. They found they had to go to others to get their questions answered. This may have undermined her leadership, making it easier for team members to defy her. Second, the team members believed Pilar was a poor communicator: "It's been communication problem after communication problem and one thing we agreed on is squashing communication problems," said Libby, one of the more outspoken members, in a full team meeting. Third, team members also felt that Pilar tended to be rigid when it came to applying the rules to individual families; other supervisors might bend the rules to help a deserving family, but the workers felt that Pilar was closed to the idea. Fourth, they said she was defensive and lacked the capacity for personal reflection. Esme recounted that Pilar had told her that she was filling in her time sheet incorrectly; Esme checked with the administrator responsible for timesheets and was told she was doing it correctly. Esme told Pilar this but said that Pilar did not acknowledge her error.

Finally, team members were angry that Pilar refused to reveal any details about her private life. The team leader admitted she was adamant about her boundaries: "This is a professional setting. . . . There are other things that you don't need to know. I mean this is not a social club." She went on, "I am still the supervisor. I am not [their] friend. I am not their parents either. I mean seriously, I'm not." Debbie, the team's manager, said this conflict had "taken on a life of its own" and that both sides had dug in. Debbie felt that "given that she refuses to say anything, then your curiosity has [been] piqued that much more." If Pilar were to answer a few questions—about her age, whether she was married, where she lived—Debbie felt the tension would dissipate and the team members would lose interest. Pilar may have had ample justification not to divulge personal details, but her refusal exacerbated tensions with the team.

Pilar had her own criticisms of the team members. She felt she was trying to involve the team members in processing conflict but when she did so, the members did not engage. In one case, she had disagreed with several of the workers about whether to return children to their parent. She revisited the discussion at a later meeting but the worker that had been most opposed to the decision remained silent, thwarting Pilar's attempt to talk it through. Further, though she generally felt their casework was up to par, they were always behind on compliance with updating their notes about their cases. She also criticized their writing, particularly the court reports they had to write if a family was court-involved (because the agency had decided to remove their children, for example). According to her, the reports were riddled with grammatical errors, which she pointed out to them. The team members resisted making the changes, saying that was her job. In general, she felt their oppositionality came from their immaturity.

Finally, as discussed earlier, Pilar raised another concern that directly relates to race and ethnicity: she felt that these issues were critical to understanding families but that the team members overlooked them. She had ultimately given up this fight, given the range of other conflicts she faced. Grace gave her perspective on this, which suggests some resistance, as part of a larger concern that Pilar was "extremely particular." Grace continued, "So, if you're doing a closing summary—a closing summary that would have been okay in my old unit is not okay here. So, it's given back to me, and it's like all the specifics—race, ethnicity—that's fine, but we already know all that. We've had the case this long; go into dictation, look at it, you know? That is all stuff we know."

As noted earlier, Debbie, the office manager, was quite involved with the team. She often sat in on their weekly meetings and her office was right next to the team's, so team members would often ask her advice. She would often play a role in resolving conflicts between the team leader and its members, which may have undermined Pilar's authority. When asked how she saw the team, Debbie said, "The biggest problem, I think so far, really has been the lack of trust and the lack of professional respect between the workers and the supervisor," calling it a "schism." She had criticisms of Pilar—she was too involved with cases, she wasn't helpful in individual supervision because she followed her own agenda rather than responding to the needs of her workers—and the teaming consultant said there was tension between the two of them. Debbie had concerns about the workers as well, however. Esme she described as "sarcastic, abrupt, and disrespectful" and felt she was influencing newer members of the team, especially Jasper. She felt that everyone was contributing to the team's problems. "If you asked me a couple of months ago, I probably would have been more—that the problem was just with the team leader. But, it's not. It's definitely both [the leader and the members]." Debbie acknowledged the role of the workers, but her criticism of Pilar may have led her to allow the open defiance of team members, something she could have used her authority to temper.

The contention, though, was not only between the team members and Pilar. Several members brought up a time when team member Dolores, who joined about a year after the team had begun working together, said that she felt isolated because other members seemed to have more interaction with each other than with her. Esme described her reaction: "And I said, 'I'm going to, kind of, call you out right now and say that you don't volunteer to do any teaming things. You don't ever say, 'Esme, can you come' or if someone asks you, you're not always, like, volunteering." Libby concurred. She said the other team members said to Dolores, "We feel like you're sometimes out of the team because you don't offer to do stuff as much as we do, and you never ask us to go out on a home visit with you, and this is sort of where things are at." Dolores also described the incident, saying, "It was kind of hard to actually say it" to the rest of the group. When asked how the group responded, she said, "I think people were a bit defensive." In this case, the team members all point to someone else as the source of the problem. This stands in stark contrast to the discussion on Team North about the time Antonia chose not to speak about a problem she was having to some team members she knew less well. In debriefing that conflict, the members actively tried to understand each other's perspective and their own contributions. Team East's members resorted to defending themselves.

Therefore, unlike Team North, which profitably engaged differences, Team East had continuous and counterproductive conflict, from early on in its life, that team members were unable to resolve. In fact, rather than striving toward mutuality, individuals became locked in their positions, unwilling to acknowledge that they had something to learn from those who disagreed with them.

Team East attempted experimentation, the second learning behavior, but was unable to make any new approaches stick. The most striking example was the team's incapacity to create a formal way of partnering on cases and thus fulfilling the mandate it had been given as part of the teaming pilot. The other teams managed to move, at least in part, from working solo to working in pairs or trios, but Team East never did. Team East members tried some other experiments early on including creating a "face sheet" for every case that would include the most important information so that everyone on the team could get quickly up to speed if they were called on to help; they also considered creating a standardized list of tasks for each worker. They gave up on both these experiments, however, and basically worked as any other unit would, except that they met weekly to discuss cases.

Finally, evidence of self-reflection or constructively reviewing errors, as we saw, for example, in Team North's discussion of its work with fathers, was scant. When the interviewer asked whether the team engaged in reflection about its work or team processes, most members flatly said no. In response to this question, Libby did give an example of how she and Pilar had had a conversation about one of Pilar's practices that Libby objected to, but it was basically a confrontation, not a time for mutual deliberation: "So, I thought I'm going to do it [address the practice] this time, right here, right now and just said to her it was very irritating . . . that I was very mad about the situation; that it felt like she didn't have confidence in the ability of me to be able to do my job . . . it wasted my time, and that I didn't understand why it happened." Libby reported that Pilar eventually apologized though it was unclear whether her behavior changed as a result.

Both Pilar and Debbie seemed to contribute to the team's lack of learning behaviors. Pilar brought years of clinical experience and was seen as an astute clinician, but we have no examples of Pilar reflecting on her behavior as team leader, as we saw Katie from Team North do when talking about her transference issues with a client. We also know that Pilar was also seen as rigid and by the book when it came to casework. These characteristics could contribute to a stifling of learning on the team. However, it is possible that she, a leader of color in a white-dominated organization, felt that she was under greater scrutiny than white higher-ups and therefore had to be much more careful about taking risks. Significant research, including Rosabeth Kanter's pathbreaking work on tokenism, suggests that leaders different from the norm endure greater scrutiny and visibility.[2] If Pilar herself felt at risk, it is more understandable that she would act in a defended and insular way, rather than one that was open, inquiring, and flexible. That could not only inhibit experimentation, but open self-reflection as well, given that explicitly admitting mistakes or weaknesses can make one more vulnerable. But even if Pilar was unwilling to reflect or bend the rules because it could make her vulnerable, her not doing so could still suppress the team's learning.

Like Pilar, Debbie had a lot of influence on the team. She seemed leery about giving up too much of her authority, even though that was a prerequisite if the team were to truly begin taking responsibility for its own work.

In Debbie's first interview, she said, "I may tend to allow a process on issues in the teaming unit that . . . other units don't get that opportunity for. But if a decision needed to be made, ultimately it's mine to make." This may have contributed to the team feeling that they were stymied in their attempt to make the team more self-managing.

Debbie's firm grip could also have undermined Pilar's ability to project authority to the team. Ultimately, at the request of the director, she gave the team more latitude, but the problems may have been too deeply embedded at that point. We also never saw Debbie engage in the kind of reflective practice that Harriet, her counterpart on Team North, displayed.

Given the intractable team conflict and its members' inability to experiment or reflect as a team, we are closer to understanding why the team avoided conversations related to race and culture. In some ways, its lack of such discussions seems very surprising: most team members and the team leader brought knowledge, awareness, and interest to the topic. If team members are unable to bridge differences of opinion, however, if they are truly unable to come together as a unit, then it seems quite reasonable that they would evade issues that could heighten conflict, including questions related to fraught issues such as race and ethnicity. This could be even more the case given the history of interracial conflict in the office, something we explore in greater depth in the next section. In fact, the conflict in the office and on the team suggests that both psychological safety and identity safety were severely compromised.

Safety Climate

Both psychological safety and identity safety were largely absent in the team, but the dynamics were different. The lack of psychological safety was openly and widely acknowledged by team members, but explicit concerns about identity safety were fewer and more subtle.

Pilar herself suggested that team members may not have felt psychologically safe: she described trying to process disagreements but that people remained quiet, perhaps because "some of the staff are afraid of speaking up." She also recounted two team meetings with the teaming consultant, when he had asked the group generally how things were going, but the members simply said "OK" or were silent. He suggested to her privately that team members didn't "trust each other yet."

Esme described an incident in which she brought up some concerns and then found her commitment to the team questioned. "At the last teaming meeting . . . I was very vocal in saying that, 'Something needs to give. I am not happy, I'm frustrated. Where are we going with this?'" She was asked at that meeting "if [she] was ready to give up," to which she said no. At the following meeting, Debbie, the team manager, began a conversation, without naming names, about whether team members were fully dedicated to the team. According to Esme, Pilar said to the group, "'If you're not committed to moving forward in this team it's understandable. It's been a long haul. Let us know because we need committed members on this team, and we can make sure that we'll find someplace for you to go.'" Esme asked whether the discussion was prompted by her remarks at the earlier meeting and was told it was. She was angry: "And I said, 'I don't think it's fair for you all to question my commitment when I've been at practically every meeting. I've stuck in here. I've come in here with ideas and thoughts. And, you know, I've shown my commitment since I've been here.'" This is a classic example of an unsafe environment—in which someone took a risk by airing concerns and subsequently found her motivation and engagement doubted.

Another team member, Libby, felt that sometimes her team members did not give her the benefit of the doubt and, rather than taking things at face value, felt that she was out to protect her own interests. "I feel like sometimes people interpret [others' intentions] versus ask what people's intentions are around things, and that can be complicated," she said. Later in the interview, she was asked, "Is there anything that either enables or inhibits you from speaking up, or asking questions or taking action on the team?" Libby responded that "sometimes the team dynamic will do that," continuing, "I think that's where people making their own decisions about why people do things, versus taking things at face value and that kind of stuff, so that impacts me to sometimes sit back or not choose to say things." Libby was saying that she felt enough discomfort that she sometimes chose to withhold her opinions, a hallmark of an unsafe team.

In fact, she was correct that others questioned her motives. Another team member, Isabelle, referring to Libby, said, "Sometimes I feel like . . . one person . . . knows how to work the system for herself and I kind of feel like she knows how to play the game and then I feel like I'm being taken advantage of and I don't appreciate that." Isabelle's comment grew out of a larger concern that Libby was favored, which meant that she was "seen as the better social worker [and] her way is the right way."

Isabelle also said, straight out, that the team was not a safe place to bring up concerns:

> INT: Do you think people can generally bring up tough issues?
>
> ISABELLE: No.
>
> INT: How do you think people would react if you brought up tough issues or—?
>
> ISABELLE: I mean they might say it's not there. And put it back on you.

Isabelle added that bringing up tough issues would raise the "risk of being seen a certain way or you know, kind of like you're being labeled . . . like, maybe the troublemaker or you know what I mean?" She felt that while people might not say anything explicitly or call her out by name, "they all look at each other or whatever." She kept trying to contribute, but it was difficult: "I try not to shut down and to share my opinion. It's kind of hard . . . it's frustrating." Overall, Isabelle felt that differences related to personality and work style among the team members negatively affected the team: "I think it affects the team, yes, it affects the team because if I feel like I can't trust you, I'm not going to want to help you."

All told, these examples suggest a significant lack of psychological safety on the team, related both to their superiors and to their teammates.

In addition, at least two members felt concerns about identity safety as well. Isabelle's concern about being labeled a troublemaker connected to her belief that her superiors found her too "ghetto." This meant, to her, that her work style was not sufficiently professional or fully cleansed of her background, growing up poor in a low-income neighborhood of color. At the same time, Isabelle felt Libby's race may have had something to do with the fact that she was favored, though it wasn't primary.

> INT: Do you think people are treated equally?
>
> ISABELLE: No.
>
> INT: Can you say more?
>
> ISABELLE: Just the favoritism.
>
> INT: Do you feel like the favoritism is race-based or . . . ?
>
> ISABELLE: I think it's both personality, work ethic, like work style, and that race makes it a little easier. I don't think it's a huge issue but I think it does come in somewhat.

For her part, Libby felt that sometimes being white on a team that was majority of color meant that she could sometimes be dismissed, though not in a malicious way:

> We were having a conversation, and it was about race and that kind of stuff, and somebody else on the team asked me my opinion, and the other person had said, "Well, she's just a white women." So, I said, "Well, I guess I don't have anything to add. I'm just a white woman." I just brought it into a humor so that the person could hear what they had just said. . . . And it instantly changed. Like, "no, wait." Somebody said, "I want to hear what you have to say about it." And it didn't become this heated discussion where it could have easily become that. But to me, I don't think it was meant in malice or anything. I think it was meant in a misunderstanding.

Of greater concern to Libby were issues related to other aspects of identity. As noted, she felt that racial and ethnic issues tended to be overemphasized compared with "sexual orientation, or gender identity, or religion. I think people have a harder time with those things." She elaborated regarding her concerns about religion: "The way I practice my religion is just different than other people; I mean, I'm Christian, and that kind of stuff, but how I look at religion, and how I look at religious groups is very different than people in my unit. . . . I think sometimes people aren't aware that when you talk a lot at work about your religion, or mention God a lot, that you're talking about your religion, and what sort of implications that can have for other people." This appeared to be a reference to Isabelle who described herself as a "born-again Christian" and said that her religion affected her work, including her attitude toward homosexuality, "Homosexuality like, I'm not going to hate you because of this. It's just I don't believe that it's God so . . . I'm sensitive and I don't treat you any different but if you ask me, I believe it's not right, you know what I mean?" Libby didn't disclose her sexual orientation to the interviewer, but she clearly took the issue seriously and could have found Isabelle's attitudes threatening. Therefore, both she and Isabelle expressed concerns that social identity groups that were important to them did not feel fully welcomed in the team.

A final potential piece of evidence regarding safety, though it is difficult to interpret, is Pilar's refusal to share even basic facts about her personal life with team members. In her interviews, she simply said that she felt this information was out of bounds for a work context, as her earlier quoted statements suggest: "This is a professional setting. . . . There are other things that you don't need to know." But it is possible that there were details about her life that she felt might put her at risk in some way. Some research suggests that people of color at work are put into a double bind about whether to disclose personal information. On the one hand, not disclosing information can make one seem distant or unfriendly. On the other, employees may be reluctant to do so if disclosing information might reinforce negative stereotypes.[3] For that reason, it is not uncommon for people of color to be seen as aloof or not part of the team.[4] Again, we don't know Pilar's motivation. Whatever the reason, it is also plausible that team members picked up Pilar's refusal to disclose as signaling a lack of comfort or at least a lack of connection with the group, which then perhaps made them feel less at ease.

Finally, working in Office East probably contributed to a lack of safety on the team as well as an unwillingness to broach topics related to race and ethnicity. As we noted earlier, Office East had recently experienced severe conflict, stemming from the racial incident involving the black doll as well as the merger of two offices. Team members described an office that was still full of discord despite efforts to address it. For example, the new office director, Sonia, a Latina, was being accused by some of favoring other Latinas, echoing the charges against the previous white director. Team members, both white and of color, also noted a tendency to race-based cliquishness in the office as a whole. Isabelle said some people tended to "stick with their own kind," adding that some felt "'oh, you're white; you don't know what you're doing or you don't understand.' " Debbie, the white manager, also believed that intergroup relations were somewhat tense. Moreover, Pilar gave a vivid account of conflict at a meeting of all the supervisors in Office East, though she did not connect this with intergroup tension: "I couldn't believe it. . . . I mean these two supervisors went at it. I don't know if you ever watched a cock fight, but I grew up with cock fights. And I have to say, I said to myself, 'My God, if this would have been private sector they would had called security and escorted them out.' It's a miracle that there was no hitting." The office sounds like a battleground.

In sum, it appears both the team and the office environment contributed to a daunting lack of safety for team members, which then would have made it harder for the team to engage in learning behaviors—and all the more difficult to take up issues related to race and culture. This is all in clear contrast to Team North.

Why did Team East engage in an evasive racial-cultural practice? Given the mostly color-cognizant individuals in the team, the incubator is likely the main contributor. It combined a noxious office atmosphere with a rancorous and polarized team dynamic that stifled team learning and left multiple members feeling unsafe. Team South would prove a different story.

~ Chapter 6 ~

Color-Hostile Practice: Team South

The members of Team South were laughing and joking as they waited for their weekly meeting to start. It was a cold January day and they began by appreciating the warmth in their offices, which were unlike some other parts of the building. "Our heat comes from the top, we're lucky," said Dan. This led to other thoughts about their space: "I like our unit the best," said Bridget. "We're in the cave." The team leader, Bob, responded, "We couldn't be over there [in the main part of the office], they'd be all yelling at us—'too loud!'" Everyone laughed: they were known as a boisterous group and while sometimes chastised for this, they wore it as a badge of honor. Bob turned to the agenda. "February is 'love everybody' month, that's the [Aware] month." A Portuguese-speaking worker, Ana, immediately rejoined, "Me and Radhi have nothing to do with that!" Radhi was the daughter of Indian immigrants and the only team member of color. She and Ana, who was bilingual, were the only workers on the team who were eligible for Aware membership. Radhi did not respond, but Bob, a white man, said sarcastically, "I'm trying to join." The group discussed two Aware events coming up. The first was a costume and flag contest. "We got to dress Radhi up in something," said Bob, which was followed by a burst of laughter. Bridget told Ana that Ana had said she would wear her Portuguese dress, but Ana refused: "I was ten years old, you think I can fit into that dress? It would be a miniskirt on me now." "We would win!" said the team leader. Radhi said, "I'm not wearing no sari," in a tone that suggested she was trying to be funny but nonetheless indicated some discomfort. Hilarious bursts of laughter had accompanied most statements, but no one reacted to this remark. Ana noted, "We did India last year, we do Portugal this time." Bob objected: "Yes, but we'll have lots of competition with Portugal." Radhi rejoined, in an exasperated tone, "What do you want to do, do India again?" Without making a decision, they moved on to the second event, in which employees brought desserts from their cultural background. After some discussion of what to bring, Dan said, "I'll bring a can of corn. . . . I protest this whole thing. I hate being told I have to go to this crap." A few moments later, he added, "Do these guys ever do any social work?" When Bob asked whom he was referring to, Dan responded, "The people who run these committees." After a couple of chuckles, Team South moved on to another topic.

This opening vignette provides a compelling contrast with both Team North and Team East. Team North's members thought about Aware as a resource to which to turn in their desire to provide appropriate services to their families. Team East invited a representative from Aware to speak with the team, even if its members remained largely silent during her presentation. It's highly unlikely that Team South would have done either of these things. Instead, it criticized, both implicitly and explicitly, Aware-sponsored events and used them as an opportunity to make fun of Aware as a whole. The team also had another conversation in which it castigated affirmative action. For this reason, we call the team *color hostile*. Understanding this dynamic is the goal of this chapter.

The Backdrop

The small city in which Team South was located was majority white and included a large community of Portuguese families, both newly arrived and long-standing. It also had pockets of Hispanic and African American families. The office caseload was roughly 75 percent white, with another 15 percent or so split between black and Latino clients. The team had been an assessment unit, which meant that once a case had been screened in, team members were responsible for creating an assessment and a service plan for the family. Normally, the case with the service plan would then be transferred to another ongoing unit that would then implement the plan with the family. However, Team South, like Team North, proposed that it take cases from start to finish, from investigation through ongoing. Unlike Team North, it did so.

The team was majority white during the entire period of data collection, and included one member of (Asian) Indian descent and one of Portuguese descent, who was trilingual, speaking Spanish in addition to Portuguese and English. The team leader, manager, and office director were all white men.

Team South met once a week and, like the other teams, spent much of its time discussing cases, though the team leader, Bob, also gave updates about things happening in the agency or the team's office. He also regularly reviewed team statistics, which included its percentage compliance with the rule that every client had to be visited at least once a month, and compared these numbers with other units. Meetings were noisy and full of teasing and banter, often exploding in uproarious laughter.

Team Racial-Cultural Practice

Team South rarely discussed race and culture in team meetings—only three times during the period of data collection. In one instance, culture came up as part of a case discussion. The other two conversations were, as noted, related to organizational issues about race and culture and could be seen as disrespectful or even denigrating to workers of color.

The case conversation was about a Portuguese family involved with the agency because of domestic violence: the mother had threatened the father with a knife, in front of the children, and one of the children had been cut, though not badly. The team discussed how the two workers on the case had different perspectives—and even different loyalties—because the Portuguese worker, Ana, was working with the mother and the other worker, Bridget (of English and Irish descent), was working with the father. The most pressing question was which parent would get temporary custody of the children while the parents were separated. Drawing on her knowledge of domestic violence within the Portuguese community, Ana argued for the mother, though she recognized that the mother had wielded a knife against her husband. She noted that the mother had been abused for years by the father, something she felt Bridget was downplaying. Bridget felt that both parents were equally at fault and that the agency should be neutral in the decision that ultimately would be made by a judge.

The team's other two conversations were not related to cases, but to organizational practices. In the first, relatively brief, conversation, the members were discussing a supervisor position (the first step up on the management ladder, supervisors oversaw the work of four or five workers) opening up in their office and who would be considered for it. The team knew that Bridget, one of its senior members, was looking to move up, but Bob, the white team leader, warned her that another worker would likely take precedence because she was a worker of color: "She's a minority. . . . She's vice president of Aware, you don't think that helps?" The team reacted with surprise. One person said, "Stop!" and another said, "Oh my God!"—both in disapproving tones. Bridget vowed, "Trust me, if I wanted that position and she got it over me . . . Let me tell you, that would go right up to [the commissioner.]" Bob assured her that she "would be my top candidate but you never know."

Their second conversation was the context of the vignette about the two upcoming Aware events, described earlier. Ana's quick insistence that she and Radhi—the two workers on the team eligible for Aware membership because Ana was a Portuguese speaker and Radhi was Indian—had "nothing to do with that!" makes it clear that she and Radhi were not involved in Aware. Her remark also suggests that she assumed the team members would disapprove of the events and therefore wanted to distance herself and Radhi from them.

However, despite Ana's effort, the assumption was that either she or Radhi would be their unit's representative regarding costume, though Radhi immediately begged off: "I'm not wearing no sari." After some discussion, they moved on to the dessert event in which Dan said he "hated" being told to attend this kind of event and made insulting remarks about the people who planned it.

After Dan made his point, the group moved on to joking about a calendar outside the conference room with a couple of staff birthdays noted for that month, which was January. Bridget noted, "They have [staff member's] birthday and [staff member's] birthday on there, handwritten." Ana responded, "You're kidding me! All the [Aware] people? Mine's not on there! Guaranteed— I don't go to a meeting!" Bridget rejoined, in a sarcastic tone, "You need to complain," but Ana said, "They'll say 'you never come to a meeting.'" Ana pointed out that Radhi's birthday was in January, so it should have been posted as well, but Radhi noted that she didn't attend their meetings either. Ana joked, "Next time they ask me to come to [Aware] meeting, I'll tell them 'you didn't put my birthday up there, so I'm not coming.'" This was followed by a huge burst of laughter from the group.

In sum, Team South's racial-cultural practice was different from that of the other teams. It was the only team in which we witnessed conversations that were disrespectful to workers of color and to Aware in particular. Dan's particularly disparaging comments were not challenged by anyone else in the meeting. Altogether, we call Team South's practice color hostile.

Individual Racial-Cultural Practice

As we describe in detail, most team members espoused a color-blind perspective that manifested in their lack of attention to such issues in their work. This was in marked contrast to Teams North and East, in which most members were at least culturally cognizant if not racially cognizant as well. However, we also show how Team South's members did implicitly suggest an awareness of race and ethnicity, even as they explicitly denied their importance. We begin with the white workers because they dominated the team, then move to the one worker of color and to the team leader. The data come largely from individual interviews.

White Members

Team South's white members largely claimed a color-blind perspective. As we elaborate, however, in some ways they, at least implicitly, seemed quite aware of race and culture. In their spoken remarks, however, they downplayed both. In fact, when asked in a team interview whether the agency should be racially and ethnically diverse, only one person, Dan, responded, saying yes; the others remained silent. This was a radical departure from interviews with other teams, in which that question received a chorus of yesses. Even Dan then elaborated by saying, "Everybody brings their own experiences and knowledge to the job. It's not necessarily cultural—people go through different things, learn different things, see different things, and that affects the job." In this explanation, Dan immediately diminishes the role of race and culture, arguing more for the importance of individual differences. Another team member implied that color cognizance was a sign of being less evolved: "It's hard to focus that much on diversity when you just have moved beyond that, kind of, in a sense. . . . Like when you can see beyond the diversity, and you're not like always aware of, oh, 'this person is different from me.' . . . You're just working and working. Every person, the problems are the same, and that kind of thing."

This color blindness was also borne out in their descriptions of their practice. None of the team members suggested that they could harbor any bias. Moreover, most of the white members denied that they drew on their background in any way, as suggested by this exchange with Bridget, a white woman.

> INT: Uh huh. And there's no way in which you draw on it [your cultural background] in how you think about how to do the work?
>
> BRIDGET: No.
>
> INT: How you make decisions? How you think about families?
>
> BRIDGET: No, not really.
>
> INT: Anything like that?
>
> BRIDGET: No.

The interviewer had a similar exchange with Dan.

> INT: Do you think being Italian has any impact on how you do your work?
>
> DAN: Not at all.
>
> INT: Do you draw on it in any way? Values? Principles?
>
> DAN: No. Because I think that since the people we work with are individuals, everything has to be looked at on its own basis, so I try not to draw from my own stuff at all. I try to draw from their situation.
>
> INT: Okay. So, any way in which it makes your job easier or harder?
>
> DAN: I don't even think about it when I'm here.

Dan seemed to suggest that if he doesn't think about something, it has no impact on him. That may be the case; we cannot know for sure. On the other hand, being Italian and white aligns him with the dominant group—in his team, office, organization, and larger society—and therefore its impact may be invisible to him. Facets of ourselves that align with the dominant group are often invisible to us, though we saw how some white members of Team North had worked to make them visible by, for example, acknowledging their bias.

One white member, Rita, did say she drew on her Italian background, which made her family oriented. She said that when she first met a client, "I like to ask people about their families, what it was like growing up. You know? Where are their brothers and sisters now? If they don't have good relationships, well, what happened? Because I always find that family supports are wonderful. So, I'm always looking for that; there's no question." She also felt that she had gained "moral values" because "my father was a very hard worker." So, she asked her clients who weren't working, "Well, why aren't you working? What kind of stopped you?" If the client had a disability, "What kind of disability do you have? I mean, is this something that is definitely a forever thing, or is there something that you can do, you know?" This ability to connect with her cultural past does distinguish her from most of the other white members of her team. However, her moral values could be rooted in a basic bootstrap belief that people from all backgrounds face the same kinds of hurdles and share a similar ability to overcome them, rather than in recognizing the particular challenges faced by nonwhites as, for example, Chris on Team North did when he wondered whether a black father was being treated more harshly than a white father would have been.

Consistent with their claims of color blindness, the team members gave few examples of how they took race and ethnicity into account, even when working with families whose heritage was different than their own. In fact, they generally said that they worked the same with families, regardless of their background. One white worker said that she often worked with black families but when asked, "So, is there any way in which you work with that case differently than you work with any other case?" she responded, "No. Actually. I don't think so at all. Not at all, honestly." She did say that on occasion she would bring a bilingual worker if she needed to speak with someone who did not speak English, but that was the only thing she would do differently. One of the quotes from the beginning of chapter 3 is from Dan who, in response to the question, "So, any way in which you might try to get information about the cultural background of these folks, talk to people [from the same background as the family]?" said, "No. It's all the same." Compare this with Arlo, from Team North, actively seeking information about the cost of hair care for a black teenage boy.

As far as learning from others' cultural backgrounds, the answers here were thin and sometimes contradictory. One worker denied any such learning at all. When the interviewer asked, "Have you learned from other people's backgrounds in terms of how they do their work, and how you might do your work differently? Is there anything?" she responded, "No, I mean aside from individual differences. I don't see them as really culturally driven." Two members of the team did express appreciation for the knowledge and perspectives brought by Ana, the Portuguese worker, though it was expressed in general terms. For example, Rita said, "It's nice now, because I think we have a different perspective on things with Ana being bilingual. I think it makes a big difference on some of those cases, and I can understand probably why she looks at things a little differently, because she understands exactly where people are coming from with the whole cultural piece with the Portuguese families."

However, other comments suggest that team members believed that Ana's cultural knowledge came with a cost and might even be detrimental. This came up in reference to the Portuguese case described earlier, involving the wife who wielded a knife against her husband, which Ana was working on with Bridget, another team member. Ana was working more closely with the mother and Bridget with the father.

Bridget had mixed feelings about Ana's cultural knowledge. She began by saying, "It certainly helps to have Ana on the case," but then noted, "It could go against us in the case . . . just because of the strong feelings [held by Ana] that I'm kind of overlooking the cultural aspect of that case. Because I think that the facts are not so much culture-driven." She also felt that Ana could become "overly involved" when working with Portuguese cases and ascribed this to Ana's Portuguese background: "I think a lot of it is cultural, because they are Portuguese-speaking, and she's Portuguese." Bridget admitted, "I have to kind of step back and acknowledge that she knows the functioning of this family well, because it's her own upbringing." However, she then downplayed the significance of this cultural knowledge: "At the same time, cultural issues aside, facts are the facts to me, and I'm very clear that . . . I don't care about the details. . . . The fact is these parents are fighting viciously in front of the kids. Bottom line: Changes need to be made on both sides." Ultimately, she felt that Ana was "totally not objective" and noted that her intern felt the same way. "It helped to have my intern do a visit last week, where she said [to Ana], 'Wow, it's pretty clear who you side with.' You know? So, she's very— she gets very involved in certain cases." In other words, Bridget felt that a cultural perspective was not that helpful because culture was not significantly implicated in the dynamics. She went on to suggest that Ana's familiarity with the culture was problematic because she became too involved in the case and could no longer be objective. In fact, when asked whether she had learned anything by working on the case with Ana, Bridget said that she had not.

Bridget was not the only one who felt that Ana was not able to be objective. Rita, whom we quoted earlier saying she valued Ana's cultural expertise, referred to the case: "[Ana], you know, is from the Portuguese culture, and [Bridget's] not. And this case happens to be a Portuguese-speaking family, and it was a real cultural kind of issue. . . . And I think Ana kind of really could align with that. Whereas, Bridget, I think she was being a little bit more objective about things, and saying you know, 'I understand the cultural piece, but you know, this is the issue that we have.'" Rita seems to believe that not having knowledge of the family's culture can enhance objectivity, and that having such knowledge can taint it. Bridget seems to agree with this as well: because her background was English and Irish and because her family had been in the United States for several generations, she saw herself and was seen by Rita as neutral, instead of being influenced by her background just as Ana was.

This is where their claims of color blindness start to unravel. They implicitly acknowledged background as important, but saw the dominant culture as the neutral norm and any deviation from that as potentially biased. This has two consequences. First, it positions explicit connection with racial or ethnic heritage as problematic rather than enriching. The white members of Team North never suggested this. Moreover, this perspective purports to argue for objectivity but doesn't recognize that all of us come from some kind of cultural perspective and all of us are influenced by it. Exploring the ways that race and culture affected all of them—for example, as Dave on Team North did when he discussed his Italian background—would help them understand how their backgrounds can both enhance their work and create blind spots.

Ana's viewpoint on whether she brought something special to the case was notably contradictory, a form of what we've called color minimization. On the one hand, she did assert that her cultural knowledge gave her insight into the case. "This particular case is Portuguese. I'm Portuguese. It's a cultural case," she said. "I just think, because I know what the Portuguese culture is all about, some of this stuff is accepted in the Portuguese culture, [like] domestic violence, where he's being abusive and how he's not admitting [what he did wrong]." However, she then denied that it had an impact on her work with the family:

> INT: So, do you feel like you're—the fact that you have a Portuguese background, does that mean that you approach the case differently than [Bridget] does?
>
> ANA: [Pause] I don't think so. I just know what's more normal as far as Portuguese families. I know what's more accepted. I know the whole—I know the drinking, the domestic violence—all that stuff is pretty cultural, and I think that that's why [the wife] has remained as long as she has in that relationship, because it's more acceptable.

Ana also gave examples of how she had drawn on her cultural expertise in the past: "I've worked with other Portuguese families, where these were the issues. And I was able to talk to the batterer in the sense—get him to recognize his own faults." But after giving these examples, she said no when asked "Are there ways in which you draw on your cultural identity—in this case being Portuguese—in how you think about doing your work?" Antonia, on Team

North, or Esme, on Team East, never manifested ambivalence. They felt very rooted in the knowledge and expertise that came from their backgrounds.

Despite her inconsistencies, Ana seemed unaware of her team members' ambivalence about her cultural knowledge. She believed they valued it: "I think that they [the other team members] value what I have to say about how I grew up, and how I'm looking at things with other families that I get, and stuff, and why I want to somewhat educate them a little bit on what's right and what's wrong. . . . They never criticize me about any of that."

Altogether, the white members of Team South stand out in the entire sample and in particular contrast to Team North. Unlike most of the other participants, they claimed color blindness, even though some evidence indicates that they took cultural background into account, if implicitly and perhaps even unconsciously. Ana was different from her teammates because she was aware of the impact of her background, including the knowledge she gained from it. Even she, however, was strikingly conflicted about whether to embrace that expertise, which may be a by-product of the team's overall response to cultural considerations. The team norm that denied the role of race and culture, which is also a broader societal norm, may have made it difficult to acknowledge or feel positively about using a cultural lens.

Indian Member

Radhi, of Indian descent and the lone worker of color on Team South, did acknowledge the impact of race in her life and her casework. She seemed accustomed to racist remarks. "Being Indian—there's always something that somebody says, and you just have to shrug it off, and you deal with it. And I don't dwell on it." When a client, on first meeting Radhi, said she did not want to work with her because the client mistook Radhi for being Iraqi, the team discussed whether Radhi should come off the case. "But I wanted to see what was going to happen. . . . And then all of a sudden, she just kind of came around, and she mentioned to Bridget that 'that wasn't very nice of me' or something like that. . . . But it never became an issue after that again. She was never rude, or disrespectful or any of that."

Radhi didn't see her background only as something that could trigger discrimination or prejudice, however. She believed it had an impact on her work, just as everyone's background had an influence: "Everybody carries their own background—cultural background—whether you're Portuguese, whether you're Italian. Any of that," she said, in contrast to most of her white teammates who denied the influence of their heritage. Describing how being Indian affected her casework, she said, "I think sometimes when you're working with a family that's culturally diverse . . . you can understand a little bit more as to maybe why they did what they did, not that it was right, but you can maybe understand what they were thinking." She described how she applied this to families dissimilar from her own, in this case Cambodian families: "I used to have a lot of Cambodian families that I worked with in the adolescent unit. And a lot of these kids were truant, you know? And for them, a lot of these parents were like, 'well, you know, we went to the fields, and we worked, and we didn't go to school, and for us yes, it [school] is important, but it's not that important.' I think it just makes you more aware, you know?"

However, she also suggested that culture mattered only with what she called diverse families, which meant families of color. "I think it's just if you work with a diverse family, you just have that [culture] in the back of your mind. . . . Maybe that's why they did what they did. But then again, when you're working with somebody that's of Caucasian descent, you think—it's not cultural maybe, but it's something else; maybe it can be generation to generation. Something that may have happened over time within the family, and that's how they've always done things." This quote suggests that, for Radhi, culture was relevant only with families of color and, further, that though generational influences may be present in white families, they are somehow completely divorced from race or ethnicity. Members of color in Teams North and East would have disputed this.

Moreover, though Radhi seemed clear that race or culture mattered, at least for some families of color, she didn't think that such families should be approached differently: "I mean, everyone has issues, whether they're Caucasian, Hispanic, African American. It doesn't matter. . . . We treat them all the same. . . . We don't make it any different, because they're a different race, anything." Like some of the workers we quote in chapter 3, she seemed to see "treating families differently" in purely negative terms, as a sign of bias, rather than as a way to adapt to a family's needs that might be partly informed by their racial or ethnic heritage. This contrasts with a number of her counterparts on the other teams, such as Jasper on Team East, who took culture into account when he approached disciplinary issues with his families.

Overall, although Radhi showed more color cognizance than her other teammates, she had hesitations. She seemed to see race and ethnicity as isolated or separable influences rather than as fully woven into a family's experiences, no matter the race of the family. She believed that families should be treated the same, regardless of background. Moreover, her manner when discussing these issues tended to be tentative and unsure. Given the attitudes of her teammates, this may not be surprising. We explore later in this chapter how her team's intergroup incubator also likely contributed to her hesitation.

Team Leader

A white man, Team South's team leader, Bob, espoused consistently color-blind views about the role of race and ethnicity in casework. For example,

INT: So, do conversations about race and ethnicity, the effect on a
       particular case, do those happen?

BOB: It does, but I think it's more based on whatever points are brought up. It's not so much on race, it's more on, it's because of this, this, and this, you know? Yeah, they happen to be black or they happen to be this, but they still did A, B, and C. They need to do this and this to get beyond that.

Such views were not unknown among the other workers in the dataset, but Bob went beyond any other participant—and certainly more than the team leaders of Team North and Team East—in stating some resentment against workers of color and the Aware group in particular for having opportunities that he felt had been denied him and other white workers.

He seemed to have learned some of this from his family growing up. Bob described his background as Irish Catholic; he recalled growing up in a small city that was roughly half white and half Latino. He felt this experience had helped him connect with people from all backgrounds, "I never see myself as a racist person and, I don't know, I think that it helped me growing up in a community like that. I couldn't speak the language, but I had friends who were Hispanic, I had friends who were black. Maybe I was color blind, I didn't really see it as that, as an issue." However, his father had been a leader in the town at a time when it was pursuing affirmative action among public employees, a period his father had found difficult. This made an impression on Bob.

My father was the deputy chief of the fire department and it was during the time that they were integrating. Civil service was really strong and you had to hire so many minorities in different things. I remember him saying, "Oh, Jesus, you know, you couldn't hire your brothers and sisters anymore" because that's how it always was and how difficult that was for him. . . . He was also on the school committee, so I also saw a lot about hiring of teachers and how much race played a role in that during that time. So I think I was well educated on that.

This experience may have influenced his later views, because he had concerns about Aware's influence in the agency. "It's a segregated group. It's this group to work on issues to help people overcome some of the obstacles within an agency, barriers, things like that. And I agree with that, but at what cost? . . . What does that mean for the white social worker out here or somebody who doesn't quite fit the need of that? What role are they going to play in the hiring of certain people?" He felt Aware was "getting stronger" partly because of the commissioner's support and partly because he felt there were a number of people of color in leadership positions who were not prepared and therefore needed more training. "I think what's happened is they have had people in color or different race in positions and they could not maintain it, so what needs to change, what trainings have to be instilled or what has to—so that they are qualified to do those jobs. So . . . I just think that, again, you're having a group of people who are not trained in managing something like that who are now holding power in these groups."

He felt that this same trend was limiting his opportunities, referring to the notion of reverse racism: "Does that mean I'm going to be discriminated against because I am a white male and it's kind of reversing itself a little bit." He named two other white men in his office, both in leadership positions, that he felt had lost opportunities for promotion because of their race. He also seemed to carry a suspicion that when he was denied something, affirmative action was the cause. He described applying to an agency leadership training course but, during an interview, was told he was "overqualified" because he was "already seen as a leader." But, he said, "I didn't kind of buy that. . . . It's to really help out minorities within the agency to get to a point where they could take over those positions." Ultimately, he felt less willing to volunteer for different activities within the agency: "But it's like that's discouraging me a little bit only because I feel like, you know what, I volunteer for all this. . . . And it's like some days you ask yourself, well, 'should I put myself out there anymore?'" In fact, though Bob claimed color blindness, he seemed quite aware of race and, in particular, how, from his perspective, race was curtailing his opportunities given the agency's policy of affirmative action.

Individual Contributions

With Team South, we not only have to explain why the team rarely discussed race and ethnicity, we also have to understand why it had two denigrating conversations about Aware, the agency's internal caucus for people of color and bilingual workers. This review suggests that we can look, in part, at the impact of individual belief and practice, especially given the noticeable contrast with the color cognizance of the other two teams.

As team leader, Bob likely had a disproportionate impact on the group. He espoused strong color-blind views though he actually did seem quite aware of race in his antagonism to programs like affirmative action that attempt to level the playing field for people of color. He felt his own future in the organization held less promise as a result of these policies. He also believed that the agency was creating leadership development programs because leaders of color were not as competent as their white colleagues and needed additional training. He also believed that Aware had a damaging effect on the agency. This helps us understand his actions in the two meetings when the team discussed Aware. Although he avoided direct criticism, he did nothing to stop others' aspersions and, indeed, helped fuel the fire. He did not defend the agency's affirmative action policy and he joined in making fun of Aware's events: indeed, he led off the discussion calling February "love everybody month." Moreover, he said nothing in response to Dan's especially pernicious comments: Dan said he "protested" these events and that he "hate[d] being told I have to go to this crap." Dan also disparaged the workers who planned these events, asking, "Do these guys ever do any social work?" Bob let these comments go without comment, which is noteworthy, and helps explain the team's open hostility to Aware.

Given Dan's comments, it is important to highlight his racial-cultural practice. Dan said nothing so denigrating in his team or individual interviews, but he did seem resistant to thinking about racial or cultural differences. He denied any impact of his background, which was not that uncommon, but he was also adamant that cultural differences were irrelevant: "It's all the same," he said. Although he was the only person to say yes when the interviewer asked in the team interview whether the agency should be racially and ethnically diverse, he then immediately undercut the point. Bridget held largely similar views, and both she and Rita suggested that Ana's cultural background led to bias rather than insight. All these perspectives diverged from those of most of the white workers on Teams East and North.

Ana and Radhi, the two workers eligible for Aware membership (though neither joined), diverged from their colleagues. They both gave credence to the importance of racial and cultural background, but neither was a strong voice. The contradictions expressed by Ana, the Portuguese worker, when discussing her beliefs and behaviors seem to reveal decided confusion about whether it was appropriate to draw off cultural background. Her marked inconsistency seems more understandable given the team's resistance to taking such backgrounds seriously, including questioning her objectivity. It's easier to understand why Antonia on Team North betrayed no such contradictions: her cultural insights were embraced by her teammates.

Although Radhi was not particularly contradictory, her words and manner were hesitant. Just as she seemed to shrug off racist comments toward herself, as we noted in her description, she may also have tried to shrug off the hostile conversations about Aware in the team meetings. As the only person of color on the team, she may have felt it was something she had to deal with rather than an opportunity to advocate for herself and her point of view. This seems entirely sensible: she did not mention her teammates' antipathy to Aware and to broader color-cognizant practice, but she had to be familiar with it. Her caution—in contrast to members of color on Teams North and East—is quite understandable.

Given the individuals on the team, it is not surprising that the group as a whole rarely discussed race and ethnicity and was sometimes disparaging when it did so. We can't underestimate the importance of context, however. In any team, the members and the team as a whole are in a constant cycle of mutual influence: the individuals shape the team even as the team shapes its members. For that reason, in the next section we investigate the intergroup incubator, the overall team and office context that can both draw out and stifle individual leanings. This portrait emerged from analysis of team and individual interviews and observation of team meetings.

Intergroup Incubator

Team South had planned to make the most significant changes in practice of any of the teams and had largely done so. Because it took cases from the point at which allegations were first investigated, it was able to speed resources to the families even before the investigation and assessment periods were completed. The team and the agency felt that this resulted in better outcomes for families and quicker closing of cases, though no formal outcome-based evaluation had been undertaken. Therefore the agency decided that all existing teams, and new ones joining the program, should adopt the Team South model. These changes were just starting implementation when the data collection came to a close.

This model had largely been developed by the team's manager, who had taken the lead role in developing the proposal for the team, which was rare—most of the other proposals were developed by team members. The manager, Mark, conducted an intensive nine-month research and planning process, much more in-depth than any of the other teams. Both the teaming coordinator and the teaming consultant working directly with the team believed that it was this upfront planning work that had made the team so successful. They also felt that Office South was a positive environment for the team. Like Office North, it was generally regarded as a well-run office that did excellent casework. The team leader felt that the office was much more cohesive than others, and most team members agreed that morale was good.

Overall, therefore, the picture of the team, from both external observers and team members, was quite rosy: the team was seen as quite effective and indeed, saw itself that way as well. However, a review of their learning and safety dynamics suggests a more complicated picture.

Learning Behaviors

Straightforwardly and constructively resolving conflict, experimenting, and reflecting on practice are the three key learning behaviors. Team South engaged to some extent in all three.

Team members reported disagreements on the team but felt they were generally low-level and productively resolved. The team leader described one case in which two workers assigned to the case disagreed but engaged in continual discussion: "I think it opened the eyes to what each other is thinking. But I think that's healthy. . . . And, you know, we talk openly. We actually brought that case to supervision because I think those are the types of things that people need to hear as a group." Ana said people were open to feedback from each other: "I don't take offense . . . because they're very receptive to what I have to say about them, so—and I'm receptive to what they have to say about me."

However, the team appeared to have more conflict than this sunny picture suggests, including conflict that was not always resolved constructively for everyone involved. Several members described a team discussion during which they aired concerns that Radhi wasn't quite pulling her weight. A couple of members said they had discussed it with her individually. The team leader also raised the matter at a meeting, the only time he brought something like this to the full group. He said in an interview that he decided to do it at the meeting both because other workers had been coming to him about the problem and because he wanted Radhi to have an opportunity to present her point of view. Radhi apologized to the group. Those who felt Radhi wasn't doing her fair share said the conversation had gone well and a couple said that they had seen a change in Radhi since the meeting. No one, however, expressed concern about how Radhi herself was doing as a result of the conversation. Radhi did not explicitly name this particular discussion but she did refer obliquely to it, criticizing herself: "I mean, like you want to be a really—you want to be a good team member, but then I think you know automatically when you didn't get that [a task] done. You know yourself, like—and to me that's the worst. You don't want to let anybody down. . . . You feel bad, like I didn't get it done." Although most team members thought that the resolution had been productive, the impact on Radhi was left unexplored.

Moreover, other conflicts—also related to Radhi—came up in other more indirect ways and seemed resistant to resolution. Rita described a particular dynamic.

> RITA: You know, [Radhi] is laid back. [Ana] is very on top of things and wants everything done just right, and so Radhi will be like, "Well, what are you whining for?" And Ana's like, "You know, you need to get—you know?" But I don't think that they've come to an even way to resolve some of that. . . . Maybe it's just a personality conflict between the two of them, but it's pretty fun to watch. When we went paintballing [as a team activity], that was one of the biggest things—Ana really wanted to shoot Radhi, and have some fun. And Radhi felt the same way. [*Laughter*]
>
> INT: Oh, that's interesting. And that was seen as fine?
>
> RITA: Yes.
>
> INT: As opposed to—you know, unexpressed aggression, or—I don't know?
>
> RITA: Well, we're all kind of saying who we're going to target and who we're going to take it out on. So, it was kind of all made in fun. But they definitely were the team leaders that needed to be on these different teams.
>
> INT: That's interesting.
>
> RITA: It was interesting.

> INT: So, I could imagine that that could get unpleasant, but it's your sense that that's not been the case?
>
> RITA: It hasn't. Not for me to feel uncomfortable.

The desire of Radhi and Ana to "shoot" each other may have been a productive way to blow off steam, but Rita herself acknowledged that the two hadn't come up with a way to resolve their disagreement.

Additionally, concerns about Radhi doing her fair share again seem implicated: Rita describes Radhi as "laid back" and Ana as "very on top of things." It is striking that Radhi, the one person of color on the team, was seen as problematic and unable to pull her weight—this on a team largely hostile to collective efforts by people of color in the organization. Research on group dynamics suggests that "the most vulnerable and weakest group member becomes the focal point of negative and harsh interactions."[1] We explore this dynamic at greater length later when we discuss psychological and identity safety on the team.

Radhi was not the only focus of conflict; team members described other conflicts that seemed to rankle. Bridget said that she and the team manager were sometimes at odds. "Mark and I have absolutely had our issues, because we're both very headstrong people, over the years. We have had our issues. . . . Once he makes his decision, he sticks his feet in the mud, and I do the same thing." In fact, she noted, "We actually have an issue that came up yesterday. I'm still not talking to him, because I'm really mad at him."

In short, the team's image of itself as productive conflict resolvers was belied by some of their own descriptions of events, which suggested a more checkered reality. They did make these claims, however, and credited their ability for constructive conflict resolution to their team cohesion, which they reported as very high. The team is "so close and so bonded," said Bridget, "We have a mutual obligation to each other and that's really strong." Rita agreed, "I think . . . every single one of my team[mates] would say we're here because we have such a solid team." As an illustration, one member at a team interview pointed to their happy and boisterous dynamics at a recent all-team reflection meeting: "I mean we were the loudest in the whole room. There were like a hundred-something people there. We had a great time."

It was this cohesion, they believed, that allowed them to straightforwardly address conflict. In a team interview, Ana made this point and Bridget agreed:

> ANA: Everyone in the office kind of sees that we all get along so well with each other, and we can, you know, we can say whatever to each other, and we're fine.
>
> BRIDGET: And we do [say whatever to each other]. We do it all the time. [*Laughter*]

However, like their claims about productive conflict, their claims about cohesion may also have been overstated. We've already noted conflicts within the team that had not been constructively resolved and documented how team members criticized other team members, especially Radhi. Their insistence on their cohesion is therefore noteworthy. We believe the team had a strong investment in seeing itself as cohesive even if that didn't fully square with reality, which we explore in more detail. For now the important point is the team's avowal of its closeness, for a couple of reasons.

First, this avowal seemed to be rooted in an in-group–out-group dynamic— the team against everyone else—that could inhibit learning from others. In some psychological circles, this is called *splitting,* an unconscious psychological defense that creates a dichotomy between good and bad and then splits off the bad into another entity that in turn bolsters its feeling of goodness.[2] Team South saw itself as strong and capable and other groups with which it interacted as problematic. This dynamic was present in regard to the other teams in the program as well as with other employees in Office South. (They also, as we note later, may have been splitting Radhi off as well.)

Referring again to a recent quarterly reflection meeting where all the teams were present, members in a team interview said that their obvious enjoyment of each other bred resentment among members of the other teams. "People see—'wow, it's working. They're happy. They get along.' . . . I mean we cheated on a couple of things, but we had fun. [*Laughter*]. . . . The other teams were going, 'you cheated.' You know what—so what. We had fun. . . . I could see the look on some people's faces that they resented that or envied— I don't know what it was. But it's working for us," said Bridget. The team members seemed to have no awareness of how their behavior, including cheating, could affect other participants in the meeting. It seems that their investment was to see themselves in a favorable light; reflection might create a more nuanced view.

The in-group–out-group dynamic was also present when comparing themselves with other workers in their office. They felt that other units in the office didn't like them, also because of "resentment" because they were seen as a "preferred or specialty unit." One recalled that several fellow employees had recently said that they wanted to "smash" the mug that the team member had received at a recent quarterly reflection meeting. The vividness—indeed violence—of the comment suggests the team may have been viewed with a heated dislike. The team dismissed these kinds of concerns, however. Their dynamic bordered on arrogance. At the all-team reflection meeting, Team South's members could see "how much further along we are compared [with the other teams]." They said the other teams might need to assess their team dynamics, but "we don't talk about the process anymore because we're so beyond that."

A second notable quality about their claim of cohesion is that it was based on their similarity; this in conspicuous contrast with the other teams, who were much more likely to stress their diversity. As Bridget said, "We finish each other's thoughts at this point." Rita noted, "We really all do have similar visions in our social work styles." Dan reflected on changes he had made since joining the team: though he had a different approach to cases when he first started: "I think now our styles are so close that I haven't seen that in a long time, and if—I couldn't even give you an example about that in the beginning. It's just been too long." Dan's insistence on similarity went further. When asked whether there were any differences on the team that stood out for him, he said no, there were no such differences, the only participant in the study to say that about his or her team. (When prompted with a restatement of the question, he noted age differences on the team.) Learning, however, often happens through the expression and integration of difference, not through an emphasis on similarity. This suggests another potential barrier to team learning, including learning about race and ethnicity.

As noted, learning from conflict is one of several learning behaviors, which also include experimentation and self-reflection and review of errors. Team South had, as we explained, experimented with more dramatic changes in case-work than the other teams, changes that the agency felt were exemplary. These were led by the team's manager, however, though the team leader and members had to implement them.

We did see the team engage in useful self-reflection at several points. Unlike any of the other teams, Bob regularly brought in comparative statistics, so they could, in relation to other units in the office, track their caseload numbers, how well they were doing at closing cases, whether they were complying with the agency mandate to visit every family on their caseload at least once a month, and the like. Team members also engaged in discussions when they felt their work was not as good as it should be. In one case, the supervisor raised a case in which removing a child from a home "should have gone smoother than it did." In another instance, a team member reflected that the current approach of emphasizing the strengths of a family wasn't working as well with families in which substance abuse was a problem and suggested that the team revisit its practice on this. Such self-reflection is meaningful and promising but seemed limited to some aspects of the task and was virtually absent from interpersonal dynamics, including those within the team as well as its relationships with outsiders.

Overall, the team had some capacity for learning, including self-reflective behaviors, as well as some ability to address conflict straightforwardly. Certainly its members were more like Team North than Team East. The picture of Team South that comes from careful analysis of member dynamics departs from the fully rosy portrait its members claimed. However, there was more conflict, including unresolved conflict, than team members acknowledged. Their in-group favoritism fueled by their belief in their fundamental cohesion and similarity, so different from Team North's promotion of its diversity, could actually erect barriers to growth and development. These characteristics could potentially undergird their color-hostile practice. A group so invested in its internal sameness is likely a group that resists differences. Race and ethnicity raise the specter not just of benign difference but also of potentially charged and divisive differences. We address this dynamic at greater length later. Here we want to seed the idea that the group may have found difference so challenging that it manifested in color hostility.

The team's attitude toward difference may also have contributed to the safety climate on the team. Members generally indicated a sense of safety, though Radhi, the team's lone member of color, was something of an exception.

Safety Climate

Most of the team's members indicated that they generally felt welcome and comfortable on the team. This exchange with Dan is illustrative.

INT: Would you say that you feel accepted on the team?

DAN: Oh, yes.

INT: Is there any piece of you that you feel like you can't totally be yourself?

DAN: No. There never has.

Rita, in response to the same question, said, "I feel like I'm a respected member. People listen to me."

Many members credited Bob with creating a climate of safety. "He can give you kind of constructive feedback in a joking way. And it's never critical. And he makes it kind of light," said one. Bridget felt that he had their back: "He is a very strong advocate for us, which we totally appreciate."

These comments suggest that Team South's safety climate was more like Team North's than Team East's. However, a wrinkle in Team South diverges from Team North's experience. Radhi's more hesitant comments about her place on the team stand out from those of her white teammates. They are particularly important because she was the team's only member of color. She intimated, though somewhat obliquely, that she did not feel particularly safe in the team. Radhi was by far the quietest member of the team, speaking rarely in their meetings and team interviews. She noted,

> Sometimes I am more on the quiet side. They [her team members] wouldn't think that, but you know, sometimes maybe if I don't know how to say "this is how I feel"—that I kind of keep it to myself. Like, if I don't think it's going to come across right, or if it's not appropriate—like it's not going to work, then I just don't say it. . . . I'm that type of person [that] I don't look for conflict. . . . I'd rather not be looking for any conflict and kind of just do what I have to do.

This comment is a useful window onto Radhi's experience as a team member. She was the only one to suggest any kind of reticence in speaking up; all the other members said they felt no inhibition about participating in group discussions. She also seems to blame herself: she chooses not to speak up when "it's not going to come across right or if it's not appropriate." Therefore, she is self-critical rather than seeking some explanation in the larger team dynamics.

Finally, in her reference to conflict, she suggests that she may be less likely to speak up when she feels her opinion would cause conflict because it would be different from those of the others. She noted this dilemma at another point as well: "What if you have a—you don't agree? Like, you know, what if you—you don't want to cause conflict, yet you want to voice your opinion." The heart of psychological safety is the willingness and ability to speak up precisely when one's opinion is different from the others. Yet Radhi clearly worried about doing so. The team emphasis on similarity may have contributed to her reticence to speak up, particularly when she is aware that her comment may raise a different perspective.

Further, although she did not explicitly indicate any concerns when asked whether she felt valued and heard, she used a curious, somewhat awkward locution style that seemed to undermine the stated content of her comments. When asked whether she felt that her opinions were valued, she said, "I think so. Yes, I definitely think so. I don't think that your opinion is not valued. I think that it is. You know? I never feel like it's not." First, she said "I think so" rather than the more emphatic *yes* that we heard from other team members. Second, she then turns her response into a negative—rather than about feeling valued, she makes it about being not valued. She also uses *your* in her initial response ("your opinion is not valued"), which can be a form of distancing, though she does use *I* in the next sentence ("I never feel like it's not"). When asked whether she has ever felt unheard she said no because "you do get your point across," which again uses the *you* construction.

She might have felt less safe than others on the team for a number of reasons. Bob had already raised, in a team meeting, her teammates' reservations about whether she was holding up her share of the work. She thus knew that team members had some doubts about her, which, as we note, clearly made her feel terrible. She elaborated:

> RADHI: If you didn't do something, then you feel bad yourself, you know. . . . You felt bad, like nobody needs to make you feel bad. You already know it yourself, like "oh jeez, I should have done that."
>
> INT: How do you know?
>
> RADHI: I think just being conscious of it. Like nobody needs to say—you know, you take it pretty hard when . . . you needed to do something, and it didn't happen. . . . Like I just know, if I let my team member down, I may not show it, but I do

know inside. And I don't like that. Like I just want to be a
good team member . . . you know what I mean?

Not only did she already feel badly about this, Bob had decided he needed
to bring up another issue with Radhi—that "she's working on the assessment
the day it's due instead of having it almost ready. Same thing with the service
plan or something, working on it at the eleventh hour, you know?" He felt
it was necessary to raise this at a team meeting because he had been hearing
"little things here and there" from other team members and "I don't want it
to snowball into a resentment thing, you know?" Whether or not his and the
team members' concerns were valid, hearing this kind of criticism from both
her supervisor and her teammates could easily make her feel less comfortable
and less welcome on the team.

In addition to these concerns, which could affect her sense of psychological safety, she may also have experienced a feeling of identity threat, being
the only person of color on a team that not only expressed largely color-
blind views but also explicitly denigrated Aware, its leaders, and the agency's
interest in developing and promoting people of color to leadership positions.
Although she never said anything about this in so many words, it is possible
that these conversations left her feeling isolated and vulnerable, even fearful.
She may also have felt a terrible conflict between identifying with a team to
which she clearly wanted to belong and rooting herself in her identity as an
Indian American, a person of color, and the daughter of immigrants. Her
team members seemed to have no awareness of the bind they were putting her
in—a bind that Antonia and Teresa on Team North did not face because their
teammates did not force them to make a choice. Radhi herself never spoke of
such a bind. She may have sensed it however—consciously or unconsciously.
We don't know whether Radhi was doing her fair share, but if not, it could
be that unexpressed anger toward her team members made her less willing to
give her all, resulting in less engagement with her work.

Summarizing Team South's incubator is more difficult than doing so for
Team East and Team North. This is largely because what members of other
teams said about their team was similar to the conclusions drawn from our
analysis. But Team South members made very positive claims that were par-
tially belied by more careful parsing of their language and by investigating
Ana's contradictions and Radhi's hesitation. We also have to explain why the
team's racial-cultural practice was not just evasive, but actively hostile.

The team had an image of itself as a happy, boisterous, homogeneous group
that far surpassed its peers in the quality of its work and the tightness of its
bonds. In some ways, the cohesion and self-confidence of team members were
rooted in their insularity, in their clear delineation between themselves and
everyone else. They defined themselves not only in terms of who they were
but also in who they were not: they were not other teams still struggling to
find their way, they were not other workers in their office who envied their

esprit de corps, they were not a fractured unit split by differences. They were a tenacious, interconnected group of similar individuals who outpaced the competition.

This picture has some plausibility. Team South did have a capacity for learning. It had succeeded in making significant changes in practice, more than any other team. It did reflect on past practice and regularly compared its performance with those of other units in their office. It had some record of directly addressing conflict. Looking at the team as a whole, it appeared to be largely safe for its members—certainly that was what they said.

The give-and-take of their dynamics does not fully support this perspective, however. The members prided themselves on being able to address conflict directly, but some of them felt this was not fully accurate. We know that one member, Radhi, withheld comments that might contradict others' opinions and generally was much quieter than her teammates. The team did not appear to see that its insularity had an arrogant tinge to it that might have undercut relationships with others in the office on whom they depended to carry out their work. Also, the group seemed eager to disregard the diversity on the team—in work style, in gender, in race and ethnicity—rather than dig into it. Indeed, while the members of Team North and Team East painted pictures of their teams that acknowledged difference and recognized flaws, Team South seemed invested in its assured and uniform image of itself. Why this was so is not clear, but it does suggest that any challenge to that perspective could have been seen as threatening or dangerous.

This has serious implications for its learning about race and culture. A group that accentuates its homogeneity likely lacks the awareness or the skill to appreciate and investigate what heterogeneity brings. In fact, a group with a deep investment in its cohesion and camaraderie may find such exploration virtually inconceivable, especially with charged differences like race and ethnicity. Not surprisingly, for the most part, the team denied that such explorations could be useful and simply avoided related conversations altogether. When topics related to racially conscious organizational policies did come up—regarding affirmative action and the cultural events sponsored by Aware—the team was highly critical and even mocking. Team members exhibited not neutral disinterest, but actual hostility. This suggests that such topics were not just unimportant but threatening. The color blindness of team members was not just a political ideology but instead connected to their sense of themselves as a fully united entity, unriven by significant differences or discord.

This could create particular burdens for Ana and Radhi. Staying true to their beliefs and life experiences might mean puncturing the basic narrative and identity of the team. They reacted in different ways. Ana could not deny her life experience and so provided numerous examples of cultural insights, though at the same time denied their benefits. The pressing need for the team to champion its similarity may have imposed a requirement for conformity that could explain Ana's seesawing between two opposing points of view.

Radhi was in a tougher position as the only person of color on the team. She brought difference into the room with her darker skin tone. Simply by being a member of the team, Radhi thus challenged the self-image of others in a potentially troublesome way. Although Radhi never expressed doubt that racial and cultural differences matter in individual interviews, she did not bring that perspective to team discussions and, indeed, either played along or remained silent during the team's conversations about Aware. She said that she tended to be quiet when her beliefs conflicted with those of others. As she was already under scrutiny as the one team member who others felt was not pulling her weight, it may have felt impossible—and not worth the potential retribution—to openly challenge her teammates on the difficult terrain of race and ethnicity.

It is also possible that the group may have unconsciously placed Radhi in a distinct role that served the group's larger functioning. We already discussed how the team may have engaged in splitting with other teams in the teaming program and with other units in the office, seeing itself as all good and the other groups as all bad. A similar dynamic may be operating within the team, where Radhi and her perceived problematic work behaviors are split off from the group to maintain its sense of competence and cohesion. In other words, they made her a scapegoat. A scapegoat "performs a central function in counseling groups by channeling tensions and establishing a type of unity among group members."[3] Creating a scapegoat and depositing all that is bad in one person can provide a sense of cohesion and harmony for the group, though it often masks deeper conflict and tension that are too threatening to address explicitly. The role of the scapegoat is often given to a person perceived to be vulnerable. We will never know, but Radhi's vulnerability may have come, at least in part, from her being the lone person of color on the team.

Ultimately, what accounts for Team South's color-hostile practice? Its members' individual leanings are a significant piece of the picture. Its white members called themselves color blind but did see color. Bob bore resentment, as a white man, to efforts intended to level the playing field; Dave was openly denigrating of employees of color who championed racial and cultural awareness; and Bridget and Rita seemed to see whiteness as a neutral norm and divergences from it as lacking objectivity. The incubator also played a role, however. The professed camaraderie and cohesion belied deeper anxieties and disturbances. These more subterranean dynamics not only resulted in real barriers to engaging racial and cultural difference, they also likely contributed to the team's racial-cultural practice.

A direct comparison between Teams South and North is instructive. They had some remarkable similarities. Their office contexts were largely positive or at least benign. They both had white team leaders and memberships that were almost all white, with one member of color (Antonia in Team North, Radhi in Team South). They both reported to white managers and white office directors. They also each had a white worker who was bilingual (Teresa, a Latina who racially identified as white, in Team North and Ana in Team South). Both teams had at least some capacity to constructively confront conflict and reflect on their own practice. Yet their approaches to difference, and to racial and cultural differences in particular, could not have been more different. Team North's members actually enjoyed their diversity: they claimed it, championed it, explored it. This was true for differences of opinion, work style, gender, or race and culture. Team South's members downplayed their heterogeneity: they dealt with it when they had to resolve an open conflict but otherwise tried to ignore it, whatever its source. In fact, the team used the conversations about Aware and race-conscious organizational policies to brandish its cohesion, to signal a unified front against racial or cultural awareness, seemingly oblivious to the impact on Ana and Radhi. Given this fundamental distinction between the two teams, we can better understand why Team North was color cognizant and Team South was color hostile.

Our goal in this and the previous two chapters was to explain racial-cultural practice by drawing rich and detailed portraits of the three teams. Each illustrated how that practice was intimately intertwined with individual, team, and office dynamics. In the next chapter, we simplify and synthesize by providing a schematic explanation of racial-cultural practice, a model that we then apply to each team.

~ Chapter 7 ~

An Explanatory Model of Racial-Cultural Practice

Much of the management scholarship on managing diversity as well as the sociology and psychology research on race in organizations focus entirely on aspects that are clearly and directly related to race and ethnicity: the representation of people from various racial groups at different levels of the organization, EEO or affirmative action policies, diversity training, and the like. We argue, though, that more general features also play a critical role in how race and ethnicity are addressed, particularly the capacity for learning and the degree of safety. A team's racial-cultural practice is part of the fabric of team life: it can only be explained by viewing the team as a whole entity that exists within a broader office and organization context. In our study, all the teams are within one organization, which means that organizational characteristics are of limited value in understanding differences across teams. Because the teams were positioned within different offices around the state, however, we can assess the impact of the office environment, as well as the effect of the team as a container for what happens within it. We call this team and office context the intergroup incubator. Like any incubator, it broods something—in our case, the racial-cultural practices of the individual members. The ultimate result is the team-level racial-cultural practice.

In the end, we have three teams that ranged along a continuum of approaches to racial-cultural practice. Team North had a color-cognizant practice; as we've noted earlier, this is not the same as a culturally competent practice, but it is a step toward that ideal. Team North had broken the color bind. The other two teams had not, though they were constrained in different ways. Team East had a color-evasive practice. For the most part, its members brought a strong degree of interest and some knowledge and skill to their team. The team as a whole, though, largely sidestepped conversations related to race or ethnicity and completely avoided any detailed investigations. Team East could not overcome the impediments—a lack of safety and of a learning orientation—to these conversations. Finally, Team South was not just evasive; most members had an antipathy to acknowledging the weight or impact of race and culture in their work, except when it in some way threatened them. We have dubbed them color hostile to indicate that the team was not color blind at all, though most members claimed they were. This team had no interest in breaking the color bind. In fact, the color bind gave them cover: it allowed them to largely avoid conversations about race because they could claim the neutrality of color blindness while attacking their agency's color-conscious policies.

Our goal in this book has been to understand why the teams took such very different paths. We began, in chapters 4, 5, and 6, by providing thick descriptions of Teams North, East, and South, making contrasts among the teams along the way. In this chapter we more systematically compare the teams. To do so, we use an explanatory model of racial-cultural practice generated from the analyses of each team. We provide a general model in both narrative and graphic form and then a specific model for each team that summarizes its particular dynamics. A description and model of a fourth team, Team Southwest, are detailed in appendix C, which appears at https://www.russellsage.org/publications/color-bind.

A team begins as a group of individuals. These individuals bring with them attitudes about the role of race and ethnicity in themselves, their world, and their work. A few may have a strong ideological stance, though most will hold these beliefs implicitly. Regardless, the beliefs will influence how much they take race and culture into account as they go about their daily tasks and as they discuss their responsibilities with their colleagues. Those with a more color-blind approach will largely sidestep these issues and those who are color cognizant will consider their impact.

Teams are more than simply a set of individuals, however. In working together, they create expectations and protocols that become relatively stable and therefore powerful. These patterns will either reinforce or contradict the predispositions that each group member brings, including personal interest in delving into race and culture. Therefore, whether an individual actually expresses those inclinations depends a great deal on the team's climate and routines. Two team characteristics are critical: the degree to which members feel safe, comfortable, and welcomed and the extent to which they engage in practices that encourage the airing and integration of differing views, experimenting with new ways of working, and reflecting on team processes and performance. These characteristics are influenced by the team's leadership as well as the larger office and organizational environment and its interest in or defense against learning and curiosity. Together, the team and its larger context create an intergroup incubator, which broods the individual inclinations of team members.

This brooding engenders a singular set of roles and relationships that characterize the team, which we describe in this chapter. Those roles and relationships then have a huge impact on the team's racial-cultural practice.

Figure 7.1   *An Explanatory Model of Team Racial-Cultural Practice*

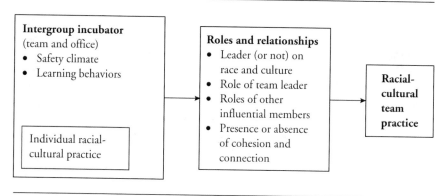

Source: Authors' compilation.

Several aspects of roles and relationships stand out. First, the presence or absence of a leader on racial and cultural issues is important, someone who was both willing to spearhead raising these issues and was seen by others as a resource. Second, we focus on the role of the team leader as either facilitator or suppressor of learning and safety more generally as well as of conversations related to race and ethnicity. Third, we identify other team members who seem to carry particular weight on the team that would affect its racial-cultural practice on the team's dynamics. Finally, regarding relationships, we highlight the team's overall cohesion and connection among group members, or lack of them. We describe the roles and relationships for each team below.

Figure 7.1 is a graphic depiction of our argument. The model may be deceptive in its simplicity. We know that teams or work groups are messy entities impossible to reduce to a set of boxes and arrows. However, we deliberately make the model as parsimonious as possible to better highlight the key characteristics that we believe make a difference. Moreover, the model suggests something of a linear relationship, but in reality it is difficult to identify what comes first and what comes later. We see each team's approach to addressing race and ethnicity as fully bound up with other team dynamics; its forthrightness or fear in addressing race and ethnicity would have a feedback loop affecting the team's larger sense of safety and learning as well as its roles and relationships.

Team North

Most of Team North's members, white and of color, brought not only interest in, but also knowledge and awareness of, race and culture to their work. As such, each carried out her or his own color-conscious way of working. These individual approaches were positioned in a largely constructive environment—

the intergroup incubator—that was both relatively safe and learning-oriented. Team members felt that they could bring their full selves to the team, that they could speak up even if their opinions contradicted those of others, and that their racial or ethnic identity did not put them at risk. The team was comfortable with conflict and difference; it dug into them instead of avoiding them or polarizing as a result. Team members were capable of reflecting on their own thoughts and actions and asking for help and insight from others.

This combination—of individual predispositions toward color cognizance existing within a safe learning container—is what sets Team North apart from the other teams. Its incubator, acting on individual practice, created a unique set of roles and relationships that ultimately resulted in a team-level color-cognizant practice. Three members played key roles: Antonia, a Latina; Katie, the white team leader; and Dave, also white. The relationships on the team were characterized by a dynamic cohesion that cultivated rather than suppressed difference. This cohesion included a cross-racial partnership committed to cultural cognizance.

Antonia, of Mexican background, had a leadership role regarding race and ethnicity in the group, acting as a cultural broker. She saw herself as an advocate for Latinos as well as for people of color more broadly. She offered valuable insights and expertise based on her cultural knowledge, such as the knowledge she gained about how the Dominican community operated. Other team members expressed strong and clear-cut appreciation for her contributions and what they had learned as a result. We've already seen that when members of other teams tried to play a similar role—like Pilar on Team East—they were not met with the same interest or commendation.

Antonia's leadership also took the form of admitting her faults. Twice in team settings she mentioned how she had learned from Katie that she had to check her prejudices when working with poor Latino families. She also owned, in a team interview, to making a major error and naming her tendency to act first and think later. Her willingness to make herself vulnerable may have made it easier for her white colleagues to acknowledge their own biases and shortcomings.

Moreover, Antonia could point to a time when she had learned from a white person about race: she asked a white team member for advice when she was experiencing hurdles working with a well-off white family. This is noteworthy because it challenges a commonly held belief of both whites and people of color that the latter hold both the expertise about and the responsibility for race and culture. If whites are to be color cognizant, if they are to engage on these issues, they have to claim their own racial or cultural expertise. At the same time, people of color have to allow for the possibility that they can learn from whites about race, that whites may know something that they do not. No other person of color mentioned learning anything specific about race or culture from their white colleagues. To the extent there was influence at all, it was unidirectional, from people of color to whites. Altogether, Antonia was a major contributor to the team's discussions and learning about the role of race and ethnicity in their work.

Katie, the team leader, also contributed, but in a different way. She set a general tone of openness and reflection on the team. She brought up topics that could be contentious at team meetings, such as whether workers should engage in hands-on activities like cleaning children of lice. She raised incidents where she felt the team had fallen short and encouraged the group to revisit them, such as the series of three removals that the team discussed. She reflected on her impulses and limitations, including her counter-transference related to a client. She encouraged experimentation, such as their team meeting practices, and, as the meeting leader, kept the practices going. Although not a leader on race or ethnicity, she took on a facilitator role: she encouraged discussion of such issues when others brought them up at team meetings and occasionally raised issues herself. No other team leader played a similar role.

Dave also stands out as a contributor to team dynamics. He made himself vulnerable and raised tough issues over and over. He said in his interview for an opening on the team that he felt he needed to work on his ability to become interdependent, to ask for help. He named that multiple times in later team interviews and team meetings. Dave identified gender dynamics as an issue on the team, prompting multiple discussions. He encouraged the team to try to focus more on tasks, challenging the team to be its best self. He raised issues with the team leader about her practice. His impact on the team was less related to race and ethnicity; instead, he contributed to its general dynamism, approach to learning, and ability to discuss gender issues.

Altogether, the relationships on the team were characterized by an animated cohesion. Team members felt connected even as debates and differences kept bubbling up. Because the connections were not based on similarity, the team could withstand and indeed learn from the varied approaches that continued to surface. Out of this set of key individuals, other team members, and their distinctive interconnections grew a mutuality regarding race and ethnicity. Others acknowledged Antonia's influence but did not cede their responsibility. Multiple team members, of all backgrounds, felt responsible for ensuring that these issues informed their practice. In fact, the team created a cross-racial commitment for color cognizance. The consequences of that commitment were revealed in their team meetings: they used a racial or cultural lens to understand a wide range of issues, from disciplinary techniques to understandings of mental illness to their capacity to support Antonia. (For a graphic depiction of this argument, see figure 7.2.)

Team East

Like their counterparts on Team North, the members of Team East individually attended to issues related to race and ethnicity, but, unlike Team North, we never saw them as a group delve deeply into these issues. We suggest that the intergroup incubator is the major culprit here, stifling these leanings, rather than growing them. Altogether, we have evidence of a noxious office environ-

Figure 7.2   *A Model of Team North*

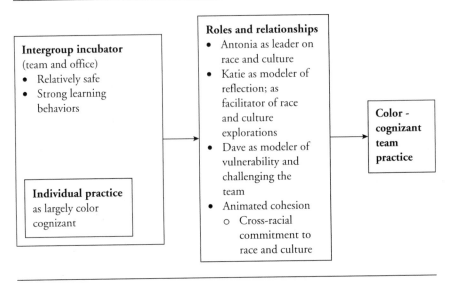

Source: Authors' compilation.

ment with significant tension, including intergroup tension, and therefore a distinct lack of safety, especially as related to relations among racial and ethnic groups. Some psychoanalytic theorists would suggest an insufficient holding environment in which workers could try out new behaviors and ways of being while still being supported.[1] We have a pernicious team context as well: not only was the team unable to learn more generally, several members stated they felt some lack of safety, including two who suggested a lack of identity safety.

This incubator acted on the individuals in the team to create Team East's unique set of roles and relationships that ultimately led to a color-evasive team practice. Both Pilar, the Puerto Rican team leader, and Debbie, the white team manager, played important roles. The overall relationships on the team could be best described as polarized and schismatic.

Pilar as team leader probably had the most impact on the team's dynamics. As the team's formal leader and someone devoted to issues related to race and culture, she would have been the likely instigator of team-level conversations, but she was so disliked and mistrusted by the team members that this was impossible. In fact, Pilar could be characterized as a failed leader: she saw herself as a model and teacher of how to attend to these issues, but the team never granted her that authority. Debbie, Pilar's direct superior, seemingly color cognizant, never encouraged such conversations in team meetings nor participated in them when they did occur. She was a nonleader in this arena.

Figure 7.3   *A Model of Team East*

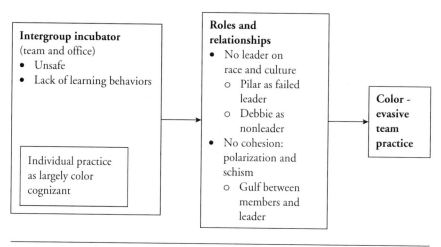

Source: Authors' compilation.

It's important to point out that regardless of Pilar's and Debbie's approaches, it would have been very difficult to broach racial or ethnic topics, given the office context. Home to an ugly racist incident not long before the teaming pilot began, the office continued to experience racial tension, including charges of racial favoritism.

The team's lack of discussion, though, was also related to the overall set of relationships on the team. The group was characterized not by cohesion but by polarization and schism, anchored by the gulf between the team members and Pilar. With such a divide, the team stagnated; it could not resolve conflict or move forward. Given this atmosphere, there was no incentive for the team to investigate territory, like race and ethnicity, which could create more conflict. If it could avoid a potential source of conflict, it would—leading to a color-evasive practice.

In sum, it may not be so paradoxical that, in Team East, we have a group of color-conscious individuals who created a team practice that was largely color blind. In fact, given the team and office climate, the surprise may be that they ever mentioned it at all. (For a graphic summary of this argument, see figure 7.3.)

Team South

Team South brings a unique positioning. Team East held the seeds for color-cognizant practice in that most of their members were interested and knowledgeable; they just needed the right incubator. But Team South would have to undergo a major transformation for such an approach to bloom.

The team did engage in learning around aspects of its task but was strikingly closed to learning about race and culture. It may appear that the culprit is individual practice. After all, most members espoused a color-blind perspective in their casework, including the team leader who was particularly forceful on the topic, and the two members who were more color cognizant were either contradictory or hesitant. Therefore, the virtual absence of using race or culture as a diagnostic lens in their case discussions is not surprising. However, the incubator appears to be a powerful force that did not just reinforce a color-blind team practice, but also ultimately reinforced the desire of the majority of team members to largely suppress discussion of race and ethnicity as it allowed the voicing of resistance to efforts such as affirmative action and cultural events. Like the other teams, the way the incubator acted on the individuals in the team produced a singular set of roles and relationships. We look at the roles played by Bob, the white team leader; Dan, a white team member; Ana, a team member of Portuguese descent; and Radhi, a member of Indian background. We characterize the overall relationships on the team as cohesive but insular.

Bob, the team leader, held a contradictory positioning. He encouraged a learning approach to the team's casework, and the team did reflect on past practice. He was firmly closed to learning about race and culture, however. He claimed color blindness, but this gave cover to a resentment toward color-conscious policies, such as affirmative action, and toward the collective efforts of Aware. Given his animosity and influential position as leader of the group, it is likely that Bob suppressed race- or culture-related conversations. Dan also played a particularly active role in signaling animus to exploring the role of race and ethnicity in the team's work: his remarks about Aware and its leaders were particularly insulting. It is likely he also suppressed discussion in the group.

Ana and Radhi, the two members eligible for participation in Aware, are also important players. In her individual interviews, Ana did speak for the insights gained from her cultural awareness, though she then immediately denied these claims. Therefore, she was too conflicted and equivocal in her beliefs to be a strong advocate; if she had any inkling in that direction, she was likely discouraged by the strong color-blind beliefs of her white colleagues, including the team leader. Although Radhi was more sure about the importance of culture, her participation was generally muted. Radhi said that she often held back from voicing opinions that she felt might conflict with those of others. She would have been very hesitant to take on what would have been quite a battle. At the same time, it's noteworthy that Radhi was singled out as the member others felt was not doing her fair share. In fact, Radhi could have been serving as a scapegoat, a role that may have enabled the rest of the team to feel more connected.

The team's relationships were largely characterized by a cohesive insularity—us against the world—based on the members' sense of themselves as funda-

Figure 7.4   *A Model of Team South*

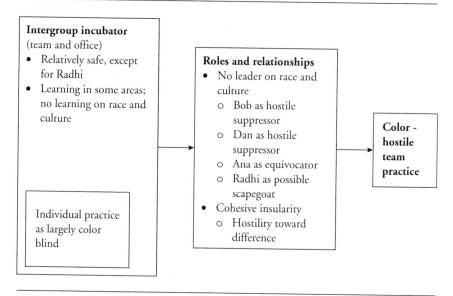

Source: Authors' compilation.

mentally similar. This seemed to include Radhi as well—at least no one said anything about Radhi's being less a part of the group, even though they could be critical of her. The team's insistence on its closeness, however, likely made it impossible for Radhi or anyone else on the team to actually face their fissures. Ultimately, the group's color hostility seems firmly rooted in its aggressive claims of internal cohesion: difference in any form was threatening, and racial or cultural difference especially so. (For a graphic summary of this argument, see figure 7.4.)

These models stand as summaries of the core characteristics of each team. Such summaries are fruitful for two reasons. First, they provide a clear picture of each team: they enhance our understanding of team dynamics and their relationship to each team's racial-cultural practice. Second, they enable us to suggest points of attention and intervention as organizations consider how to develop more color-cognizant practice among their members and work units. Having created these models, though, we now want to complicate them. The teams, as well as members on each team, harbored multiple inconsistencies that sometimes made the task of creating clear labels challenging. But just as those labels can be fruitful, contradictions can be too. We explore the generativity of contradiction in our next chapter.

~ Chapter 8 ~

The Nature of the Terrain:
Flaws and Contradictions

Over bagels and cream cheese at its morning meeting, Team North was discussing other teams and feeling competitive. Team South, said Katie, "is a little further ahead than us" when it came to ensuring that the team met at least weekly. "It has to be part of the regular routine," she said. "I don't like losing!" said Antonia. Teresa joined in, "I know! We need to be the best team!" After noting that Team South's manager was more actively driving the team than their own manager, the team members turned to their cases, including that of an Arab father and his children. The mother had recently left the family and the father was raising the children on his own. Teresa, the caseworker, wondered whether it was time to close the case. Eliza felt it was: "He's making good decisions about his kids." Teresa added, "And I have to say, he is awesome with the kids. . . . They adore him. [He has a] good relationship with them. Which I thought was interesting, being from his culture." She went on to note that the client wanted to get remarried in his home country and "he wants to bring his wife back and he wants to have the kids then, so that she can take care of them." Eliza quipped, "Can't you just mail a wife for that? I thought there was a program" to some laughter before the team moved on to another case.

Team North, though far ahead of the other teams in its willingness to broach topics related to race and ethnicity, was far from perfect. Certainly this discussion of the Arab father was not a model of cultural sensitivity. Teresa seemed to presume that men like him generally do not have close relationships with their children, whereas Eliza appeared to draw on a stereotype about the basis of marriage in Arab cultures. None of the other team members challenged these representations. Nor was this the only time they played into stereotypes or made obtuse comments. But, for us, that shouldn't consign them to being dismissed or condemned. Like many of us, Team North harbored contradictions in how it thought about issues related to race, ethnicity, and culture. Like all of us, Team North was flawed. Unlike most of us, it was willing to broach the topic, which meant that the possibility of learning lay open to them in a way it cannot if we are fully silent.

In this chapter, we explore the flaws and contradictions that are the nature of this terrain. We begin by more deeply exploring the shadow side of Team North, exposing how it contained multiple impulses, even as—perhaps because— it delved into this territory far more than any other team. We then illustrate another facet of Team South, which, despite its color hostility, showed a commitment to looking at the strengths and potential of the parents they worked with rather than just their liabilities. We don't disavow our earlier representations of these teams, but we do bring in another slant that adds complexity to their portraits.

We continue by revealing some of our blind spots—and the conflicts that brought them to light—that we faced as we collaborated to interpret the data and write this book. We are a diverse team, just like those we write about, though our team has only two members. Tamara is a professor of counseling psychology and Erica teaches about management and organizations. Tamara is also a clinician, with a private therapy practice. Erica is not. Tamara is African American. Erica is white. We tussled at a variety of points along the way. Ultimately, we created a shared understanding of the evidence, but even as we put the finishing touches on the manuscript, well-worn disagreements continued to emerge. By sharing some of our debates, we highlight not only our arguments, but also our foibles and some of the insights that resulted from talking through our differences.

We conclude by framing flaws and conflicts as one manifestation of the contradiction and inconsistency so often found in this arena. Many others have pointed out how contradiction and ambiguity related to race and ethnicity seem embedded in our nation's DNA as well as in individual psyches as we wrestle with these issues. We explore how embracing—rather than suspecting— this lack of coherence can be generative.

Team North: A Model of Imperfection

One of Team North's toughest cases was the refugee family from an African civil war, which we've highlighted several times in this book. We've chosen previous excerpts from their discussions to illustrate ways in which the team was using culture as a lens to understand better what might be happening with the young boy and his family members. However, at times team members referenced culture in a way that could have stereotyped the family.

At several points, team members described the family's culture as sexist or male dominated. For example, Dave, the lead worker, noted in one conversation, "Just now [the boy] was talking about witnessing sexual abuse stuff in Africa. He talks about, not in these words, but it was a male-dominated culture. How the men treated the women, stuff like that." Although Dave acknowledges that he is not directly quoting the child, he does use the term *male-dominated,* which may evoke particular concerns or images in the minds of other team members that don't align with what the boy was actually trying to say. This matters because it could make it more difficult for them to understand or work with him. In fact, later in the same conversation, they return to the same theme:

> TERESA: He's [the boy] coming from this male-dominated culture where—
>
> ANTONIA: Chauvinist.
>
> TERESA: Wasn't he considered special?
>
> KATIE: He was.
>
> TERESA: He was probably treated in a way that—
>
> ARLO: That's not that unusual. I've got a bunch of kids, young adults from Africa [like that].

Here again team members use the words *male-dominated* as well as *chauvinist,* a term laden with meaning for many Americans that may not accurately capture the boy's culture and customs. Further, Arlo then sweeps together huge swaths of territory and hundreds of different ethnic groups when he states that male dominance is "not that unusual" among young adults from Africa.

It is possible that the culture the boy came from was a traditional or patriarchal one with a gender hierarchy and relatively fixed gender roles that favored men. Regardless, the team members were using well-worn Western tropes to understand a boy from a very different context. At another point, they were discussing his household's lack of cleanliness. Katie noted that household members used to just "throw things on the floor," which she also saw as cultural: "That's how you are in Africa." Team members were happy that a local social service agency was sending in a "cleaning crew every other week to clean, do laundry," and "teach them how [to clean]." Perhaps team members were correct in their characterization of the family's habits, but ascribing their routines to a continent-wide approach to taking care of the home is strikingly ignorant at best and racist at worst. Moreover, no one expressed any doubt about the conclusions they've drawn, even though, as shown in another description of this case in chapter 1, they were well aware of the limits of their cultural knowledge when it came to this family.

These examples bring to light the downside of color cognizance: we can be conscious of the importance of race and culture but evoke them in stereotypical or ethnocentric ways that, far from furthering understanding, simply reinforce harmful images. In fact, these illustrations help us make the distinction between color cognizance and cultural competence that we described earlier. Whereas color cognizance is a simple cognitive awareness of the impact of race and culture and the presence of racism and discrimination, cultural competence encompasses knowledge, attitude, and skill and is a lifelong pursuit.[1] No one is fully culturally competent. But one cannot pursue such competence without color cognizance; it is a foundational element because it motivates open discussion.

Team North was largely color cognizant but not always culturally competent. Although many times its members were thoughtful and perceptive about the potential impact of culture or race, the examples in this chapter show how they could also wield them as crude tools that may have done more harm than good. But that is the point. It is tempting to dismiss Team North as ignorant or racist, but at least it was on the path—groping and stumbling, it is true, but making its way nonetheless. Members of other teams likely also harbored stereotypes about the families they worked with but because they stayed largely mute, these beliefs stayed underground. If these simplistic assumptions come to light, they can be challenged.

In fact, it is impossible to be on the path without stumbling—if not falling down altogether. We're back to our dilemma of probity versus generosity. We have to empathize with those who, like Team North, are on the path; at the same time we have to be willing to call out where we think others (or ourselves) have erred. We have tried to strike the right balance in writing this book, but we recognize that at points we may have fallen short. Perhaps our biggest challenge has been how to think about Team South.

Team South: Taking a Strength-Based Perspective

Honestly, we have had a tough time with Team South. In previous chapters, we described it as color hostile, because it had two conversations in which it disparaged Aware, the organization for workers of color and bilingual workers. These conversations couldn't help but put Ana, the Portuguese-speaking worker, and especially Radhi, an Indian American and the only worker of color, in a difficult position as the two members eligible for Aware membership. In our attempt to be empathic to those two workers, we have treated the rest of the team with a level of rectitude that may not have been appropriately weighted with generosity. Here we want to explore another facet of the team that complicates the picture and perhaps restore some balance to our portrait of the team.

Team South saw itself as a team that did everything it could to keep children in the home, using what was called a strength-based approach that sought to begin with the capabilities of the family rather than its limitations. This was in line with the agency's recently codified values, one of which was strength-based practice. So Team South was by no means alone, but team members felt that their commitment to this approach stood out. As we've described, Team South could be self-congratulatory about its work, and given that we did not view interactions between workers and families, we cannot speak to how different its practice was from other teams. We do have evidence, however, from descriptions of one case, which suggests its depth of allegiance to these precepts. These descriptions come from a team member, the office director, and a report from an external observer.

The case involved a young mother with a five-week-old baby. One morning, the child's four-year-old sister woke her mother, saying that her brother was bleeding badly. The mother discovered that several of the boy's fingers were badly damaged and that one was severed. The child was rushed to a children's hospital; the case was referred to the agency and the team given responsibility for the investigation. The mother had several strikes against her. She had had an infant who had died previously, apparently from SIDS, but the death cast a taint of suspicion. She had a history of depression. She had also grown up in the agency's care because of significant problems in her family of origin.

The hospital's child protective team, including doctors, administrators, and social workers, demanded an emergency removal of the children. The team resisted. The infant was in the hospital, being cared for, and the four-year-old could stay with a friend, so neither child would be in immediate danger. They had time to gather information rather than "rush to judgment," as they felt the hospital was doing. According to Bridget, the lead worker on the case, "One of the social workers was so critical of mom, and I look at her, and I said, 'Did you have the chance to sit down and meet with her?' 'No. I haven't met her yet.' I said, 'You haven't met her yet?' And she's making all this judgment calls, and looking at facts on paper." The team collected information from a variety of sources, including the children's pediatrician, the older child's school, and the mother's therapist—"a thorough investigation," according to the office director. All testified to the mother's strong care and parenting for her children. Although the doctors believed that the wound was from a rat bite, the child protection team at the hospital continued to press to remove both children from the mother. Given the evidence they had collected, the team felt that the children were safe with their mother and instead focused on getting the family into new housing. According to the report, written about a year after the incident, from the external observer, "The story has a happy ending. The family has a new place to live. The children are at home; both are fine. The case is stabilized."[2]

We can't testify to whether the team took appropriate action, though the office director and external observer both believed that it had. Regardless, it does show both the team's determination to gather facts rather than jump to conclusions, and a desire to try to see strengths where others would see limitations. For example, as Bridget described, "She [the mother] has been through a lot in her life. She grew up in the system of [this agency], which most people would hold against her, but actually she came out of it with a world of knowledge and experience."

This story doesn't take away from the team's aversion to Aware or its in-group insularity, but it does suggest that team members have some awareness of how easy it is to prejudge clients and discriminate against them. In fact, Erica, when she first collected the data that included this story, was shocked and jumped to the same conclusions as the hospital. It was only after hearing the story several times that she was able to shake her assumptions about the fitness of the mother. Ultimately, she learned something from the team about how to approach these families with an open mind.

Team South leaves us with this question: can we treat the team the way it treated this client—by starting with its strengths rather than its deficits? Our driving goal is how to establish color-cognizant practice, and this story doesn't change our overall argument: that teams need color-conscious individuals as well as a learning-oriented climate that is safe for everyone. Team South fell short on all those scores. Also, we don't know the race of the family, so we don't know whether the mother's race played a role in how the team treated her. Given team members' awareness of some kinds of discrimination, however, the story does raise the possibility that team members might be nudged toward a broader understanding of prejudice, including that based on color and culture. At the same time, it poses the potential of what the team could teach others, including ourselves. How do we need to be nudged?

Team Tamara and Erica: Being Cognizant of Our Blind Spots

The term *blind spot* suggests how easy it is to overlook our own flaws: if we are blind to them, how can we see them? In our case, it was often through our conflicts. We write here of several times we had to resolve disagreements that arose from one of us pushing back on what the other was taking in (or not taking in) from the data.

In one case, though it was clear we weren't seeing eye-to-eye, it wasn't clear for a long time what we were disagreeing about. It took several exchanges, both written and verbal, to bring the issue into focus: we were having very different emotional reactions to the evidence we were analyzing.

The disagreement first surfaced on an early chapter draft describing Team East. Erica had written the draft and Tamara was commenting on it. In the chapter, toward the end of a long description of Team East's members and dynamics, Erica described how Office East had suffered a serious racial incident in which a defaced black doll was found on the desk of a Latina worker (for a fuller description, see chapter 5). In the margin, Tamara wrote, "It sounds like a setup for failure. . . . This is a CRISIS and has tremendous effects on the culture." In a later draft, Tamara wondered whether the incident should be put at the beginning of the discussion about Team East, rather than the end: "It makes me rethink the entire case," she wrote. Both times, Erica felt that Tamara was implicitly and unfairly criticizing her for not taking the issue seriously enough. Erica felt she did recognize its implications: that was why she had included the incident in the first place. However, she never raised this concern with Tamara.

A month or two later, the two of us were on the telephone discussing the dynamics of Team South, particularly the impact of its disparaging conversations about Aware on Radhi, the team's only member of color. Tamara became frustrated, saying that Erica did not understand the devastating effect such conversations could have on the worker. She added that Erica also seemed equally ill-attuned to the impact of the doll incident on Office East. Tamara said she found these incidents very emotional because they were an expression of the ugliness that people of color anticipate—and not infrequently encounter—at work. Erica said that she did see how destructive such incidents could be but that in her case it was more intellectual than emotional or visceral. This was our first serious fight and so we each wrote notes after the call, both to document what happened and to explore our contributions and reactions.

In her notes, Tamara wrote, "Erica and I had our first real fight over the data today. I was so frustrated that Erica seemed so analytical and lacking in emotion about the lone Indian woman [Radhi] who is on a team that is basically hostile toward POC [people of color], disguised by their denigration of the multicultural group [Aware]. . . . This is the first time that I have honestly been heated and felt angry toward Erica around this book project." Erica, in the meantime and without seeing Tamara's notes, was starting to understand why her reactions were so distressing to Tamara.

> Writing this now, I feel like I understand better what is going on. I am so focused on what these events mean for the teams and how they will affect our argument, that I don't see them as real incidents that hurt real people. I am focused on them as *data,* I care about them as data, they are important to the extent that they can help us create our argument. I don't feel personally affected by them and I also don't really take in how they affected people that I had a relationship with, even [if] it was just a researcher relationship. I wonder whether this is what Tamara has been trying to tell me and whether she has been reacting to something in my manner that is very dispassionate and removed.

We shared our notes with each other. Tamara wrote in the margins of Erica's notes, "Yes, this is exactly how I feel. It can feel like you acknowledge it but the impact that it might have on people is missing in some instances." She went on to apply this understanding to herself: "I'll have to think if I, too, may do this when in the researcher role [on other studies]."

About a month later, we discussed the argument again as well as what we had learned from reading each other's notes. Tamara said that she was no longer angry especially because Erica had come to recognize what it was that was making her frustrated. She also referenced a "Modern Love" column in the *New York Times*[3] that had influenced her change of heart. In the column, a white American woman writes about a long-term relationship with a British Jamaican. She feels fully committed to the relationship but he breaks it off. She does not give his reasons but uses the column to reflect on her white identity and what it meant to be in a biracial relationship. Race was "part and parcel" of their connection: "Daniel and I talked about race a lot." The author says that "Daniel didn't teach me that race matters. . . . I was raised to think critically about such things." But she also acknowledges that "regardless of my relative awareness of the racist structures I lived within, it was hard for me—it's hard for white people, period—to feel racism personally. Racism can matter to us, make us angry, but it usually isn't personal. Personal is yourself, or your mother, or your child." Tamara said this had helped her understand why Erica's reactions might be more intellectual and removed than emotional and visceral. Erica had read the same column and found it intriguing, but hadn't connected it with her and Tamara's dispute. She appreciated that Tamara had seen the link, used it to reflect on her reactions, and shared that with Erica.

A second disagreement concerned one of the major premises of our argument: the difficulty of talking about race. Erica had made this claim boldly in a couple of early drafts, such as "Americans are terrified of talking about race." Tamara had pushed back, saying that whites might be scared of talking about race but that people of color talked about it all the time. In response, in a later draft of chapter 2, Erica still made a vivid claim: "Americans are frightened—often terrified—of talking about race" but noted a couple of sentences later that "that is a generalization that requires some nuance." She proceeded to note several refinements, including that whites had more trepidation about this than people of color did. She felt this responded to Tamara's concern. So she was annoyed when she read Tamara's comment, "I think we could lose credibility by making this statement [that Americans are terrified of talking about race] even though you provide the nuance below. Black people talk about race all the time and racial socialization is part of ongoing discussions with their kids." At another point in chapter 2, Erica wrote, "[Color cognizance] is hard because it involves talking about racial and cultural differences, which we've all been taught not to do." Again, Tamara wrote, "I think this statement is too general. I'm not sure that many people of color have been taught not to talk about race."

Although Erica felt defensive, she also knew that Tamara was probably onto something. As she thought about it, she realized that she had been using the term *American* to mean white American, that she had generalized from her racial group to an entire population. In the service of arguing for a color-cognizant perspective because it allows us to explore and learn from difference, she had erased difference, using the white experience as the norm, the neutral, the "unnamed, universal moral referent."[4] If Tamara hadn't pushed back, Erica would not have recognized how she was contributing to that dynamic. At the same time, Erica found it hard to give up what she saw as the clarity and boldness of the original statement. As you see in chapter 2, we came to agreement on language that encompasses more varied experiences and reactions to talking about race. We negotiated up until the final draft, however. We recognize that the disagreement is not fully resolved between us and will continue to arise in our work together.

Erica was not the only one who had to catch herself. Tamara recognized that she was also drawing from personal experience. In one of her comments, she wrote, "OK, now that I've said this [that black people talk a lot of race] I need to think about my own lens. I was raised in a household in which we talked about race all the time—my sense is that my other black friends did too but I should be sure of this. Also, I do race work and teach race classes, so this [saying that all people avoid talking about race] just runs counter to all my experience." In other words, Tamara understood that her experience might also not fully translate to everyone from her background.

At another point, Tamara recognized something else she needed to watch for, in response to some back and forth with Erica. When describing individuals in the sample, we sometimes disagreed about how to understand what was going on with them. One instance came up related to Team Southwest, a team we didn't include in the narrative but is described at length in appendix C. Mary, the team's manager, was African American and also president of Aware. Based on her reading of the data, Erica characterized her as someone who recognized and worked against racism and discrimination in the agency in her role as Aware president, but seemed uninterested or unversed in how race and ethnicity could be useful in diagnosing and working with clients. Erica ascribed this to Mary's personal point of view. Tamara initially suggested other explanations. At one point, she commented that Mary's role with Aware might be relevant: "She may feel that she's known because of her role for advocating for these issues so that on the team she doesn't want to continue to push the issues." At another point, remarking on a quote from Mary that read, "I just always felt a person was a person was a person and race didn't enter into it. . . . We all bleed red and we all have the same blood types," Tamara wrote, "So I wonder how/if the organizational context is pulling for her to take a different position. For example, is there a pull in the environment for people of color to take on these roles." Later, after a fuller picture of Mary emerged, Tamara acknowledged that Mary's disinterest in the role of race in casework did seem to be at least partly about Mary's personal level of racial identity development. In fact, a complete understanding of Mary or anyone else in the study does require looking beyond the individual, but Tamara seemed resistant, initially, to considering that individual inclinations might play any role at all. After a number of such volleys, Tamara told Erica in a telephone conversation that she needed to keep her sympathy for people of color in check: she would often jump to defend them, which could impede her ability to see the full picture.

This issue continues to percolate between us. Tamara noted toward the end of our writing process that "for people of color I would look to broader systemic issues to account for their negative behaviors . . . but I don't think I [would be] as likely to pursue the context with whites probably because I know that the context is typically not discriminatory toward them." Erica would agree that organizational contexts generally privilege whites and disadvantage those of color, but would still argue that looking to context is equally important for both.

We could keep going—there are certainly more examples we could share. This, however, is not about making a full confession. Instead, we wanted to name some of our blind spots and illustrate that, through a combination of probity and generosity, we learned from them. Ultimately, the question is not whether any of us will fall short on this demanding terrain; it is what those flaws say about us. If we see them as evidence of our monolithic inadequacy, we will walk away out of shame or impotence. If we see them as part of a contradictory self, with both magnanimous and miserly impulses, we have a shot at doing better. We can see inconsistencies as fissures of possibility. As Leonard Cohen wrote, "There is a crack in everything. That's how the light gets in."[5]

The Fertility of Contradiction

Work in sociology, political science, and psychology has also documented the decades-long presence and importance of inconsistencies and ambivalence as Americans try to make sense of race.[6] Richard Merelman, Greg Streich, and Paul Martin write of "unresolved dilemmas" in their study of community conversations about race. Participants could not come to agreement about whether unity, a shared national identity, or diversity, ethnic and racial pluralism, better captures the American experience. Instead, they kept cycling through the same arguments, even, in some cases, after weeks of discussion. The researchers found evidence of "individual cycling," or individuals promoting both unity and diversity, "sometimes even in the same utterance." They also documented group cycling: "Typically, small group conversations progressed until most of the conflicts of American identity appeared. When the conversation reached this point, one could sense an almost palpable pause, as people attempted to digest the dilemmas and move forward. Group cycling refers to the fact that most groups could not pass this point." That is, the issues remained unresolved.[7]

This seesawing between poles also occurred in a different set of community dialogues about race. "The participants express a *range* of sentiments about the proper balance between unity and racial difference. . . . People are deeply ambivalent about the tensions involved." Katherine Walsh found that the members of these dialogue groups undertook "the task of clarifying a complex identity of people who desire the noninterference of color as well as an awareness and respect for racial difference."[8] Mica Pollock, in her intensive exploration of "race talk" at a diverse American high school, named six "dilemmas" that characterized such talk, including "we don't belong to simple race groups but we do" and "race doesn't matter but it does."[9]

Psychological exploration of "white dialectics" explores the intrapsychic vacillations that many whites engage in as they try to make sense of race and their own role in the racial order. In a study of white counselor trainees, Nathan Todd and Elizabeth Abrams identified six tensions, such as the pull between feeling "I am advantaged" and "I am not advantaged" or self as white versus self as not white.[10] Eduardo Bonilla-Silva's analysis of interviews with whites about issues related to race such as whether they supported affirmative action, shows they engaged in common "sematic moves" including "Yes and no, but." He writes that not only was their language often contradictory, but also even "rhetorically incoherent" to the point of being "incomprehensible." "Digressions, long pauses, repetition, and self corrections were the order of the day."[11]

Some believe that this back-and-forthing—whether at the individual or communal level—simply obscures what is, at bottom, simple racism. Bonilla-Silva asserts that "a common way of stating racial views without opening yourself to the charge of racism is apparently taking all sides on an issue."[12] In another article, he and Tyrone Forman write that these contradictions, what they call "'color-blind racism,' allow Whites to appear 'not racist' . . . preserve their privileged status . . . blame Blacks for their lower status . . . and criticize any institutional approach—such as affirmative action—that attempts to ameliorate racial inequality."[13] Howard Winant argues that a "white racial dualism" that is "contradictory as well as confused and anxiety-ridden" has arisen in the United States. Although it may hold the possibility of progressive change, it has largely been used to reinforce the racial hierarchy.[14]

Other work suggests that many of us are genuinely confused about what to believe. Bonilla-Silva himself acknowledges that "This incoherent talk is the result of talking about race in a world that insists race does not matter." Though, he continues, "since it is so preeminent, it must be included as part of the linguistic modalities of color blind racism."[15] Others agree: "[Diversity training] participants may be confused about programs that emphasize racial or gender differences when they had been taught in the past to be *color blind* or *gender neutral.*"[16] We also agree. Many Americans may have been taught color blindness but sense that it offers too simplistic a solution. We're apprehensive about what could happen if we open Pandora's multicolored and multicultured box. We don't feel we have the skill to handle the debates and interactions that might ensue. We may feel caught in what is, in fact, a false choice between unity and diversity and can't make a decision.

Given this confusion, some argue ambivalence and contradiction, if explored, are potentially generative. "Historically, scholars of public opinion have viewed ambivalence over political stances or issues as a function of lack of information or of a less-than-sophisticated ideology," writes Walsh. However, she argues, drawing on Jennifer Hochshild, that "ambivalence is actually a cause for 'cautious optimism'. . . . The presence of ambivalence and disjunction in individuals signifies awareness of, rather than obliviousness to, the complexities of the political and social context."[17]

Todd and Abrams suggest that only by holding the tensions generated by white dialectics are whites able to develop an "authentic whiteness," using the term *authentic* to mean "individuals are congruous within themselves and in multiracial relationships."[18]

We believe that both understandings of inconsistency and ambivalence are valid: they can mask a deeper, bona fide racism and they can be fertile ground—even at the same time. We also recognize, though, as have others, that they are only generative if they are explored. Pollock argues that the only way to transcend the six dilemmas of "race talk" that she identified is to explicitly discuss them: that is, to talk *"about how we talk."*[19] Todd and Abrams take this tack when thinking through how to work with white counseling trainees: "Struggle with ambiguity is central to the process of change and, in fact, is central to a progression through the stages of change. . . . Educators could point out the contradictions and ask students to struggle thoughtfully with these tensions."[20] For example, students could be asked to write about ways in which they see themselves as white and as not white.

Walsh and Pollock have also named some of the conditions necessary for such conversations, conditions that should sound familiar. They both reference, in their own ways, the need for what we would call learning behaviors—the ability to both voice one's perspective and attend to others—or, in Walsh's words, the "dual tasks of listening and argumentation."[21] Pollock says, "We each need a willingness to listen sometimes while others talk and to talk sometimes while others listen."[22] Walsh noted further that rather than presuming that such conversations might have "members of marginalized groups talk and members of dominant groups listen . . . we have seen people of a variety of racial backgrounds engage in both of these acts."[23] In other words, everyone needs to claim a voice on race as well as heed others' voices.

Both authors also refer to the importance of safety, though they temper this with a concern that it not lead to pablum. Walsh recounts the attempts by dialogue organizers and facilitators to create a relatively safe environment by encouraging respect and civility. Guidelines for discussion included items such as "dialogue, not debate" and "When disagreement occurs, don't personalize it." However, she noted that in practice some of the most productive moments came with confrontation: "It is when people scrutinized each other's claims that they most clearly seemed to convey respect for one another."[24] Pollock also indicates the importance of basic ground rules: "All participants [must] trust that their comments will be both respectfully engaged and put to use." She also says, however, that these conversations must "mix a desire for interpersonal harmony with a drive for analytic sophistication." She notes that, ultimately, we should acknowledge upfront that "every speaker will make mistakes" and that our best hope is to "muddle through" together. We hear both authors, like us, calling for both rectitude and empathy.[25]

Our purpose in this chapter was to showcase the presence of inconsistency and ambiguity as Americans address race and ethnicity. We also hoped to model some ways of living with those contradictions and making them generative by adding complexity to the story we've written thus far and by holding our limitations up to the light. As we bring the book to a close in the next chapter, we suggest how our insights can enhance research and practice in a variety of fields and disciplines.

~ Chapter 9 ~

What We've Learned
(and Still Need to Learn)

At bottom, our argument is very simple. Race and culture are potent facets of the American landscape—shaping where we live and go to school, whom we befriend and with whom we partner, how we get sick and whether we heal, how much we earn and what we own, how and where we work—and yet are largely undiscussable in most workplaces. Though many scholars and practitioners call for talking about race, it's rare. It's rare because it's difficult. It raises thorny issues, triggers strong emotions, and challenges those who benefit from the status quo. Many work groups are caught in the color bind— even if team members think talking about race and culture could be fruitful, some may be scared of the conflict that could erupt and others may be resistant to the further-reaching implications that could emerge.

What, then, can break the color bind? Two basic ingredients are needed.

First, a work group needs at least some members who are color cognizant— who believe that race and ethnicity have weight and consequence—as opposed to color blind. Second, those individuals need to exist in a larger context, an intergroup incubator—that includes their team and office—in which they feel relatively safe and in which they learn together about their work and how to do it better. From our work, it appears that both elements must be in place.

Connections with Previous Research

We begin with our colleagues from what we think of as macro disciplines, such as sociology, political science, economics, and policy. Scholars from these fields have done the critical work of documenting the dramatic inequities that face people of color in American society, from lower income and less wealth to shorter life expectancy to higher levels of housing foreclosure.[1]

Many of these scholars then assert the need to address these inequalities, including by having tough conversations. After thoroughly mapping the racism in the criminal justice system, Michelle Alexander challenges us: "We need to talk about race openly and honestly. We must stop debating crime policy as though it were purely about crime. People must come to understand the racial history and origins of mass incarceration—the many ways our conscious and unconscious biases have distorted our judgments over the years."[2] What enables those conversations? Most work at the macro level ends without thinking about how to overcome the barriers to such discussions.

As scholars who plumb micro dynamics, such as individual and team sensemaking and behavior, we see this as our charge. We realize we can't understand the difficulty of these conversations without assessing the impact of encompassing phenomena like the discourse of color blindness and racial injustice. Those larger influences, though, don't tell the whole story. We also need to understand how individuals relate to their colleagues, the nature of group interaction, and the climate of their offices and organizations. What we've tried to do here is illuminate what might be required for work groups in any context to broach these topics and successfully navigate them.

Valuable research at the micro level in the psychology lab focuses on intergroup relations and the importance of color cognizance, but much less does so on what enables such a perspective. Moreover, by definition, this research stops short of investigating such dynamics in real-world work groups and therefore can't unearth the densely interconnected web of dynamics that such groups inevitably house. Lab research also usually overlooks the role of the office or organizational context.

We also offer additional understanding to those interested in the broad dialogue about unity and diversity, often manifested in the debate between color blindness and color cognizance. The contestation between the two models has been well documented in a variety of settings, including high schools,[3] community dialogues about race,[4] neighborhood debates over gentrification,[5] student dialogue groups,[6] and our political order.[7] Little work, however, has explored how the models are manifested in work settings, though both are certainly present. Some organizations tend to take a color-blind orientation by trying to avoid discrimination against employees while assuming that employees of all backgrounds will assimilate to the dominant culture.[8] Many organizations, though, influenced by the managing diversity movement, say they want to go beyond simply avoiding discrimination to actually integrating the diversity in their midst—a more color-cognizant approach—because they believe it can result in increased organizational performance in a variety of domains.[9]

Workplaces are an important context for several reasons. First, they not only reflect societal inequities, they also actively contribute to them through job segregation and employment discrimination.[10] Second, unlike many other contexts in which these discourses have been explored, employees actually have to coordinate their work. Unlike members of community dialogue groups, students, or even neighbors, work colleagues need to develop collective goals, negotiate how to accomplish the job, and create a division of labor. Therefore, it could be particularly important, as well as especially challenging, to create a color-cognizant way of working.

A second broad audience comprises scholars from clinical and social service fields where practitioners provide services to other individuals, such as psychology, social work, medicine, and education. Recognizing that societal forces such as discrimination and racism affect individuals seeking services, academics in these fields conduct research about how to skillfully work with patients, clients, or students from widely varying racial and cultural backgrounds. In psychology, social work, and medicine, these conversations tend to fall under the rubric of cultural competence.[11] In education, they are more likely framed as part of multicultural or antiracist practice.[12] Some fields have created comprehensive rubrics of the knowledge, skills, and attitudes necessary for culturally competent practice, including awareness of the impact of one's background, knowledge of other cultures, and the capacity to broach topics related to race and culture.[13] Little of this work has systematically explored how broader societal discourses such as color blindness and color cognizance influence attitudes, beliefs, and outcomes.

Moreover, relatively little attends to the role of organizations and work groups. Some research has identified frameworks for organizational, rather than individual, cultural competence.[14] Very little though has explored the mediating role of work teams. It is more common for scholars from clinical fields to systematically think about the role of the family than about the workplace environment of agencies, clinics, or schools. Organizations and their subunits—departments, programs, teams—often create worlds of their own that are more or less permeable; while all breathe in the societal culture that surrounds them, some may build internal cultures with their own tenets and etiquette that are relatively impervious to outside influence. These customs then profoundly shape the group's collective product as well as its impact on individual practice. Therefore, an understanding of both organizational and group dynamics helps us discern how to provide culturally competent care.

Our work also contributes to research in clinical fields because it documents the actual racial-cultural practice of service providers (in our case, child welfare workers). Theory building about how to develop cultural competence has far exceeded research that actually assesses whether these practices are happening. Field research is necessary for building evidence-based practice. We also offer constructs from other disciplines, including psychological safety and learning behaviors, for enhancing cultural competence. These could be helpful for training new clinicians.

Finally, we offer a set of insights for researchers in management, organization studies, and organizational psychology. Research on diversity in teams and organizations is copious and insightful, but several paths remain largely unexplored. First, much of this work tends to downplay or ignore entirely the impact of the larger social and political context. True, authors often acknowledge that the attention to organizational diversity has been driven in large part by demographic changes in the United States, and some work acknowledges the racial power imbalances that help structure our society and thereby interfere with effectiveness.[15] In-depth attempts to comprehend team and interpersonal dynamics by connecting them with societal phenomena, such as the discourses of color blindness and color cognizance or widespread discrimination and injustice, are rare, however.

This is partly because the vast majority of this research is quantitative. Such work is critical when it comes to documenting disparate outcomes, such as pay discrimination or inequitable career opportunities, as well as testing causal models, such as what predicts more and less effective outcomes for diverse teams. It cannot, however, explore the micro-interactions that take place in work groups, how they may be influenced by the impact of difference on team relationships, and how those interactions may feed off societal dynamics. This literature therefore tells us less about how the inequitable outcomes it reveals have an impact on the day-to-day functioning of work teams.

Similarly, work on teams more generally, not just diverse teams, has skillfully documented the connections between safety, learning behaviors, and performance, but little of it is qualitative.[16] So we don't really know much about what safety or learning looks like in daily practice. Moreover, much of this literature distinguishes broadly between teams that learn and teams that don't, rather than looking more closely to see whether teams may be learning in some domains and not in others. Team South did bring something of a learning orientation to thinking generally about its work but was largely closed to any kind of learning about the role of race and culture.

Although the literature on teams, including diverse teams, does bring in the group task, it rarely explores the nature of the task in any depth. Most of this previous work explores how group dynamics affect task performance.[17] A subset investigates whether the nature of the task—usually dichotomized as complex and creative versus simple and routine—helps determine whether diversity is beneficial or harmful to team outcomes.[18] Very little work examines how the group frames its task and how it understands the connection between its own diversity, its diversity ideology, and the work it carries out. A deeper connection between a team's make-up, its interpersonal dynamics, and its task is also rare.

Finally, the large majority of work on race and culture in organizations—whether found in the management, organizational psychology, or sociology literatures—attends only to features that are obviously related to race and ethnicity, such as organizational demography, affirmative action programs, promotion opportunities for different racial groups, and the like. But how an organization or a work group manages its own diversity—whether it explicitly considers and draws on race and ethnicity when thinking about its task or its internal processes—is entirely bound up with how it does everything else.

In this study, we've linked racial-cultural practice to two broader aspects of the environment: its safety and its learning orientation.

Breaking the Color Bind at Work

For the last several decades, managing diversity has become an imperative—at least an espoused imperative—across the United States. More recently, the language is changing: the term *inclusion* is on its way in.[19] The fundamental premise is the same, however: organizations need to create a more diverse workforce at all levels and a more inclusive culture. In fact, it is hard to find established companies or government departments or NGOs that do not have some kind of program, however meager, meant to address this charge. In many cases, those programs are only window dressing. Some organizations, though, truly want to make change—and fail anyway. This is true for multiple reasons. One cause, often overlooked, is that the color bind may be so strong that it is impossible for people—both of color and white—to talk openly and candidly about their experience at work and the impact of various formal and informal practices. Instead, avoiding these conversations, workplaces simply implement policies they have heard about elsewhere or bring in consultants with a canned set of steps to follow. Many never do the internal talking and listening necessary to really understand what is afoot in their particular sphere of action and craft an approach that is right for them.

Any kind of organizational change is hard. It is impossible if people can't talk about the issues such change represents. Attending to the color bind—that is, enabling honest conversations—is necessary for work groups or organizations as they embark on an effort to make themselves more diverse and more inclusive. It is by no means sufficient, but it is essential. Work groups in social service agencies and classrooms, clinical care organizations, start-ups, and global corporations have to be able to talk about race. Our research suggests clues that should be relevant for all these contexts and others as well.

Presume Multilevel   When we would describe the findings of this research to various audiences, we were often challenged. If we began by describing the inclinations of individual team members, people would interject, "But it's really about what the team allows, isn't it?" If we began by illustrating team differences, we would hear, "But doesn't the organization really set the tone?" If we described the agency's approach, people would ask, "But doesn't it really depend on what the team members believed?" The answer is yes! Creating a color cognizant practice depends on all three, as expressed in our model that looks at how the intergroup incubator, encompassing both team and organization, influences individual preferences.

Individuals will bring their perspective, and their practice—with customers or clients as well as with their work colleagues—will bear this out. People who tend to color blindness will likely avoid the territory; those more color cognizant will broach the topic more often. Therefore, if an organization is truly committed to creating a color-cognizant way of working, it will help recruit and hire a workforce with the same motivation. Motivation is not always easy to identify. Moreover, requiring adherence to a simplistic standard is likely to backfire. However, hiring processes are increasingly creative and newer approaches find ways that require applicants to think aloud about complex issues, for example, by asking them to respond to a vignette. The goal is not to see whether applicants come up with the correct answer—indeed, the best vignettes have no correct answer—but rather to see how they approach thinking about the problem. This approach could be adapted to see how applicants think about difference more broadly as well as about racial and cultural differences in particular, including their own backgrounds.

Of course organizations have to go beyond their recruitment processes. They also have to think about how to encourage all employees to think more deeply about their racial-cultural practices. This often involves training, but training is perhaps the least effective method to change thinking and behavior.[20] That certainly depends on how the training is done, and we write more about this later. Nonetheless, organizations have to go beyond education to structural modifications. Research suggests that performance reviews are one of the best methods to encourage behavior change in general as well as change related to employee diversity. There is no stronger way to signal an organization's commitment than to regularly and systematically remind employees about what matters and then appraise them on that basis. Organizational leaders also have to model what they want their employees to do. No amount of exhortation will make up for what workers might perceive as hypocritical behavior. That means, for example, that organizations have to ensure that people of color hold high-level leadership positions and that organizational practices reflect a diversity of cultural approaches.

Group practices are also critical to shaping individual behavior. Most employees, whatever the setting, work in some kind of unit—if not a team, then a department or program or division. Recent work has shown that establishing a norm can be a powerful inducement for behavior change. People are more likely to engage in an activity if they believe most of their colleagues or neighbors or other community members are doing the same.[21] Therefore, group members are more likely to engage in color-cognizant practice if they see others doing so.

Our work also indicates that the overall learning orientation may be just as important as individual preferences. If the team, the office, and the organization combine to create a relatively safe environment as well as one that encourages self-reflection, experimentation, and integration of different perspectives, it may help embed a more color-conscious approach. For organizations to make that a reality, they need to think beyond their racial-cultural practice to the kind of overall climate they create. In this endeavor, leadership makes an enormous difference.

Leadership Creates the Thinkable Discussing difference—especially racial and ethnic differences—is often unthinkable. "Race is unspeakable," notes Bill Ayers, an education scholar.[22] Therefore, it has to be made speakable—and thinkable. The single best way that can happen is through modeling. People talking about race shows that people can talk about race. Cross-racial conversations—both rarer and scarier—show that people of different backgrounds can broach the topic and not just survive but learn. That modeling comes through leadership, not just by higher-ups, but from peers as well. "For multicultural groups to work productively . . . they need to have some members . . . who have a level of self-esteem and self-confidence, who are open to dealing with differences, and who have some awareness of how their behavior affects others."[23]

Positional leaders—that is, those who are seen as leaders because they are in positions of authority—play an essential role. Employees judge what is acceptable by what they see their leaders do. Leaders talking about race will sanction talking about race. These leaders need to go beyond well-worn phrases and predictable slogans, however. It is not enough to say that the organization welcomes racial and cultural diversity or even that it believes that such diversity leads to better outcomes. Leaders need to illustrate how race and ethnicity have an impact on the day-to-day work of the organization, even if—particularly if—such connections may be hard to see on first view. They need to visibly explore whether race or ethnicity might underlie some kind of conflict in the organization. They need to talk about their racial background and how it might influence the way they see the world or lead the organization.[24]

Workmates can be leaders here too. Watching a colleague wonder aloud about whether race or ethnicity might be related to a task she has to carry out or to a debate she is having with a coworker shows that such considerations are possible. Seeing teammates regularly make the connections demonstrates a racial-cultural lens can be one of a number of different lenses used to further understanding. For the greatest impact, however, both whites and people of color need to raise these issues. When white members, as part of the dominant racial group, speak up, it shows they are not remaining silent out of fear or ignorance or resistance. When people of color raise these issues, they demonstrate that they are willing to speak up despite the possibility of risk—or at least believe the benefits outweigh the costs.

Therefore, when both whites and people of color model that these issues matter and are discussable, it sends potent signals to other members of both groups, who may have an incipient desire to be involved but are anxious—perhaps for different reasons—about doing so. For whites, seeing other whites participate signals that they can and should contribute. It's not uncommon for white people to feel not only that they lack the standing to take part in such a discussion but also the expertise to enrich it. Although this is understandable, ultimately it abdicates their responsibility to engage. However, if whites only see other whites taking up these issues, they are likely to wonder why people of color are not participating. It might suggest a racist or discriminatory flavor to the discussion. Or they could worry that perhaps white people should not mention race. A 2008 lab study showed that whites were much more likely to mention race when discussing a race-related issue when a black confederate did so. If the black confederate did not mention race, the white subject generally did not either.[25] Therefore, it could signal greater safety to white people to see people of both backgrounds contributing.

At the same time, people of color who are interested but concerned about participating need to see people from their own group taking part because it signals that the environment is at least relatively safe. They may also need to see whites participating. If only people of color are engaged, it could be a cue that whites are not interested or are even threatened by the conversation. White participation also gives the imprimatur of the dominant group. When people of color bring up issues related to race, it can be seen as self-interested or as "playing the race card."[26] When whites do so, however unfairly, that concern diminishes. This could make it easier for people of color, understandably wary, to participate. Finally, both white members and members of color need to see that mixed-race conversations can be fruitful and constructive rather than angry or bitter. They also need to see that learning about race can go both ways: that whites can learn from people of color and that people of color can learn from whites. Therefore, seeing a cross-race team of colleagues having productive conversations about race and culture is a compelling sign for all employees that such discussions are, in fact, thinkable.

Exploring, Not Training   Diversity training is common in for-profit, nonprofit, and public organizations alike,[27] despite the fact that it is widely criticized and relatively ineffective.[28] Formal, organizationally sponsored conversations—whether in the form of training, small group conversations, departmental workshops, or the like—related to race and ethnicity are essential, both as a strong cue that leaders care about these issues and to send more specific messages about how such concerns are relevant to the organization's work. Although structural changes may be far more effective, organizations need to explain to their employees why they are making these changes. Therefore, such sessions are not going away soon, nor should they. Our study suggests ways to make such sessions more useful and more engaging.

Most important, we suggest these workshops focus on exploration rather than training. Some didactic portion may be necessary to frame the event, but a session that is focused on exhorting employees to think and act differently will likely fail. Many people already espouse a belief in the value of difference and additional admonitions will probably not make a difference. Instead, they likely believe something quite complex and contradictory. We would suggest finding ways to surface contradictory beliefs by reflecting on their own practice or on a vignette, to normalize the contradictions by making it clear that such ambivalence is quite common, and to invite participants to think through both the consequences of such inconsistency as well as ways to learn from the tensions they hold. The more that people actually express the tensions, rather than feel inhibited by them, the likelier they are to work with them and see their potential.

Areas for Future Learning

There is much more to know about how work groups can break the color bind. Based on what we've learned from this endeavor, new avenues of research emerge.

First, we need to understand more about how the professional or occupational context influences the ability of work teams to develop a colorcognizant practice. Our research took place in a child welfare agency. This is a very particular context with its own ramifications, but we believe it holds broader lessons.

A common assumption is that race and ethnicity are more relevant in child protection work than in many other contexts. The field focuses on dynamics in the home, on intimate details of family life and child rearing that are broadly understood to be culturally informed. Moreover, the profession of social work and the subfield of child welfare explicitly acknowledge the importance of race and culture in understanding individuals, families, and communities. The National Association of Social Workers charges social workers to pursue cultural competence and has developed detailed guidelines for practice.[29] Given this emphasis, it may seem that race and culture are more often topics of conversation in a child welfare context than in many other workplaces. However, as this book relates, that doesn't mean they are commonly discussed. In fact, most of the teams we studied—even in this context—talked about race and ethnicity both rarely and superficially.

In any case, just because race may be more salient in child protection work doesn't mean it is more relevant than in other contexts. Employees in many organizations engage with diverse clients or customers and participate in heterogeneous work groups. Even organizations operating in relatively homogeneous environments could still have good reason to explore. In fact, race and culture often have a profound impact on an organization's work but because of the color bind employees never engage in the work of finding out. Further, as we note in chapter 4, whether race and ethnicity are seen as relevant is determined much more by the beholder than by inherent qualities of the work. Those with color-blind perspectives are much more likely to downplay their weight; color-cognizant individuals more likely to investigate. For all these reasons, we believe the child welfare context may not be as different from other professional or industry contexts as many assume. However, research in other work arenas is essential to testing that belief as well as to understand how the color bind may work differently in different fields.

Second, in addition to the professional or occupational context, the organizational environment will also have influence. Because all our teams were in one agency, we can shed little light here. The new commissioner, in addition to launching the teaming pilot, also brought renewed emphasis on racial and ethnic diversity and cultural competence, as described more fully in chapter 2. At the same time, in two of the offices we studied there were serious intergroup tensions. According to the president of Aware, many workers of color felt that their chances for promotion were fewer and the likelihood they would be cited for an infraction much greater than for white employees. The particulars in these areas will depend heavily on organizational context and, therefore, research in other workplaces is essential.

Third, as with all research, our dataset had its limitations. Ours was an intensive, exploratory study of a small sample. A strength of this kind of comparative case design is that it can explore multiple levels. We can trace the impact of specific group members as well as dyadic interactions, full team dynamics, and the office environment. These fine-grained analyses bring to life aspects of our work that may seem petty and mundane. It is, though, these very workaday details that, building on each other or acting at cross purposes, construct our experiences on the job. Ultimately, whether we feel welcome and valued, whether we build close connections with colleagues, whether we do our best work, whether we feel enlivened or deadened all come down to the humdrum course of our days as much as from broad organizational policies and practices. The portraits we can draw from our qualitative, ethnographic data can be more telling, in many ways, than large quantitative analyses. We are also sensitive to what is beyond our scope, however. Our approach enabled us to build a theoretical model but not to test it. Nor can we assess how broadly the model might apply.

Moreover, our data collection did not extend to the families these team members worked with. A fuller understanding of the team's racial-cultural practice would include not only their conversations about their families but also how they interacted with them. It would also include the insights of the clients about their experiences with the agency.

Fourth, we do not link color cognizance to effectiveness or other outcomes. Given the quantity of previous research, reviewed in chapter 2, which testifies to the positive consequences of an approach that recognizes rather than suppresses race and ethnicity, we think it is plausible that that would be the case in the context of this agency, but we cannot make that claim. However, future work could investigate the relationship between racial-cultural practice and different kinds of outcomes.

Finally, we have to acknowledge the limitations of our own backgrounds and racial-cultural practices. Our grounding, socialization, and education have trained us to notice some things and blinded us to others. Although we are an interracial research team, we do not claim a purely objective or omniscient standpoint.[30] Further work done by larger and more diverse groups of researchers could add new insights into what enables color-cognizant practice. It could also suggest different questions altogether. We believe, just as a color-cognizant lens would suggest, that the wisdom and expertise of people from a wide variety of racial-cultural backgrounds are necessary to fully understand the complex dynamics of race and ethnicity in organizations.

A Final Note

In her book about community racial dialogues, Katherine Walsh ultimately argues that, though both unity and diversity are critical, it is only through attention to difference that a unity of wholeness as opposed to a unity of sameness or oneness can be forged.[31] Team North was striving for a unity of wholeness though it fell short of the ideal. It was headed in the right direction. In contrast, Team South embraced a unity of sameness, without considering the ramifications for those who brought difference into the group, or, indeed, the implications for the team as a whole.

A unity of wholeness is very difficult to achieve. One thing is certain: it cannot be realized without breaking the color bind. This may feel daunting. There is good news, however. Any time anyone raises race as a topic to be explored, the bind loosens up just a bit and the path toward color cognizance is etched a little deeper.

~ Appendix A ~

Further Detail Regarding Methods

In chapter 2, we describe the research site and our data collection and analysis. In this appendix, we amplify by providing more detail in a number of areas. The material here is related to the material on pages 28 to 36 of the narrative.

Taping, transcribing and field notes: All the team and individual interviews (except for two individuals who did not wish to be taped) and all of the team meetings were taped and transcribed. Erica also wrote field notes about details and dynamics in the interviews and meetings that would not be caught on tape, such as descriptions of the space, nonverbal communication, side conversations, and the like.

Team stakeholders: Erica interviewed four stakeholders for each of the teams. These included the team's manager (the immediate superior of the team leader), the director of the office in which the team was located, a teaming consultant working directly with the teams, and the coordinator of the teaming pilot. These two latter stakeholders were familiar with all the teams.

Organizational meetings observed: These included meetings of the executive staff of the organization as they planned several organizational changes, including the teaming pilot; meetings of the teaming pilot coordinator and the teaming consultants hired by the agency to work with the teams; and several all-day meetings and trainings for all of the members of all of the teams. These meetings were not taped but were documented in extensive field notes.

Archival material: This included materials handed out in team meetings; reports by a consultant hired by the foundation funding the teaming pilot; internal organizational documents on the pilot as well as other change processes underway including memos to staff, letters to funders, reports to state legislators, and emails; and materials developed by the teaming consultants and teaming coordinator.

Data on team members' color cognizance and color blindness: We were interested in both espoused and enacted approaches to the role of race and ethnicity in the work. Therefore, we asked questions, in both individual and team interviews, about team members' beliefs and the specific cases they were working on, and observed team meetings. The interview included the following questions: asking team members to name the dimensions of diversity on their team that seemed particularly salient to them and asking them whether these differences helped or hindered (or neither) their team's work; asking more broadly about intergroup relations on the team; asking members about their racial, ethnic, and cultural backgrounds and about whether and how they drew on their backgrounds in thinking about their work; asking whether (and, if relevant, why) it was important for the agency to be racially diverse; providing a brief case scenario related to race and asking for their reactions; and asking members to discuss a recent case in which race or ethnicity was an issue. We also observed team meetings for the four in-depth teams. Because these meetings were where workers thought together about how to approach their cases, as well as their team dynamics, they would be the venue for an exploration of how race or ethnicity might be relevant.

Data on the context of the team's work: To understand better why teams took different approaches, we gathered data on their organizational, office, and team contexts to situate them within their environment.

For organizational context, we drew on our observation of organizational meetings; archival documents related to the organization as a whole; and interviews with the commissioner, the president of Aware, the agency's internal caucus for members of color and bilingual members, the coordinator of the teaming pilot (who had worked at high-level positions in the agency for thirty years), the office directors, and the teams' managers, all of whom had been with the agency many years and had substantive knowledge about the organization as a whole.

For office context, we relied on interviews with the office directors, the teams' managers, and the team members, including questions about office morale, issues that caused office conflict, how mistakes or errors were handled, the director's management style, and intergroup relations.

For team context, we used extensive data from the team members and the team stakeholders about team structure and processes. In interviews, we asked about clarity of direction and composition, conflict, learning behaviors, psychological safety, whether members felt they had input into how the team worked together, the degree of support from their office and organizational context, and the team leader's management style. Through observation of team meetings, we were also able to collect data regarding these characteristics.

~ Appendix B ~

Team Descriptions

The background description for Team North is in chapter 4, for Team East in chapter 5, and for Team South in chapter 6. Here we provide thumbnail sketches of the other four teams in the teaming pilot. The team names were chosen as simple monikers and have only rough correspondence with their geographic location in the state.

Team Southwest

The catchment area of Team Southwest included a number of small towns in a largely rural area. The office's clients were about 80 percent white, about 15 percent Latino, and the remainder black. An intact unit, the team decided to join the teaming pilot after the team leader brought it to them to discuss. The team had been an ongoing unit and the team proposed to continue with that work but to do it with formal and informal partnerships on cases. The unit had two Spanish-speaking workers, one a white woman who had lived in Latin America for many years, and the other a Latina. The others were white and included two men, the team leader and a team member. The team's manager was an African American woman and the office director was a white woman. Like Teams North, East, and South, Team Southwest was an in-depth team, for which we have more extensive data. For clarity and parsimony, we did not include them in the narrative. However, a full analysis of Team Southwest, which we categorized as having a color-evasive practice like Team East, can be found on the Russell Sage Foundation website (https://www.russellsage.org/publications/color-bind).

Team Southeast

Team Southeast was located in the same office as Team Southwest but was formed from an assessment unit rather than an ongoing unit. Assessment workers got a case once it had gone through investigation and been formally taken on by the agency. Workers had forty-five days to meet with the family, other relatives, and various collaterals and then create a service plan for the family. Team Southeast was formed from an existing unit interested in the teaming concept. It did not suggest any change or particular goal for their work; members simply wanted to work more collaboratively on their cases. The team members were all women and all white, except for one Latina; membership remained largely stable over the data collection period. Their manager and the office director were also white women.

Team West

Office West was situated in a largely working-class suburb located about thirty minutes west of a large metropolitan area. Its caseload was about 70 percent white, the rest split between Latino and black families. Team West was created for the teaming pilot; it was not an intact unit, though some members had some familiarity with each other. The office director had created the proposal and then worked with several higher-level employees to create a designated teaming unit. The team experimented with combining assessment and ongoing work; by the end of data collection, it was beginning to include investigations as well. The team's membership was largely white women, though two Latino members participated during data collection, one man (the only man on the team), and one woman. Its leader, manager, and office director were all white women.

Team Northwest

Office Northwest served a community, largely of color, in a large city. The community population was about two-thirds black, the remainder roughly split between whites and Latinos. The leaders of Team Northwest had decided to use the teaming pilot as a way to focus on working with families with mentally ill parents. They approached the unit that would become Team Northwest to assess interest in participating. The members were game. Its make-up was the most stable over the three years of data collection and was quite diverse: the team was about one-third white, one-third African American, and one-third Latino. The team leader was white, as was the team's manager and the office director. All were women except for one white team member and the team's manager.

~ Notes ~

Chapter 1

1. When necessary, we remain deliberately vague about a family's country of origin to better preserve its confidentiality.
2. Tatum 2007; Zane 1997; Shelton, West, and Trail 2010; Richeson and Shelton 2007.
3. Yanow 1996; Ladd 1997; Apfelbaum, Sommers, and Norton 2008.
4. Frankenberg 1993; Yoshino 2007; Schofield 1986; Winant 1997.
5. Omi and Winant 1994; Alexander 2012; Knowles et al. 2009; Fine et al. 1997.
6. Crenshaw 1989; Markus, Steele, and Steele 2004; Ely, Padavic, and Thomas 2012.
7. Richeson and Shelton 2007; Shelton 2003; Apfelbaum, Sommers, and Norton 2008.
8. Edmondson 1999.
9. Steele, Spencer, and Aronson 2002; Davies, Spencer, and Steele 2005.
10. Edmondson 1999; Homan et al. 2011; Argote, Gruenfeld, and Naquin 2001.
11. Weber and Khademian 2008; Poppelaars and Scholten 2008; Van Bueren, Klijn, and Koppenjan 2003.
12. Blackman et al. 2006.
13. Stone, Patton, and Heen 2010.
14. This term is adapted from Frankenberg 1993.
15. This term is also adapted from Frankenberg 1993.
16. Many thanks to our colleague Sonia Ospina for this term.

Chapter 2

1. CNN, "Kids' Test Answers on Race Bring Mother to Tears," May 18, 2010, http://www.cnn.com/2010/US/05/18/doll.study.parents/index.html.
2. Derman-Sparks, Ramsey, and Edwards 2011; Aboud and Doyle 1996.

3. Brown et al. 2007.
4. Vittrup and Holden 2010.
5. Day-Vines et al. 2007; Juby and Concepcion 2005.
6. Trawalter and Richeson 2008.
7. Singleton and Linton 2005; Tatum 2007.
8. Holder 2009.
9. Nagda and Zuniga 2003; Nagda, Tropp, and Paluck 2006.
10. Alexander 2012; Day-Vines et al. 2007; Saguy, Dovidio, and Pratto 2008; Knowles et al. 2009.
11. Frankenberg 1993; Bell and Hartmann 2007; O'Brien 2000.
12. Strictly speaking, color cognizance could be seen as any recognition of racial differences, including explicit justifications of a racial hierarchy, like white supremacy. For that reason, we very deliberately include in our definition that color cognizance condemns racism and discrimination. Other authors use similar terms to convey the same idea, such as color consciousness (Omi and Winant 1994).
13. Alexander 2012; Tatum 2007; Nagda 2006; Richeson and Shelton 2007; Markus, Steele, and Steele 2000.
14. Marx 2006; Chubbuck 2004.
15. Cornell and Hartmann 2007, 25.
16. Jones 1999, 467; Hannaford 1996; Painter 2010.
17. Bonham, Warshauer-Baker, and Collins 2005.
18. Fine et al.1997; Omi 2010.
19. Cornell and Hartmann 2007, 24.
20. Cornell and Hartmann 2007, 24; Fredrickson 1999, 23; Hannah 2011, 47.
21. Carter 1995.
22. Hannah 2011, 47.
23. Helms and Cook 1999, 19.
24. Guarnaccia and Rodriguez 1996; Miranda, Nakamura, and Bernal 2003.
25. Helms and Cook 1999.
26. Maddox 2004; Maddox and Gray 2002.
27. Ely, Padavic, and Thomas 2012; Crosby 1997, 188.
28. Crenshaw 1989; Holvino 2001; Strolovitch 2007; Hancock 2007.
29. Thomas 1989; Tatum 2007.
30. Berrey 2005; Plaut 2002; Spencer 1994.
31. Correll, Park, and Smith 2008; Richeson and Nussbaum 2004; Wolsko, Park, and Judd 2006; Crenshaw 1989. Frankenberg's influential work on the territory of whiteness traces the history of discourses on race, comparing color-blindness with what she calls race-cognizance (Frankenberg 1993, 14–15). We have adapted her term to create our own, *color cognizance.*
32. Crenshaw 1989; Alexander 2012; Loury 2002; Chubbuck 2004; Marx 2006.
33. Tatum 1997; Norton et al. 2006; Apfelbaum et al. 2010.

34. Ryan et al. 2007; Apfelbaum, Sommers, and Norton 2008.
35. Ito and Urland 2003.
36. Alexander 2012, 240.
37. Guinier and Torres 2003; Pittinsky and Simon 2007.
38. Apfelbaum, Sommers, and Norton 2008.
39. Norton et al. 2006.
40. Frankenberg 1993, 145.
41. Doane 1997, 377.
42. Chubbuck 2004, 304.
43. Giroux 1997, 286, as quoted in Chubbuck 2004, 304.
44. Fredrickson 1999, 26.
45. Doane 1997, 385; Omi and Winant 1994.
46. Saguy, Dovidio, and Pratto 2008.
47. Knowles et al. 2009, 857.
48. Hurtado and Stewart 1997, 300.
49. Alexander 2012, 204–05.
50. Pollock 2004.
51. Apfelbaum, Sommers, and Norton 2008, 930.
52. Tatum 2007, 102.
53. Omi and Winant 1994, 158–59.
54. Winant 1997; Ayers 1997; Alexander 2012; Saguy, Dovidio, and Pratto 2008.
55. Smith and Silva 2011.
56. Gushue and Carter 2000.
57. Smith et al. 1999.
58. Richeson and Nussbaum 2004; Wolsko, Park, and Judd 2006.
59. Wolsko et al. 2000; Ryan et al. 2007.
60. Hobman, Bordia, and Gallois 2004.
61. Homan et al. 2007; Ely and Thomas 2001.
62. Van Dick et al. 2008; van Knippenberg, Haslam, and Platow 2007.
63. Purdie-Vaughns et al. 2008; Plaut, Thomas, and Goren 2009.
64. Konrad and Linnehan 1995.
65. Haider et al. 2011; Sabin, Rivera, and Greenwald 2008.
66. Green et al. 2007.
67. Hannah 2011, 41.
68. Neighbors et al. 2003.
69. Wells, Merritt, and Briggs 2009; Harris and Hackett 2008; Hines et al. 2004; Roberts 2002.
70. Pedersen 1988, 1989.
71. NASW 2001.
72. Good et al. 2011; U.S. Surgeon General 1999; Carpenter-Song 2011.
73. Arredondo et al. 1996; NASW 2001.
74. Tervalon and Murray-Garcia 1998; Chang and Berk 2009; Hansen, Pepitone-Arreola-Rockwell, and Greene 2000.

75. Fuertes et al. 2002; Zhang and Burkard 2008; Jackson 2009; Atkinson, Casas, and Abreu 1992; Ponteroto, Fuertes, and Chen 2000.
76. Guerrero and Andrews 2011.
77. Hannah 2011, 40.
78. Pollock et al. 2010; Ayers 1997.
79. Winant 1997, 45; see also Knowles et al. 2009, 867; Omi and Winant 1994, 148.
80. Charles 2009; Ellen and O'Flaherty 2010.
81. Moss and Tilly 2003; Castilla 2008; Stainback and Tomaskovic-Devey 2012; Roberson, Galvin, and Charles 2007.
82. Ely, Padavic, and Thomas 2012; Van Dick et al. 2008; Hobman, Bordia, and Gallois 2004; van Knippenberg, Haslam, and Platow 2007.
83. Gibson and Vermeulen 2003; Homan et al. 2007; Ely and Thomas 2001; Mannix and Neale 2005.
84. Ely, Padavic, and Thomas 2012.
85. Page 2007, 299; Chatman 2010; King, Hebl, and Beal 2009.
86. Stewart and Garcia-Prieto 2008; Stahl et al. 2010; Joshi, Laio, and Jackson 2006; Mannix and Neale 2005.
87. Bunderson and Reagans 2011; Argote, Gruenfeld, and Naquin 2001; Edmondson, Dillon, and Roloff 2007.
88. Cook and Seely Brown 1999; Gherardi 2000; Lave and Wenger 1991.
89. Foldy, Rivard, and Buckley 2009; van Knippenberg and Schippers 2007, 26.
90. Nembhard and Edmondson 2006; Gibson and Vermeulen 2003; Pittinsky and Simon 2007.
91. van Knippenberg, De Dreu, and Homan 2004, 1011; Homan et al. 2007; Kooij-de Bode, van Knippenberg, and van Ginkel 2008.
92. Gersick and Hackman 1990; Foldy and Buckley 2009.
93. Edmondson 2002.
94. van Knippenberg and Schippers 2007, 25; Schippers, Hartog, and Koopman 2007.
95. Edmondson 1999, 354.
96. van Knippenberg, De Dreu, and Homan 2004, 1015; Mannix and Neale 2005; Gibson and Gibbs 2006; Buckley and Foldy 2010.
97. Hackman 1987; Edmondson, Dillon, and Roloff 2007.
98. Hicks-Clarke and Iles 2000; Kossek and Zonia 1993.
99. Ely and Thomas 2001.
100. van Knippenberg and Schippers 2007.
101. Homan et al. 2007; van Dick et al. 2008.
102. Bell and Hartmann 2007; Bonilla-Silva 2002; Foldy, Rivard, and Buckley 2009.
103. Walsh 2007; Todd and Abrams 2011.
104. McRae and Short 2010.
105. Alderfer and Smith 1982, 38.

106. Thomas 1989; Bunderson and Reagans 2011; Ely, Padavic, and Thomas 2012.
107. Exceptions include Ely and Thomas 2001; Ely, Padavic, and Thomas 2012; Foldy, Rivard, and Buckley 2009.
108. One exception is Earley and Mosakowski 2000.
109. Ryan et al. 2007; Verkuyten 2005; Berrey 2005.
110. Bell and Nkomo 2001; Watkins-Hayes 2009.
111. Bunderson and Reagans 2011.
112. Ely, Padavic, and Thomas 2012.
113. Markus, Steele, and Steele 2000; Plaut 2002; Steele, Spencer, and Aronson 2002.
114. Steele, Spencer, and Aronson 2002, 417.
115. Davies, Spencer, and Steele 2005; Steele, Spencer, and Aronson 2002; Foldy, Rivard, and Buckley 2009.
116. Steele 2010.
117. Shelton, West, and Trail 2010; Chatman 2010; Norton et al. 2006.
118. Steele 2010, 207.
119. Bride, Jones, and MacMaster 2007; Conrad and Kellar-Guenther 2006; Nissly, Mor Barak, and Levin 2005.
120. Wells, Merritt, and Briggs 2009.
121. NASW 2001.
122. Teasley 2005; Guy-Walls 2007.
123. Roberts 2002, 246–47.
124. Roberts 2002, 246–47; Bartholet 1999.
125. Cohen 2003; Courtney et al. 1996; Yan 2005.
126. Bartholet 1999; Bartholet 2006.
127. Rodenborg 2004; Yan 2005.
128. Maiter 2004; Pyles and Kim 2006; Uttal 2006.
129. Becker, Jordan, and Larsen 2007; Roberts 2002; Rodenborg 2004; Wells, Merritt, and Briggs 2009; Harris and Hackett 2008.
130. Foldy, Rivard, and Buckley 2009.
131. For example, Bell and Nkomo 2001.
132. For example, Weis and Fine 2000; Krauss et al. 1997.
133. Foldy 2005.

Chapter 3

1. Carpenter-Song et al. 2007; Hansen, Pepitone-Arreola-Rockwell, and Greene 2000; Pyles and Kim 2006; McPhatter 1997.
2. Wolsko, Park, and Judd 2006.
3. Apfelbaum, Sommers, and Norton 2008.
4. Plaut, Thomas, and Goren 2009; Spencer 1994.
5. Homan et al. 2007; Van Dick et al. 2008.

6. Pollock 2004; Bonilla-Silva 2002; Merelman, Streich, and Martin 1998; Has et al. 1992.
7. Foldy and Buckley 2014.

Chapter 4

1. Hannah 2011, 39.
2. Guralnik 1974, 713.
3. Edmondson, Dillon, and Roloff 2007; Gibson and Vermeulen 2003.
4. Edmondson 1999.
5. Nembhard and Edmondson 2006; Bamberger, Bacharach, and Vashdi 2005.
6. Davies, Spencer, and Steele 2005; Purdie-Vaughns et al. 2008.
7. It's possible, of course, that these differences in approach were gendered, in that women team members felt more comfortable with cleaning while the men resisted that but felt help with budgeting was appropriate. None of the team members mentioned gender so we do not investigate that here. We do investigate gender dynamics at some length later on in this section.

Chapter 5

1. Boden 1994, 53.
2. Kanter 1993.
3. Phillips, Rothbard, and Dumas 2009.
4. Bell and Nkomo 2001.

Chapter 6

1. Clark 2002, 2.
2. Sharf 2000.
3. Tokar 1972.

Chapter 7

1. Winnicott 1986.

Chapter 8

1. NASW 2001; Hansen, Pepitone-Arreola-Rockwell, and Greene 2000.
2. Author and title of report withheld for privacy.
3. Kate McGovern, "Navigating New Trenches After a Breakup," *New York Times,* May 1, 2012, http://www.nytimes.com/2012/05/20/fashion/ reorienting-after-a-relationships-end-modern-love.html?pagewanted=all (accessed September 22, 2013).

4. Girard 1997, 286, quoted in Chubbuck 2004, 304.
5. Leonard Cohen, "Anthem," *The Future,* recorded November 24, 1992, Sony Music Entertainment, compact disc.
6. Chang and Berk 2009; Has et al. 1992; Katz and Wackenhut 1986; Winant 1997.
7. Merelman, Streich, and Martin 1998, 781, 800, 801.
8. Walsh 2007, 237, 139.
9. Pollock 2004.
10. Todd and Abrams 2011, 379, 370.
11. Bonilla-Silva 2002, 58, 62.
12. Bonilla-Silva 2002, 50.
13. Bonilla-Silva and Forman 2000, 78.
14. Winant 1997.
15. Bonilla-Silva 2002, 62.
16. Nemetz and Christensen 1996, 453. Italics in the original.
17. Walsh 2007, 139.
18. Todd and Abrams 2011, 385.
19. Pollock 218.
20. Todd and Abrams 2011, 385–86.
21. Walsh 2007, 165.
22. Pollock 2004, 218.
23. Walsh 2007, 165.
24. Walsh 2007, 153, 42–43, 156–57, 236.
25. Pollock 2004, 218, 219.

Chapter 9

1. Russell Sage Foundation, "Chartbook of Social Inequality: Income and Earnings," 2012, http://www.russellsage.org/node/3432 (accessed September 22, 2013); Loury 2002; Massey and Denton 1993; McCall 2001; Oliver and Shapiro 1997.
2. Alexander 2012, 238.
3. Pollock 2004.
4. Walsh 2007.
5. Berrey 2005.
6. Nagda and Zuniga 2003; Nagda, Tropp, and Paluck 2006.
7. Omi and Winant 1994.
8. Ely and Thomas 2001; Konrad and Linnehan 1995.
9. Litvin 1997; Tomlinson and Schwabenland 2010; Ozbilgin and Tatli 2011.
10. Stainback and Tomaskovic-Devey 2012.
11. Hansen, Pepitone-Arreola-Rockwell, and Greene 2000; Yan 2005; Carpenter-Song 2011; Mederos and Woldeguiorguis 2003.
12. Martin 2001; Chubbuck 2004; Marx 2006; Wamsted 2011.

13. NASW 2001; Sue, Arredondo, and McDavis 1992; American Psychological Association 2003.
14. Hyde 2004; Guerrero and Andrews 2011; Chrobot-Mason and Thomas 2002.
15. Ely, Padavic, and Thomas 2012; Konrad and Linnehan 1995; Alderfer et al. 1980; Alderfer and Smith 1982; Foldy, Rivard, and Buckley 2009.
16. Exceptions include Sole and Edmondson 2002; Edmondson, Bohmer, and Pisano 2001; Edmondson 2002.
17. Jackson, Joshi, and Erhardt 2003; Homan et al. 2007; Webber and Donahue 2001.
18. Mannix and Neale 2005.
19. Pearce and Randel 2004; Ellemers et al. 2011; Pless and Maak 2004; Davidson 2011.
20. Kalev, Dobbin, and Kelly 2006; Paluck 2006; Bezrukova, Jehn, and Spell 2012.
21. Paluck 2009; de Rooji, Green, and Gerber 2009.
22. Ayers 1997, 131.
23. McRae and Short 2010, 51.
24. For an example, see LaMarche 2009.
25. Apfelbaum, Sommers, and Norton 2008.
26. Connolly and Noumair 1997, 328.
27. Kalinoski et al. 2012; Bezrukova, Jehn, and Spell 2012.
28. Kalev, Dobbin, and Kelly 2006; Paluck 2006.
29. NASW 2001.
30. DeVault 1990; Harding 1993.
31. Walsh 2007, 251.

~ References ~

Aboud, E. Frances, and Anna Beth Doyle. 1996. "Does Talk of Race Foster Prejudice or Tolerance in Children?" *Canadian Journal of Behavioural Science* 28(3): 161–70.

Alderfer, Clayton P., and Ken K. Smith. 1982. "Studying Intergroup Relations Embedded in Organizations." *Administrative Science Quarterly* 27(1): 35–65.

Alderfer, Clayton P., Charleen J. Alderfer, Leota Tucker, and Robert Tucker. 1980. "Diagnosing Race Relations in Management." *Journal of Applied Behavioral Science* 16(2): 135–66.

Alexander, Michelle. 2012. *The New Jim Crow: Mass Incarceration in the Age of Colorblindness.* New York: The New Press.

American Psychological Association. 2003. "Guidelines on Multicultural Education, Training, Research, Practice and Organizational Change for Psychologists." *American Psychologist* 58(5): 377–402.

Apfelbaum, Evan P., Kristin Pauker, Samuel R. Sommers, and Nalini A. Ambady. 2010. "In Blind Pursuit of Racial Equality?" *Psychological Science* 21(11): 1–6.

Apfelbaum, Evan P., Samuel R. Sommers, and Michael I. Norton. 2008. "Seeing Race and Seeming Racist? Evaluating Strategic Colorblindness in Social Interaction." *Journal of Personality and Social Psychology* 95(4): 918–32.

Argote, Linda, Debroah Gruenfeld, and Charles Naquin. 2001. "Group Learning in Organizations." In *Groups at Work: Theory and Research,* edited by Marlene E. Turner. Mahwah, N.J.: Lawrence Erlbaum Associates.

Arredondo, Patricia, Rebecca Toporek, Pack Brown Sherlon, Janet Sanchez, Don C. Locke, Joe Sanchez, and Holly Stadler. 1996. "Operationalization of the Multicultural Counseling Competencies." *Journal of Counseling and Development* 24(1): 42–78.

Atkinson, R. Donald, Antonio Casas, and Jose Abreu. 1992. "Mexican-American Acculturation, Counselor Ethnicity and Cultural Sensitivity, and Perceived Counselor Competence." *Journal of Counseling Psychology* 39(4): 515–20.

Ayers, William C. 1997. "Racing in America." In *Off White: Readings on Race, Power and Society,* edited by Michelle Fine, Lois Weis, Linda C. Powell, L. Mun Wong. New York: Routledge.

Bamberger, Peter A., Samuel B. Bacharach, and Dana Vashdi. 2005. "Diversity and Homophily at Work: Supportive Relations Among White and African American Peers." *Academy of Management Journal* 48(4): 619–44.

Bartholet, Elizabeth. 1999. *Nobody's Children: Abuse and Neglect, Foster Drift, and the Adoption Alternative.* Boston, Mass.: Beacon Press.

———. 2006. "Cultural Stereotypes Can and Do Die: It's Time to Move on with Transracial Adoption." *Journal of the American Academy of Psychiatry and the Law* 34(3): 315–20.

Becker, Marion A., Neil Jordan, and Rebecca Larsen. 2007. "Predictors of Successful Permanency Planning and Length of Stay in Foster Care: The Role of Race, Diagnosis and Place of Residence." *Children and Youth Services Review* 29(8): 1102–13.

Bell, Ella L. J. Edmondson, and Stella M. Nkomo. 2001. *Our Separate Ways: Black and White Women and the Struggle for Professional Identity.* Boston, Mass.: Harvard Business School Press.

Bell, Joyce M., and Douglas Hartmann. 2007. "Diversity in Everyday Discourse: The Cultural Ambiguities and Consequences of 'Happy Talk'." *American Sociological Review* 72(6): 895–914.

Berrey, Ellen C. 2005. "Divided over Diversity: Political Discourse in a Chicago Neighborhood." *City and Community* 4(2): 143–70.

Bezrukova, Katerina, Karen A. Jehn, and Chester S. Spell. 2012. "Reviewing Diversity Training: Where We Have Been and Where We Should Go." *Academy Management Learning and Education* 11(2): 207–27.

Blackman, Tim, Alexandra Greene, David J. Hunter, Lorna McKee, Eva Elliott, Barbara Harrington, Linda Marks, and Gareth Williams. 2006. "Performance Assessment and Wicked Problems: The Case of Health Inequalities." *Public Policy and Administration* 21(2): 66–80.

Boden, Dierdre. 1994. *The Business of Talk: Organizations in Action.* Cambridge: Polity Press.

Bonham, L. Vence, Esther Warshauer-Baker, and Francis Collins. 2005. "Race and Ethnicity in the Genome Era: The Complexity of the Constructs." *American Psychologist* 60(1): 9–15.

Bonilla-Silva, Eduardo. 2002. "The Linguistics of Color Blind Racism: How to Talk Nasty About Blacks without Sounding 'Racist'." *Critical Sociology* 28(1–2): 41–64.

Bonilla-Silva, Eduardo, and Tyrone A. Forman. 2000. "'I Am Not a Racist But . . .' Mapping White College Students' Racial Ideology in the USA." *Discourse Society* 11(1): 50–85.

Bride, Brian E., Jenny L. Jones, and Samuel A. MacMaster. 2007. "Correlates of Secondary Traumatic Stress in Child Protective Services Workers." *Journal of Evidence-Based Social Work* 4(3–4): 69–80.

Brown, Tony N., Koji Ueno, Carrie L. Smith, Noel S. Austin, and Leonard Bickman. 2007. "Communication Patterns in Medical Encounters for the Treatment of Child Psychosocial Problems: Does Pediatrician-Parent Concordance Matter?" *Health Communication* 21(3): 247–56.

Buckley, Tamara R., and Erica Gabrielle Foldy. 2010. "A Pedagogical Model for Increasing Race-Related Multicultural Counseling Competency." *The Counseling Psychologist* 38(5): 691–713.

Bunderson, J. Stuart, and Ray E. Reagans. 2011. "Power, Status and Learning in Organizations." *Organization Science* 22(5): 1182–94.

Carpenter-Song, Elizabeth. 2011. "Recognition in Clinical Relationships." In *Shattering Culture: American Medicine Responds to Cultural Diversity*, edited by Mary-Jo DelVecchio Good, Sarah S. Willen, Seth D. Hannah, Ken Vickery, and Lawrence T. Park. New York: Russell Sage Foundation.

Carpenter-Song, Elizabeth A., Megan N. Schwallie, and Jeffrey Longhofer. 2007. "Cultural Competence Reexamined: Critique and Directions for the Future." *Psychiatric Services* 58(10): 1362–65.

Carter, Robert T. 1995. *The Influence of Race and Racial Identity in Psychotherapy: Towards a Racially Inclusive Model*. New York: John Wiley & Sons.

Castilla, Emilio J. 2008. "Gender, Race, and Meritocracy in Organizational Careers." *American Journal of Sociology* 113(6): 1479–526.

Chang, Doris F., and Alexandra Berk. 2009. "Making Cross-Racial Therapy Work: A Phenomenological Study of Clients' Experiences of Cross-Racial Therapy." *Journal of Counseling Psychology* 56(4): 521–36.

Charles, Camille Z. 2009. *Won't You Be My Neighbor?: Race, Class, and Residence in Los Angeles*. New York: Russell Sage Foundation.

Chatman, Jennifer A. 2010. "Norms in Mixed Sex and Mixed Race Work Groups." *Academy of Management Annals* 4(1): 447–84.

Chrobot-Mason, Donna, and Kecia M. Thomas. 2002. "Minority Employees in Majority Organizations: The Intersection of Individual and Organizational Racial Identity in the Workplace." *Human Resource Development Review* 1(3): 323–44.

Chubbuck, Sharon M. 2004. "Whiteness Enacted, Whiteness Disrupted: The Complexity of Personal Congruence." *American Educational Research Journal* 41(2): 301–33.

Clark, Arthur J. 2002. "Scapegoating: Dynamics and Interventions in Group Counseling." *Journal of Counseling and Development* 80(3): 271–76.

Cohen, Elena P. 2003. "Framework for Culturally Competent Decision-making in Child Welfare." *Child Welfare* 82(2): 143–55.

Connolly, Medria L., and Debra A. Noumair. 1997. "The White Girl in Me, the Colored Girl in You, and the Lesbian in Us: Crossing Boundaries." In

Off White: Readings on Race, Power and Society, edited by Michelle Fine. New York: Routledge.

Conrad, David, and Yvonne Kellar-Guenther. 2006. "Compassion Fatigue, Burnout and Compassion Satisfaction Among Colorado Child Protection Workers." *Child Abuse & Neglect* 30(10): 1071–80.

Cook, Scott D. N., and John Seely Brown. 1999. "Bridging Epistemologies: The Generative Dance between Organizational Knowledge and Organizational Knowing." *Organization Science* 10(4): 381–400.

Cornell, Stephen, and Douglas Hartmann. 2007. *Ethnicity and Race: Making Identities in a Changing World,* 2nd ed. Thousand Oaks, California: Pine Forge Press.

Correll, Joshua, Bernadette Park, and J. Allegra Smith. 2008. "Colorblind and Multicultural Prejudice Reduction Strategies in High-Conflict Situations." *Group Processes and Intergroup Relations* 11(4): 471–91.

Courtney, Mark E., Richard P. Barth, Jill D. Berrick, Devon Brooks, Barbara Needell, and Linda Park. 1996. "Race and Child Welfare Services: Past Research and Future Directions." *Child Welfare* 75(2): 99–137.

Crenshaw, Kimberle Williams. 1989. "Toward a Race-Conscious Pedagogy in Legal Education." *National Black Law Journal* 11(1): 1–14.

Crosby, Faye J. 1997. "Confessions of an Affirmative Action Mama." In *Off White: Readings on Race, Power and Society,* edited by Michelle Fine, Lois Weis, Linda C. Powell, and L. Mun Wong. New York: Routledge.

Davidson, Martin. 2011. *The End of Diversity as We Know It: Why Diversity Efforts Fail and How Leveraging Difference Can Succeed.* San Francisco: Berrett-Koehler Publishers.

Davies, Paul G., Steven J. Spencer, and Claude M. Steele. 2005. "Clearing the Air: Identity Safety Moderates the Effects of Stereotype Threat on Women's Leadership Aspirations." *Journal of Personality and Social Psychology* 88(2): 276–87.

Day-Vines, Norma L., Susannah M. Wood, Tim Grothaus, Laurie Craigen, Angela Holman, Kylie Dotson-Blake, and Marcy J. Douglass. 2007. "Broaching the Subjects of Race, Ethnicity and Culture During the Counseling Process." *Journal of Counseling and Development* 85(4): 401–09.

Derman-Sparks, Louise, Patricia G. Ramsey, and Julie Olsen Edwards. 2011. *What If All the Kids Are White?: Anti-Bias Multicultural Education with Young Children and Families.* New York: Teachers College Press.

de Rooji, Eline A., Donald P. Green, and Alan S. Gerber. 2009. "Field Experiments on Political Behavior and Collective Action." *Annual Review of Political Science* 12: 389–95.

DeVault, Marjorie L. 1990. "Talking and Listening from Women's Standpoint: Feminist Strategies for Interviewing and Analysis." *Social Problems* 37(1): 96–116.

Doane, Ashley W., Jr. 1997. "Dominant Group Ethnic Identity in the United States: The Role of 'Hidden' Ethnicity in Intergroup Relations." *Sociological Quarterly* 38(3): 375–97.

Earley, P. Christopher, and Elaine Mosakowski. 2000. "Creating Hybrid Team Cultures: An Empirical Test of Transnational Team Functioning." *Academy of Management Journal* 43(1): 26–49.

Edmondson, Amy. 1999. "Psychological Safety and Learning Behavior in Work Teams." *Administrative Science Quarterly* 44(2): 350–83.

———. 2002. "The Local and Variegated Nature of Learning in Organizations: A Group-Level Perspective." *Organization Science* 13(2): 128–46.

Edmondson, Amy C., Richard M. Bohmer, and Gary P. Pisano. 2001. "Disrupted Routines: Team Learning and New Technology Implementation in Hospitals." *Administrative Science Quarterly* 46(4): 685–716.

Edmondson, Amy C., James R. Dillon, and Kathryn S. Roloff. 2007. "Three Perspectives on Team Learning." *Academy of Management Annals* 1: 269–314.

Ellemers, Naomi, Ed Sheebos, Daan Stam, and Dick de Gilder. 2011. "Feeling Included and Valued: How Perceived Respect Affects Positive Team Identity and Willingness to Invest in the Team." *British Journal of Management* 24(1): 21–37.

Ellen, Ingrid Gould, and Brendan O'Flaherty. 2010. *How to House the Homeless.* New York: Russell Sage Foundation.

Ely, Robin J., and David A. Thomas. 2001. "Cultural Diversity at Work: The Effects of Diversity Perspectives on Work Group Processes and Outcomes." *Administrative Science Quarterly* 46(2): 229–73.

Ely, Robin J., Irene Padavic, and David A. Thomas. 2012. "Racial Diversity, Racial Asymmetries, and Team Learning Environment: Effects on Performance." *Organization Studies* 33(3): 341–62.

Fine, Michelle, Lois Weis, Linda C. Powell, and L. Mun Wong. 1997. *Off White: Readings on Race, Power and Society.* New York: Routledge.

Foldy, Erica Gabrielle. 2005. "Claiming a Voice on Race." *Action Research* 3(1): 33–54.

Foldy, Erica Gabrielle, and Tamara R. Buckley. 2009. "Re-Creating Street-Level Practice: The Role of Routines, Work Groups, and Team Learning." *Journal of Public Administration Research and Theory* 20(1): 23–52.

———. 2014. "Color Minimization: The Theory and Practice of Addressing Race and Ethnicity at Work." In *Diversity Ideologies in Organizations,* edited by Kecia M. Thomas, Victoria C. Plaut, and Ny M. Tran. London: Routledge.

Foldy, Erica Gabrielle, Peter Rivard, and Tamara R. Buckley. 2009. "Power, Safety, and Learning in Racially Diverse Groups." *Academy of Management Learning and Education* 8(1): 25–41.

Frankenberg, Ruth. 1993. *White Women, Race Matters: The Social Construction of Whiteness.* Minneapolis: University of Minnesota Press.

Fredrickson, George M. 1999. "Models of American Ethnic Relations: A Historical Perspective." In *Cultural Divides: Understanding and Overcoming Group Conflict,* edited by Deborah A. Prentice and Dale T. Miller. New York: Russell Sage Foundation.

Fuertes, Jairo N., Lisa N. Mueller, Rahul V. Chauhan, Jessica A. Walker, and Nicholas Ladany. 2002. "An Investigation of European American Therapists' Approach to Counseling African American Clients." *Counseling Psychologist* 30(5): 763–88.

Gersick, Connie J. G., and J. Richard Hackman. 1990. "Habitual Routines in Task-Performing Groups." *Organizational Behavior and Human Decision Processes* 47(1): 65–97.

Gherardi, Silvia. 2000. "Practice-Based Theorizing on Learning and Knowing in Organizations." *Organization* 7(2): 211–23.

Gibson, Christina, and Freek Vermeulen. 2003. "A Healthy Divide: Subgroups as a Stimulus for Team Learning Behavior." *Administrative Science Quarterly* 48(2): 202–39.

Gibson, Cristina B., and Jennifer L. Gibbs. 2006. "Unpacking the Concept of Virtuality: The Effects of Geographic Dispersion, Electronic Dependence, Dynamic Structure and National Diversity on Team Innovation." *Administrative Science Quarterly* 51(3): 451–95.

Giroux, Henry A. 1997. "Rewriting the Discourse of Racial Identity: Towards a Pedagogy and Politics of Whiteness." *Harvard Education Review* 67(2): 285–320.

Good, Mary-Jo DelVecchio, Sarah S. Willen, Seth D. Hannah, Ken Vickery, and Lawrence T. Park. 2011. *Shattering Culture: American Medicine Responds to Cultural Diversity.* New York: Russell Sage Foundation.

Green, Alexander R., Dana R. Carney, Daniel J. Pallin, Long H. Ngo, Krista L. Raymond, Lisa I. Lezzoni, and Mahzarin R. Banaji. 2007. "Implicit Bias among Physicians and Its Prediction of Thrombolysis Decisions for Black and White Patients." *Journal of General Internal Medicine* 22(9): 2084–90.

Guarnaccia, J. Peter, and Orlando Rodriguez. 1996. "Concepts of Culture and Their Role in the Development of Culturally Competent Mental Health Services." *Hispanic Journal of Behavioral Sciences* 18(4): 419–43.

Guerrero, Erick, and Christina M. Andrews. 2011. "Cultural Competence in Outpatient Substance Abuse Treatment: Measurement and Relationship to Wait Time and Retention." *Drug and Alcohol Dependence* 119: e13–e22.

Guinier, Lani, and Gerald Torres. 2003. *The Miner's Canary: Enlisting Race, Resisting Power, Transforming Democracy.* Cambridge, Mass.: Harvard University Press.

Guralnik, David B., ed. 1974. *Webster's New World Dictionary of the American Language.* Cleveland, Oh.: William Collins + World Publishing.

Gushue, George V., and T. Robert Carter. 2000. "Remembering Race: White Racial Identity Attitudes and Two Aspects of Social Memory." *Journal of Counseling Psychology* 47(2): 199–210.

Guy-Walls, Patricia. 2007. "Exploring Cultural Competence Practice in Undergraduate Social Work Education." *Education* 127(4): 569–80.

Hackman, J. Richard. 1987. "The Design of Work Teams." In *Handbook of Organizational Behavior,* edited by Jay W. Lorsch. Englewood Cliffs, N.J.: Prentice-Hall.

Haider, Adil H., Janel Sexton, N. Sriram, Lisa A. Cooper, David T. Efron, Swoboda Swoboda, Cassandra V. Villegas, et al. 2011. "Association of Unconscious Race and Social Class Bias with Vignette-Based Clinical Assessments by Medical Students." *Journal of the American Medical Association* 306(9): 942–51.

Hancock, Ange-Marie. 2007. "When Multiplication Doesn't Equal Quick Addition: Examining Intersectionality as a Research Paradigm." *Perspectives on Politics* 5(1): 63–79.

Hannaford, Ivan. 1996. *Race: The History of an Idea in the West.* Washington, D.C.: Woodrow Wilson Center Press.

Hannah, Seth D. 2011. "Clinical Care in Environments of Hyperdiversity." In *Shattering Culture: American Medicine Responds to Cultural Diversity* edited by Mary-Jo DelVecchio Good, Sarah S. Willen, Seth D. Hannah, Ken Vickery, and Lawrence T. Park. New York: Russell Sage Foundation.

Hansen, Nancy DelVecchio, Fran Pepitone-Arreola-Rockwell, and Anthony F. Greene. 2000. "Multicultural Competence: Criteria and Case Examples." *Professional Psychology: Research and Practice* 31(6): 652–60.

Harding, Sandra. 1993. "Rethinking Standpoint Epistemology: What Is 'Strong Objectivity'?" In *Feminist Epistemologies,* edited by Linda Alcoff and Elizabeth Potter. New York: Routledge.

Harris, Marian S., and Wanda Hackett. 2008. "Decision Points in Child Welfare: An Action Research Model to Address Disproportionality." *Children and Youth Services Review* 30(2): 199–215.

Has, R. Glen, Irwin Katz, Nina Rizzo, John Bailey, and Lynn Moore. 1992. "When Racial Ambivalence Evokes Negative Affect, Using a Disguised Measure of Mood." *Personality and Social Psychology Bulletin* 18(6): 786–97.

Helms, E. Janet, and Donelda A. Cook. 1999. *Using Race and Culture in Counseling and Psychotherapy: Theory and Process.* Boston, Mass.: Allyn and Bacon.

Hicks-Clarke, Deborah, and Paul Iles. 2000. "Climate for Diversity and Its Effects on Career and Organizational Attributes and Perceptions." *Personnel Review* 29(3): 324–45.

Hines, Alice M., Kathy Lemon, Paige Wyatt, and Joan Merdinger. 2004. "Factors Related to the Disproportionate Involvement of Children of Color in the Child Welfare System: A Review and Emerging Themes." *Children and Youth Services Review* 26(6): 507–27.

Hobman, Elizabeth V., Prashant Bordia, and Cynthia Gallois. 2004. "Perceived Dissimilarity and Work Group Involvement." *Group & Organization Management* 29(5): 560–87.

Holder, Eric. 2009. "Attorney General Eric Holder at the Department of Justice African American History Month Program." Washington: U.S. Department of Justice.

Holvino, Evangelina. 2001. "Complicating Gender: The Simultaneity of Race, Gender and Class in Organization Change(ing)." Center for Gender in Organizations working paper. Boston, Mass.: Simmons College.

Homan, Astrid C., Daan Van Knippenberg, Gerben A. Van Kleef, and Carsten K. W. De Dreu. 2007. "Bridging Faultlines by Valuing Diversity: Diversity Beliefs, Information Elaboration, and Performance in Diverse Work Groups." *Journal of Applied Psychology* 92(5): 1189–99.

Homan, Astrid C., John R. Hollenbeck, Stephen E. Humphrey, Daan Van Knippenberg, Daniel R. Ilgen, and Gerben A. Van Kleef. 2011. "Facing Differences with an Open Mind: Openness to Experience, Salience of Intragroup Differences and Performance of Diverse Work Groups." *Academy of Management Journal* 51(6): 1204–22.

Hurtado, Aida, and Abigail J. Stewart. 1997. "Through the Looking Glass: Implications of Studying Whiteness for Feminist Methods." In *Off White: Readings on Race, Power and Society,* edited by Michelle Fine. New York: Routledge.

Hyde, Cheryl A. 2004. "Multicultural Development in Human Services Agencies: Challenges and Solutions." *Social Work* 49(1): 7–16.

Ito, Tiffany A., and Geoffrey R. Urland. 2003. "Race and Gender on the Brain: Electrocortical Measures of Attention to the Race and Gender of Multiply Categorizable Individuals." *Journal of Personality and Social Psychology* 85(4): 616–26.

Jackson, Kelly F. 2009. "Building Cultural Competence: A Systematic Evaluation of the Effectiveness of Culturally Sensitive Interventions with Ethnic Minority Youth." *Children and Youth Services Review* 31(11): 1192–98.

Jackson, Susan E., Aparna Joshi, and Niclas L. Erhardt. 2003. "Recent Research on Team and Organizational Diversity: Swot Analysis and Implications." *Journal of Management* 29(6): 801–30.

Jones, James M. 1999. "Cultural Racism: The Intersection of Race and Culture in Intergroup Conflict." In *Cultural Divides: Understanding and Overcoming Group Conflict,* edited by Deborah A. Prentice and Dale T. Miller. New York: Russell Sage Foundation.

Joshi, Aparna, Hui Liao, and Susan E. Jackson. 2006. "Cross-Level Effects of Workplace Diversity on Sales Performance and Pay." *Academy of Management Journal* 49(3): 459–81.

Juby, L. Heather, and William R. Concepcion. 2005. "Ethnicity: The Term and Its Meaning." In *Handbook of Racial-Cultural Psychology and Counseling: Theory and Research,* Vol. 1, edited by Robert T. Carter. Hoboken, N.J: John Wiley & Sons.

Kalev, Alexander, Frank Dobbin, and Erin Kelly. 2006. "Best Practices or Best Guesses." *American Sociological Review* 71(4): 589–617.

Kalinoski, Zachary T., Debra Steele-Johnson, Elizabeth J. Peyton, Keith A. Leas, Julie Steinke, and Nathan A. Bowling. 2012. "A Meta-Analytic Evaluation of Diversity Training Outcomes." *Journal of Organizational Behavior.* 34(8): 1076–1104.

Kanter, Rosabeth Moss. 1993. *Men and Women of the Corporation,* 2nd ed. New York: HarperCollins.

Katz, Irwin, and Joyce Wackenhut. 1986. "Racial Ambivalence, Value Duality, and Behavior." In *Prejudice, Discrimination and Racism,* edited by John F. Dovidio and Samuel L. Gaertner. San Diego: Academic Press.

King, Eden B., Michelle R. Hebl, and Daniel J. Beal. 2009. "Conflict and Cooperation in Diverse Workgroups." *Journal of Social Issues* 65(2): 261–85.

Knowles, Eric D., Brian S. Lowery, Caitlen M. Hogan, and Rosalind M. Chow. 2009. "On the Malleability of Ideology: Motivated Construals of Color Blindness." *Journal of Personality and Social Psychology* 96(4): 857–69.

Konrad, Alison M., and Frank Linnehan. 1995. "Formalized HRM Structures: Coordinating Equal Employment Opportunity or Concealing Organizational Practices?" *Academy of Management Journal* 38(3): 787–820.

Kooij-de Bode, Hanneke J. M., Daan van Knippenberg, and Wendy P. van Ginkel. 2008. "Ethnic Diversity and Distributed Information in Group Decision Making: The Importance of Information Elaboration." *Group Dynamics: Theory, Research and Practice* 12(4): 307–20.

Kossek, Ellen Ernst, and Susan C. Zonia. 1993. "Assessing Diversity Climate: A Field Study of Reactions to Employer Efforts to Promote Diversity." *Journal of Organizational Behavior* 14(1): 61–81.

Krauss, Beatrice J., Lloyd Goldsamt, Edna Bula, and Robert Semper. 1997. *Journal of Health Education* 28(6): 67–71.

Ladd, John. 1997. "Philosophical Reflections on Race and Racism." *American Behavioral Scientist* 41(2): 212–22.

Lave, Jean, and Etienne Wenger. 1991. *Situated Learning: Legitimate Peripheral Participation.* Cambridge: Cambridge University Press.

LaMarche, Gara. "Taking Account of Race: A Philanthropic Imperative." 2009. http://www.atlanticphilanthropies.org/currents/taking-account-race-philanthropic-imperative. Accessed Dec. 24, 2013.

Litvin, Deborah R. 1997. "The Discourse of Diversity: From Biology to Management." *Organization* 4(2): 187–210.

Loury, Glenn. 2002. *The Anatomy of Racial Inequality.* Cambridge, Mass.: Harvard University Press.

Maddox, Keith B. 2004. "Perspectives on Racial Phenotypicality Bias." *Personality and Social Psychology Review* 8(4): 383–401.

Maddox, Keith B., and Stephanie A. Gray. 2002. "Cognitive Representations of Black Americans: Reexploring the Role of Skin Tone." *Personality and Social Psychology Bulletin* 28(2): 250–50.

Maiter, Sarah. 2004. "Considering Context and Culture in Child Protection Services to Ethnically Diverse Families: An Example from Research with Parents from the Indian Subcontinent (South Asians)." *Journal of Social Work Research and Evaluation* 5(1): 63–80.

Mannix, Elizabeth, and Margaret A. Neale. 2005. "What Differences Make a Difference? The Promise and Reality of Diverse Teams in Organizations." *Psychological Science in the Public Interest* 6(2): 31–55.

Markus, Hazel R., Claude M. Steele, and Dorothy M. Steele. 2000. "Color-blindness as a Barrier to Inclusion: Assimilation and Nonimmigrant Minorities." *Daedalus: Journal of the American Academy of Arts and Sciences* 129(4): 233–59.

———. 2004. "Color Blindness as a Barrier to Inclusion: Assimilation and Nonimmigrant Minorities." In *Engaging Cultural Differences: The Multicultural Challenge in Liberal Democracies,* edited by Richard Shweder, Martha Minow, and Hazel R. Markus. New York: Russell Sage Foundation.

Martin, Rachel. 2001. *Listening Up: Reinventing Ourselves as Teachers and Students.* Portsmouth, N.H.: Heinemann.

Marx, Sherry. 2006. *Revealing the Invisible: Confronting Passive Racism in Teacher Education.* New York: Routledge.

Massey, Douglas S., and Nancy A. Denton. 1993. *American Apartheid: Segregation and the Making of the Underclass.* Cambridge, Mass.: Harvard University Press.

McCall, Leslie. 2001. *Complex Inequality: Gender, Class and Race in the New Economy.* New York: Routledge.

McPhatter, Anna R. 1997. "Cultural Competence in Child Welfare: What Is It? How Do We Achieve It? What Happens Without It?" *Child Welfare* 76(1): 255–78.

McRae, Mary B., and Ellen L. Short. 2010. *Racial and Cultural Dynamics in Group and Organizational Life: Crossing Boundaries.* Los Angeles, Calif.: Sage Publications.

Mederos, Fernando, and Isa Woldeguiorguis. 2003. "Beyond Cultural Competence: What Child Protection Managers Need to Know and Do." *Child Welfare* 82(2): 125–42.

Merelman, Richard M., Greg Streich, and Paul Martin. 1998. "Unity and Diversity in American Political Culture: An Exploratory Study of the National Conversation on American Pluralism and Identity." *Political Psychology* 19(4): 781–807.

Miranda, Jeanne, Richard Nakamura, and Guillermo Bernal. 2003. "Including Ethnic Minorities in Mental Health Intervention Research: A Practical Approach to a Long-Standing Problem." *Culture, Medicine and Psychiatry* 27(4): 467–86.

Moss, Philip I., and Chris Tilly. 2003. *Stories Employers Tell: Race, Skill, and Hiring in America.* New York: Russell Sage Foundation.

Nagda, Biren A. 2006. "Breaking Barriers, Crossing Borders, Building Bridges: Communication Processes in Intergroup Dialogue." *Journal of Social Issues* 62(3): 553–76.

Nagda, Biren A., and Ximena Zuniga. 2003. "Fostering Meaningful Racial Engagement through Intergroup Dialogues." *Group Processes & Intergroup Relations* 6(1): 111–28.

Nagda, Biren A., Linda R. Tropp, and Elizabeth L. Paluck. 2006. "Looking Back as We Look Ahead: Integrating Research, Theory and Practice on Intergroup Relations." *Journal of Social Issues* 62(3): 439–51.

NASW. 2001 "NASW Standards for Cultural Competence in Social Work Practice." Washington, D.C.: National Association of Social Workers.

Neighbors, Harold W., Steven J. Trierweiler, Briggett C. Ford and Jordana R. Muroff. 2003. "Racial Differences in DSM Diagnosis Using a Semi-Structured Instrument: The Importance of Clinical Judgment in the Diagnosis of African Americans." *Journal of Health and Social Behavior* 43(3): 237–256.

Nembhard, Ingrid M., and Amy C. Edmondson. 2006. "Making It Safe: The Effects of Leader Inclusiveness and Professional Status on Psychological Safety and Improvement Efforts in Health Care Teams." *Journal of Organizational Behavior* 27(7): 941–66.

Nemetz, Patricia L., and Sandra L. Christensen. 1996. "The Challenge of Cultural Diversity: Harnessing a Diversity of Views to Understand Multiculturalism." *Academy of Management Review* 21(2): 434–62.

Nissly, Jan A., Michàl E. Mor Barak, and Amy Levin. 2005. "Stress, Social Support and Workers' Intention to Leave Their Jobs in Public Child Welfare." *Administration in Social Work* 29(1): 79–100.

Norton, Michael I., Samuel R. Sommers, Evan P. Apfelbaum, Natassia Pura, and Dan Ariely. 2006. "Color Blindness and Interracial Interaction: Playing the Political Correctness Game." *Psychological Science* 17(11): 949–53.

O'Brien, E. 2000. "Are We Supposed to Be Colorblind or Not? Competing Frames Used by Whites against Racism." *Race and Society* 3(1): 41–59.

Oliver, Melvin L., and Thomas M. Shapiro. 1997. *Black Wealth/White Wealth: A New Perspective on Racial Inequality.* New York: Routledge.

Omi, Michael. 2010. "'Slippin' into Darkness': The(Re)-Biologization of Race." *Journal of Asian American Studies* 13(3): 343–58.

Omi, Michael, and Howard Winant. 1994. *Racial Formation in the United States.* New York: Routledge.

Ozbilgin, Mustafa, and Ahu Tatli. 2011. "Mapping out the Field of Equality and Diversity: Rise of Individualism and Voluntarism." *Human Relations* 64(9): 1229–53.

Page, Scott E. 2007. *The Difference: How the Power of Diversity Creates Better Groups, Firms, Schools, and Societies.* Princeton, N.J.: Princeton University Press.

Painter, Nell I. 2010. *The History of White People.* New York: W. W. Norton.

Paluck, Elizabeth L. 2006. "Diversity Training and Intergroup Contact: A Call to Action Research." *Journal of Social Issues* 62(3): 577–95.

———. 2009. "Reducing Intergroup Prejudice and Conflict Using the Media: A Field Experiment in Rwanda." *Journal of Personality and Social Psychology* 96(3): 574–87.

Pearce, Jone L., and Amy E. Randel. 2004. "Expectations of Organizational Mobility, Workplace Social Inclusion and Employee Job Performance." *Journal of Organizational Behavior* 25(1): 81–98.

Pedersen, Paul. 1988. "Four Dimensions of Multicultural Skill Training." In *A Handbook for Developing Multicultural Awareness,* edited by Paul

Pedersen. Alexandria, Va.: American Association for Counseling and Development.

Phillips, Katherine W., Nancy P. Rothbard, and Tracey L. Dumas. 2009. "To Disclose or Not to Disclose? Status Distance and Self-Disclosure in Diverse Environments." *Academy of Management Review* 34(4): 710–32.

Pittinsky, Todd L., and Stefanie Simon. 2007. "Intergroup Leadership." *Leadership Quarterly* 18(6): 586–605.

Plaut, Victoria C. 2002. "Cultural Models of Diversity in America: The Psychology of Difference and Inclusion." In *Engaging Cultural Differences: The Multicultural Challenge in Liberal Democracies,* edited by Richard Schweder, Martha Minow, and Hazel Rose Markus. New York: Russell Sage Foundation.

Plaut, Victoria C., Kecia M. Thomas, and Matt J. Goren. 2009. "Is Multiculturalism or Color Blindness Better for Minorities?" *Psychological Science* 20(4): 444–46.

Pless, Nicola M., and Thomas Maak. 2004. "Building an Inclusive Diversity Culture: Principles, Processes and Practice." *Journal of Business Ethics* 54(1): 129–47.

Pollock, Mica. 2004. *Colormute: Race Talk Dilemmas in an American School.* Princeton, N.J.: Princeton University Press.

Pollock, Mica, Sherry Deckman, Meredith Mira, and Carla Shalaby. 2010. "'But What Can I Do?': Three Necessary Tensions in Teaching Teachers About Race." *Journal of Teacher Education* 61(3): 211–24.

Ponterotto, Joseph G., Jairo N. Fuertes, and Eric C. Chen. 2000. "*Models of Multicultural Counseling.*" In *Handbook of Counseling Psychology,* edited by Joseph Ponterotto. New York: John Wiley & Sons.

Poppelaars, Caelesta, and Peter Scholten. 2008. "Two Worlds Apart: The Divergence of National and Local Immigrant Integration Policies in the Netherlands." *Administration & Society* 40(4): 335–57.

Purdie-Vaughns, Valerie, Claude M. Steele, Paul G. Davies, Ruth Ditlmann, and Jennifer Randall Crosby. 2008. "Social Identity Contingencies: How Diversity Cues Signal Threat or Safety for African Americans in Mainstream Institutions." *Journal of Personality and Social Psychology* 94(4): 615–30.

Pyles, Loretta, and Kyung Mee Kim. 2006. "A Multilevel Approach to Cultural Competence: A Study of the Community Response to Underserved Domestic Violence Victims." *Families in Society* 87(2): 221–29.

Richeson, Jennifer A., and Richard J. Nussbaum. 2004. "The Impact of Multiculturalism Versus Color-Blindness on Racial Bias." *Journal of Experimental Social Psychology* 40(3): 417–23.

Richeson, Jennifer A., and J. Nicole Shelton. 2007. "Negotiating Interracial Interactions: Costs, Consequences and Possibilities." *Current Directions in Psychological Science* 16(6): 316–20.

Roberson, Loriann, Benjamin M. Galvin, and Atira Cherise Charles. 2007. "When Group Identities Matter: Bias in Performance Appraisal." *The Academy of Management Annals* 1(1): 617–50.

Roberts, Dorothy. 2002. *Shattered Bonds: The Color of Child Welfare.* New York: Basic Civitas Books.

Rodenborg, Nancy A. 2004. "Services to African American Children in Poverty: Institutional Discrimination in Child Welfare?" *Journal of Poverty* 8(3): 109–30.

Ryan, Carey S., Jennifer S. Hunt, Joshua A. Weible, Charles R. Peterson, and Juan F. Casas. 2007. "Multicultural and Color Blind Ideology, Stereotypes and Ethnocentrism Among Black and White Americans." *Group Processes & Intergroup Relations* 10(4): 617–37.

Sabin, Janice A., Frederick P. Rivera, and Anthony G. Greenwald. 2008. "Physician Implicit Attitudes and Stereotypes About Race and Quality of Medical Care." *Med Care* 46(7): 647–85.

Saguy, Tamar, John F. Dovidio, and Felicia Pratto. 2008. "Beyond Contact: Intergroup Contact in the Context of Power Relations." *Personality and Social Psychology Bulletin* 34(3): 432–45.

Schippers, Michaéla C., Deanne N. Den Hartog, and Paul L. Koopman. 2007. "Reflexivity in Teams: A Measure and Correlates." *Applied Psychology: An International Review* 56(2): 189–211.

Schofield, Janet W. 1986. "Causes and Consequences of the Colorblind Perspective." In *Prejudice, Discrimination and Racism*, edited by John Dovidio and Samuel Gaertner. San Diego, Calif.: Academic Press.

Sharf, Richard. S. 2000. *Theories of Psychotherapy and Counseling: Concepts and Cases,* 2nd ed. Belmont, Calif.: Wadsworth/Thomson Learning.

Shelton, J. Nicole. 2003. "Interpersonal Concerns in Social Encounters between Majority and Minority Group Members." *Group Processes & Intergroup Relations* 6(2): 171–85.

Shelton, J. Nicole, Tessa V. West, and Thomas E. Trail. 2010. "Concerns About Appearing Prejudiced: Implications for Anxiety During Daily Interracial Interactions." *Groups Processes & Intergroup Relations* 13(3): 329–44.

Singleton, Glenn E., and Curtis W. Linton. 2005. *Courageous Conversations About Race: A Field Guide for Achieving Equity in Schools.* Thousand Oaks, Calif.: Corwin.

Smith, Emilie, Katrina Walker, Laurie Fields, Craig C. Brookins, and Robert B. Seay. 1999. "Ethnic Identity and Its Relationship to Self-Esteem, Perceived Efficacy, and Prosocial Attitudes in Early Adolescence." *Journal of Adolescence* 22(6): 867–80.

Smith, Timothy B., and Lynda Silva. 2011. "Ethnic Identity and Personal Well-Being of People of Color: A Meta-Analysis." *Journal of Counseling Psychology* 58(1): 42–60.

Sole, Deborah, and Amy C. Edmondson. 2002. "Situated Knowledge and Learning in Dispersed Teams." *British Journal of Management* 13(S2): S17–S34.

Spencer, Martin E. 1994. "Multiculturalism, 'Political Correctness,' and the Politics of Identity." *Sociological Forum* 9(4): 547–67.

Stahl, Gunter K., Martha L. Maznevski, Andreas Voigt, and Karsten Jonsen. 2010. "Unraveling the Effects of Cultural Diversity in Teams: A Meta-Analysis of Research on Multicultural Work Groups." *Journal of International Business Studies* 41(4): 690–709.

Stainback, Kevin, and Donald Tomaskovic-Devey. 2012. *Documenting Desegregation: Racial and Gender Segregation in Private-Sector Employment since the Civil Rights Act.* New York: Russell Sage Foundation.

Steele, Claude M. 2010. *Whistling Vivaldi: How Stereotypes Affect Us and What We Can Do.* New York: W. W. Norton.

Steele, Claude M., Steven J. Spencer, and Joshua Aronson. 2002. "Contending with Group Image: The Psychology of Stereotype and Social Identity Threat." *Advances in Experimental Social Psychology* 34: 379–440.

Stewart, Marcus M., and Patricia Garcia-Prieto. 2008. "A Relational Demography Model of Workgroup Identification: Testing the Effects of Race, Race Dissimilarity, Racial Identification, and Communication Behavior." *Journal of Organizational Behavior* 29(5): 657–80.

Stone, Douglas, Bruce Patton, and Sheila Heen. 2010. *Difficult Conversations,* rev. ed. New York: Penguin Books.

Strolovitch, Dara Z. 2007. *Affirmative Advocacy: Race, Class, and Gender in Interest Group Politics.* Chicago: University of Chicago Press.

Sue, Derald W., Patricia Arredondo, and Roderick McDavis. 1992. "Multicultural Counseling Competencies and Standards: A Call to the Profession." *Journal of Multicultural Counseling and Development* 20(2): 64–89.

Tatum, Beverly Daniel. 1997. *Why Are All the Black Kids Sitting Together in the Cafeteria?* New York: Basic Books.

———. 2007. *Can We Talk About Race?* Boston, Mass.: Beacon Press.

Teasley, Martell L. 2005. "Perceived Levels of Cultural Competence through Social Work Education." *Journal of Social Work Education* 41(1): 85–98.

Tervalon, Melanie, and Jann Murray-Garcia. 1998. "Cultural Humility Versus Cultural Competence: A Critical Distinction in Defining Physician Training Outcomes in Multicultural Education." *Journal of Health Care for the Poor and Underserved* 9(2): 117–25.

Thomas, David A. 1989. "Mentoring and Irrationality: The Role of Racial Taboos." *Human Resource Management* 28(2): 279–90.

Todd, Nathan R., and Elizabeth M. Abrams. 2011. "White Dialectics: A New Framework for Theory, Research and Practice with White Students." *The Counseling Psychologist* 39(3): 353–95.

Tokar, Edward. 1972. "The Scapegoat as Essential Group Phenomenon." *International Journal of Group Psychotherapy* 22(3): 320–32.

Tomlinson, Frances, and Christina Schwabenland. 2010. "Reconciling Competing Discourses of Diversity? The UK Non-Profit Sector Between Social Justice and the Business Case." *Organization* 17(1): 101–21.

Trawalter, Sophie, and Jennifer A. Richeson. 2008. "Let's Talk About Race, Baby! When Whites' and Blacks' Interracial Contact Experiences Diverge." *Journal of Experimental Social Psychology* 44(4): 1214–217.

U.S. Surgeon General. 1999. "Mental Health: A Report of the Surgeon General." Washington, D.C.: National Institute of Mental Health, U.S. Department of Health and Human Services.

Uttal, Lynet. 2006. "Organizational Cultural Competence: Shifting Programs for Latino Immigrants from a Client-Centered to a Community-Based Orientation." *American Journal of Community Psychology* 38(3–4): 251–62.

Van Bueren, Ellen M., Erik-Hans Klijn, and Joop F. M. Koppenjan. 2003. "Dealing with Wicked Problems in Networks: Analyzing an Environmental Debate from a Network Perspective." *Journal of Public Administration Research and Theory* 13(2): 193–212.

Van Dick, Rolf, Daan van Knippenberg, Silvia Hagele, Yves R. F. Guillaume, and Felix C. Brodbeck. 2008. "Group Diversity and Group Identification: The Moderating Role of Diversity Beliefs." *Human Relations* 61(10): 1463–92.

van Knippenberg, Daan, and Michaela C. Schippers. 2007. "Work Group Diversity." *Annual Review of Psychology* 58: 515–41.

van Knippenberg, Daan, Carsten K. W. De Dreu, and Astrid C. Homan. 2004. "Work Group Diversity and Group Performance: An Integrative Model and Research Agenda." *Journal of Applied Psychology* 89(6): 1008–22.

van Knippenberg, Daan, S. Alexander Haslam, and Michael J. Platow. 2007. "Unity Through Diversity: Value-in-Diversity Beliefs, Work Group Diversity, and Group Identification." *Group Dynamics: Theory, Research and Practice* 11(3): 207–22.

Verkuyten, Maykel. 2005. "Ethnic Group Identification and Group Evaluation Among Minority and Majority Groups: Testing the Multiculturalism Hypothesis." *Journal of Personality and Social Psychology* 88(1): 121–38.

Vittrup, Brigitte, and George W. Holden. 2010. "Exploring the Impact of Educational Television and Parent-Child Discussions on Children's Racial Attitudes." *Analyses of Social Issues and Public Policy* 10(1): 192–214.

Walsh, Katherine C. 2007. *Talking About Race: Community Dialogues and the Politics of Difference.* Chicago: University of Chicago Press.

Wamsted, John O. 2011. "Race, School, and Seinfeld: Autoethnographic Sketching in Black and White." *Qualitative Inquiry* 17(10): 972–81.

Watkins-Hayes, Celeste. 2009. *The New Welfare Bureaucrats: Entanglements of Race, Class and Policy Reform.* Chicago: University of Chicago Press.

Webber, Sheila Simsarian, and Lisa M. Donahue. 2001. "Impact of Highly and Less Job-Related Diversity on Work Group Cohesion and Performance: A Meta-Analysis." *Journal of Management* 27(2): 141–62.

Weber, Edward P., and Anne M. Khademian. 2008. "Wicked Problems, Knowledge Challenges, and Collaborative Capacity Builders in Network Settings." *Public Administration Review* 68(2): 334–49.

Weis, Lois, and Michelle Fine. 2000. *Speed Bumps: A Student-Friendly Guide to Qualitative Research.* New York: Teachers College Press.

Wells, Susan J., Lani M. Merritt, and Harold E. Briggs. 2009. "Bias, Racism and Evidence-Based Practice: The Case for More Focused Development of the Child Welfare Evidence Base." *Children and Youth Services Review* 31(11): 1160–71.

Winant, Howard. 1997. "Behind Blue Eyes: Whiteness and Contemporary U.S. Racial Politics." In *Off White: Readings on Society, Race, and Culture,* edited by Michelle Fine. New York: Routledge.

Winnicott, Donald W. 1986. "The Theory of Parent-Infant Relationship." In *Essential Papers on Object Relations,* edited by Peter Buckley. New York: New York University Press.

Wolsko, Christopher, Bernadette Park, and Charles M. Judd. 2006. "Considering the Tower of Babel: Correlates of Assimilation and Multiculturalism Among Ethnic Minority and Majority Groups in the United States." *Social Justice Research* 19(3): 277–306.

Wolsko, Christopher, Bernadette Park, Charles M. Judd, and Bernd Wittenbrink. 2000. "Framing Interethnic Ideology: Effects of Multicultural and Color-Blind Perspectives on Judgments of Groups and Individuals." *Journal of Personality and Social Psychology* 78(4): 635–64.

Yan, Miu Chung. 2005. "How Cultural Awareness Works: An Empirical Examination of the Interaction Between Social Workers and Their Clients." *Canadian Social Work Review* 22(1): 5–29.

Yanow, Dvora. 1996. "American Ethnogenesis and Public Administration." *Administration and Society* 27(4): 483–509.

Yoshino, Kenji. 2007. *Covering: The Hidden Assault on Our Civil Rights.* New York: Random House.

Zane, Nancie. 1997. "Interrupting Historical Patterns: Bridging Race and Gender Gaps Between Senior White Men and Other Organizational Groups." In *Off White: Readings on Race, Power and Society,* edited by Michelle Fine. New York: Routledge.

Zhang, Naijiian, and Alan W. Burkard. 2008. "Client and Counselor Discussions of Racial and Ethnic Differences in Counseling: An Exploratory Investigation." *Multicultural Counseling and Development* 36(2): 77–87.

~ Index ~

Boldface numbers refer to figures.